Rhetorical Drag

Rhetorical Drag

Gender Impersonation, Captivity,
and the Writing of History

Lorrayne Carroll

The Kent State University Press

KENT, OHIO

© 2007 by The Kent State University Press, Kent, Ohio 44242
ALL RIGHTS RESERVED
Library of Congress Catalog Card Number 2006016315
ISBN-10: 0-87338-882-8
ISBN-13: 978-0-87338-882-5
Manufactured in the United States of America

11 10 09 08 07   5 4 3 2 1

Earlier versions of "'Being Read with a Greedy Attention': Mather in Drag"
and "'Affecting History': Impersonating Women in the Early Republic"
appeared in *Early American Literature*.

LIBRARY OF CONGRESS CATALOGING-IN-PUBLICATION DATA
Carroll, Lorrayne.
Rhetorial drag : gender impersonation, captivity, and the writing of history /
Lorrayne Carroll.
p.   cm.
This work examines authorial gender impersonation (men writing as women) of
American women's captivity narratives from 1697 to 1849, and the connections
between gender figuration and historiography.
Includes bibliographical references and index.
ISBN-13: 978-0-87338-882-5 (alk. paper) ∞
ISBN-10: 0-87338-882-8 (alk. paper) ∞
1. Captivity narratives—United States—History and criticism.   2. Captivity
narratives—United States—Authorship.   3. American literature—19th
century—History and criticism.   4. American literature—18th century—
History and criticism.   5. Discourse analysis, Narrative.   6. Rhetoric—Sex
differences.   7. Indian captivities—United States.   8. History in literature.
9. Women prisoners in literature.   I. Title.
PS217.C36C37 2006
810.9'3538—dc22   2006016315

British Library Cataloging-in-Publication data are available.

Contents

Acknowledgments

My friend Rod DiFillipis found the Jim Beam Commemorative Hannah Duston bottle in a junk store at the bottom of Munjoy Hill in Portland, Maine, just down the street from where I live. Rod knew little about Early American Studies when he spotted it, but he, like all members of my extended family of relatives and friends, knew a captivity text when he saw it. For the nearly twenty years I've been reading, writing, and talking about women captives, I have been blessed by the support and indulgence of many, many people, each bringing something of her or himself to the conversation about women, captivity, and history.

I first encountered several of the Duston stories at Johns Hopkins University while studying with Larzer Ziff, who, over the course of countless revisions, helped me to clarify both my intellectual project and my writing about it. In these initial stages, Mary Poovey challenged me to present cogently the theoretical bases for my study and to explore the ramifications of my claims. At Hopkins and through many years since, Karen Sanchez-Eppler, Benigno Sanchez-Eppler, and Brigitte, Gerl, and Bob Giordani became lifelong colleagues and friends. I am indebted to the Johns Hopkins University for a dissertation fellowship that provided me with time and resources to conduct research early on. I wish to thank the staff at the American Antiquarian Society as well for their help as I finished the book.

From the beginning, incisive, knowledgeable, and generous—so very generous—readers have supported this project: Chris Castiglia, David Shields, anonymous readers for *Early American Literature*, and, for the Kent State University Press, Ivy Schweitzer. At Kent State, Joanna Craig and Tara Lenington allayed all the fears I had about bringing the book to press. The Society of Early Americanists has been a wonderful home; SEA colleagues such as Ray Craig, Lisa Gordis, Sharon Harris, Mark Kamrath, Anne Myles, and Dan Williams have questioned, enhanced, and immeasurably improved my thinking and writing about captive women and their captured voices. Both for their support and for their fabulous intelligence, wit, and charm, I thank my SEA sisters, Lisa Logan and Michele-Lise Tartar.

At the first SEA conference I finally met Kathryn Zabelle Derounian-Stodola, whose scholarship on women's captivity narratives makes possible this book. Zabelle's scholarship, along with her collaborative work with Jim Levernier, opened captivity narratives to a whole generation of Early American scholars, and her attention to women's narratives provides a model for subsequent feminist interventions in the field. Zabelle has read and made valuable suggestions on each iteration of *Rhetorical Drag,* from dissertation to final manuscript. Moreover, as many colleagues will attest, Zabelle's version of the Early Americanist community extends to anyone interested in the field. Her work to build a community of mutually supporting scholars engaged in intense, vital, and rigorous conversations has helped many new scholars find a space: to paraphrase the Mary Jemison account, with them is my (intellectual) home.

On another home front, I thank Liibaan Mursal Ismaacil for companionship, burritos, and teaching me (somehow) to rethink borders, national and familial. Years ago, my sister, Barbara Hickey, provided an empty desk in the Sarah Lawrence library and told me to sit down and start writing, and she has kept me at it ever since. My other sister, Marie Robinson, offers me the finest model of intellectual curiosity, always asking the most incisive questions, a practice we all learned from my father, Robert Carroll. His keen interest in history started me on my way; his love kept me going. My mother, Mary Carroll, taught me early on that teaching could be joyful, hilarious, and deeply serious. This book represents one of my attempts to infuse her spirit into all of my work. And I thank my brothers, Bobby and Richie, for years of lifting me on their shoulders to see a bit more clearly.

At the University of Southern Maine, Kathy Ashley, Donna Cassidy, Bud McGrath, and Nancy Gish have been wonderfully encouraging colleagues, as have the faculty of the Women's Studies Program, who have listened to and commented on various components of the book. Provost Wood and Dean Malhotra provided financial support for the book's production, and the library staff made research a pleasure. Although she teaches at Bates College, Erica Rand has so generously given her time to my work and to USM that I continue the tradition of making her an honorary faculty member by including my thanks to her here. Hugh English, Gabriel Demaine, and Wendy Chapkis support me with their profound joy in teaching, writing, conversation, and activism. My friend and colleague Lydia Savage invited me to housesit with her in Worcester and so made possible critical research at the American Antiquarian Society. Both Lydia and Matthew Edney, who found the map of Quaker meetings in the Brown library, encouraged me to think about the geographical aspects of these texts.

Also in Maine, Tommy Quinn provided me with my first word processor when I was writing about Hannah Duston by hand. Jeffrey Thomas insisted that I make the leap to a real computer and then gave me one. I wish to thank Eileen Monahan; her friendship has sustained me in ways I cannot explain, but she knows. Finally, I thank Joe Medley for the deeply thoughtful ways in which he practices collaboration and companionship and generously shares his path with me.

As Mary Rowlandson says, "But to return": to the beginnings of this project, when my children were young and inexplicably indulgent of my need to leave them to do my work. It amazes me to think that Meghan Quinn and Conor Quinn have lived most of their lives with this book literally in the middle of the house. They have gone from listening politely to my stories about "the Hannahs" to contributing their own considerable knowledge about rhetoric, gender theory, Native American studies, and cross-cultural practices. They have taught me how to be a good scholar and a much better teacher. When I think about the lives of the captive women I write about here, I am grateful that Meghan and Conor have always challenged me and supported me in my role as mother, community member, and teller of tales. This book is for them (and for Jai, too).

INTRODUCTION

⸎

"Particular Knowledge"

Tricky Texts

"Captivity narratives are tricky texts."[1] Surely the thousands of texts, in multiple media, that purported to tell readers/viewers/auditors the true story of Jessica Lynch's captivity and redemption in Iraq underscore Christopher Castiglia's laconic characterization of this popular genre.[2] Castiglia, in a review of captivity narrative studies, explains that "while captivity narratives suggest an immediate relation of historical events . . . they simultaneously bury their own textual history, submerging their influences, predecessors, and coauthors beneath the foundations of a fictionally autonomous 'I'" (127). *Rhetorical Drag* excavates some of the buried elements, the submerged and occluded conditions that produced several popular early American women's captivity narratives whose "I's" anchored stories of abductions, suffering, redemption, and return. By revisiting and reconstructing the textual histories of these dramatic (and melodramatic) tales, I investigate the connections between gender figuration and historiography in early American contexts.

The "tricky" practice exposed and examined in these texts is authorial gender impersonation, an act of imposture that begins with the male writer assuming the female captive's voice. This imposture encompasses an array of discursive practices that reflect and inflect contemporaneous gender regimes. Because the impersonation exceeds merely the appropriation of the "I" and depends for its success on ascriptions of gendered language and diverse rhetorical practices, I refer to this phenomenon as *rhetorical drag*. This term represents a deliberate invitation to readers to consider how we might use queer theory as well as archival research and feminist inquiry to think about the practices of authorial impersonation and its cultural effects. The analyses and interpretation here rely on a reading of rhetorical drag as a complex linguistic enactment, one analogous to Judith Butler's view of drag as a performance predicated on dynamic and elusive (and, therefore, allusive) gender constructs. "Is drag the imitation of gender, or does it dramatize the signifying gestures through which gender itself is established?" Butler asks (*Gender Trouble* x).

A series of responses to this question emerges throughout the chapters of the book, where different specimens of rhetorical drag display various functions, and the functions reflect some of the ways in which gender is instantiated. In Cotton Mather's use of Hannah Swarton's "I," for example, drag functions as an *instrument* that "spatially" extends Mather's polemical skills into the parlors of French Catholic Canada. Thoreau's third-person retelling of Hannah Duston's captivity employs rhetorical drag to establish a strange phantasmagoric *identity* between the memorialist and the captive. The narratives display different functions of rhetorical drag—transformative, exemplary, interpretive, allegorical—and often the impostures serve multiple purposes and result in sometimes contradictory or confusing representations.

These confusing characteristics first led me to investigate the provenance of each narrative. Initially, obvious grammatical inconsistencies, such as pronoun shifts, struck me as odd or dissonant. To account for these rhetorical glitches, I searched several archives and determined whose hands were at work in bringing the narratives to print, a process that uncovered the complexities of each text's publication environment. As the archival sources revealed the actual authors, some of the confusion cleared. But these revelations produced another question: why would men, in most cases men with some degree of cultural authority or those who aspired to it, write as women? Attempting to work through this problem, I began to understand how feminist and queer theories could illuminate the study. For example, once the impersonator chose to write as a woman, he had to deploy a style in which he thought a woman would write. This style necessarily emerged from the discursive regimes that governed the social organization of gender at the time of composition. Style, as a set of recognizable and replicated marks, is, after all, the heart of drag performance.[3]

Butler notes, however, that even as contemporary performances of drag rely on the ironies of gender confusion and contradiction for their cultural and political effects, they embody modernist dispositions and practices. It might appear, then, that using the term "drag" is anachronistic in a study of early American texts. Yet Butler's formulation of drag, along with Frederic Jameson's discussion of parody and pastiche, makes drag theory a useful hermeneutic in considering these earlier works. That is, even within their own historical context, as each of the captivity narratives demonstrates what a female experience should sound or look like, each produces an explicitly gendered style; each performs gender. This fabrication involves rhetorical choices about diction, direct and indirect discourse, interpolated texts, and (self) characterization, among other stylistic elements. The style of the text is thereby determined by the particular textual markers that the impersonator decides best represent "female" writing.

Authorial impersonation in the early women's captivity narratives, however, does not share with modern drag performance the parodic and ironizing effects of appropriating and then mocking the gendered styles. Deploying rhetorical drag to characterize—literally—the female captives, men were engaged in writing history and shaping their own historical moments. The examples of early American rhetorical drag in this book are not parodic because the styles produced by the impersonators do not attempt to be highly individuated; rather, the texts exhibit language that offers an almost indiscriminate version of what it meant to be female at the time of the texts' publication.[4] The irony arising from these conventionalized models of gender is that, while the authors chose to impersonate *particular* women whose *individual* experiences of captivity made them fit subjects for historical writing, they constructed the captive woman according to generalized or dominant models of "femaleness." Differentiated, then, from the often comedic and mocking parody we might find in modern drag acts, the drag performed in these narratives has the quite serious end of persuading its audience that the women's voices had important tales to tell.[5]

A crucial understanding of drag in this study depends on viewing it not solely as a set of textual markers—one traceable in syntax, allu-

sion, grammar, and tropes—but also as a generative context. As Butler, discussing Divine's performances in John Waters' films, notes, his
"impersonation of women implicitly suggests that gender is a kind
of persistent impersonation that passes as the real" (x). *Rhetorical
Drag* locates the "signifying gestures" that certify and authenticate the
"author's" femaleness. While these gestures signify a "real" woman's
voice, they also illuminate the conditions that instantiate gender as-
signment and make it possible for the impersonator to insert "her"/
himself more or less successfully within it. More than a descriptor or
imitation, then, the practice of rhetorical drag generates an environment or a disposition in the captivity narratives that makes it possible
for the impersonator to craft the experiences of gendered subjects.

Each instance of rhetorical drag in this book also signals what Marjorie Garber calls a "category crisis." In her discussion of transvestite
images, Garber argues that "the presence of a transvestite in a text . . .
indicates a *category crisis elsewhere,* an irresolvable conflict or epistemological crux that destabilizes comfortable binarity, and displaces the
resulting discomfort onto a figure that already inhabits, indeed incar-
nates, the margin" (17). Moreover, "category crises can and do mark
displacements from the axis of *class* as well as from *race* onto the axis
of gender" (17). Displacement, as a function of transvestite performance, appears in these narratives not through cross-dressing but, as
Castiglia emphasizes, through culture-crossing. Then, as a second-order
phenomenon, the men who "cross" into a woman's voice displace onto
that rhetorical construction the anxieties and expectations that their
own historical writings produce. The displacement most often emerges
from an epistemological crisis: does the woman's empirical experience
of captivity support or supplant the interpretive authority of the male
historian? The problem of how to use the experiences of conventionally marginalized persons—marginalized by their gender, and often by
their class status as well as by their suspect culture-crossing—lies at the
heart of rhetorical drag.

Accordingly, the subjects constructed by rhetorical drag interrogate
the meanings and values of experiential authority in early American
historiographical work. Jim Egan, in a brief discussion of critical work
on early American women's writing, notes with appreciation that the
recovery and study of women's texts can "make it clear that there are
'experiences' that fall outside the purview of the Anglo-male confron-

tation with another continent and preexisting culture, experience that must nevertheless be considered American" (82). Clearly, early practitioners of rhetorical drag, each for his own reasons and in his own contexts, recognized that "the purview of Anglo-male confrontation," while central or dominant, did not constitute a full historical vision. Many female captives had been taken in colonial warfare; in relating their experiences they could provide a rare view of the enemies "at home," and their tales of captivity served to justify colonial expansionist projects. As well, stories of women's experiences of capture and return helped to reconstitute a patriarchal order broken by warfare but recuperated in the histories of the wars. But, as Egan notes, some critics "too often use unselfconsciously the very terms that require historical explanation" (82), in particular the term "experience," and the use of the women's experiences by the male impersonators posed some difficulties.

Egan argues, for example, that when writers or critics mobilize experience to function as a signifying authority, they present the experiential text as a kind of truth claim based on authenticity and empirical/embodied acts and agency. Joan Scott, too, asserts that this privileging of experience has profound consequences for the work of interpretation: "When experience is taken as the origin of knowledge, the vision of the individual subject (the person who had the experience or the historian who recounts it) becomes the bedrock of evidence on which explanation is built" (81). The experiences that serve as the "bedrock of evidence" in these captivity texts are wrought through imposture; rhetorical drag both *appropriates* the body and voice of the captive woman and *explains* how her experience should be understood within the historical vision of the impersonator. The captivity narratives in this book all rely on the trick of authorial impersonation in order to construct and then recapture the women's experiences as authentic, empirical evidence for the real authors' historical claims.

Indeed, the trickery of rhetorical drag in these texts has succeeded so well that many contemporary scholars interpret the narratives as exemplary specimens of female agency and voice in historical periods comparatively lacking in women's texts. Women's captivity narratives have become major components of scholarly projects that seek to recover women's writing and to expand literary and historical canons. Ironically, scholarly consensus holds that the founding text of the genre,

Mary Rowlandson's *The Sovereignty and Goodness of God Together with the Faithfulness of His Promises Displayed,* was at least mediated by a male author.[6] Yet most studies, while noting instances of editorial intervention, or, indeed, authorial impersonation, do not emphasize its effects or its recurrence throughout the genre.[7] These impostures, however, directly shape the ways in which we might interpret representations of gender, subjectivity, experience, and authorship in the captivity narratives, and they offer compelling examples of the relationship between the writing of history and the regimentation of gender.

The link between impersonation and these representations is foregrounded in *Rhetorical Drag.* By interpreting and contextualizing significant instances of male intervention in women's captivity narratives ranging from 1697 to 1849, I demonstrate that rhetorical drag was assumed for the strategic purpose of directing readers to the writers' own interpretations of colonial and, later, U.S. history. One aim of this book is to note that, while women's captivity narratives rightly have been included in gender and women's studies curricula because women allegedly wrote them, this inclusion evinces the risks of grounding feminist research solely in the alleged experiences of a purported female body. By describing and interpreting some of the early American texts that employed gender imposture, *Rhetorical Drag* seeks to elaborate and complicate the methodological and theoretical bases for the study of gender and historiography.

"Particular Knowledge"

The specific ways in which the female captives are rendered through their speech, especially in their discussions with, and descriptions of, the Native peoples who captured them, demonstrate that the experience of captivity as a woman offered the male writers opportunities to occupy a participant-observer position distinct from the more conventionally male space of contestation. That is, the patriarchal ordering of Anglo-American society made unseemly the image of a male captive working alongside a Native woman, while a female captive's access to domestic details would be naturalized.[8] Thus, the reportage of these details—especially those describing a captive woman's work, habits, and experiences—benefits a male impersonator who wished to produce a dramatic and intimate portrait of Native, and sometimes French colonial, cultural practices.

Each use of rhetorical drag provided a means for these men to construct a captive woman who told her own tale. The image of the speaking and writing woman became a crucial component in the male author/editor's own entry into writing a history of the wars between Native Americans and Euro-American settlers of New England. The men adopted rhetorical drag because, through this mode, they could impute to their own productions the power of the female captives' empirical knowledge of both the events of captivity and the cultural practices of the people who captured her. Accordingly, following Foucault, I ask what a "sociohistorical analysis of the author's persona" entails and "what status [the author] has been given" in order to determine the value and "system of valorization" (107) that female authorship offered these men.[9] Approaching the inquiry with these questions allows me to consider how the attribution of female authorship afforded the male editor, reviser, and/or authorial impersonator "a certain mode of being of discourse" (107). In the narratives, that "mode of being" is the experience of the captive woman, who is figured as a historical informant.

We know that the texts (or rather, the sponsors of the texts) conceived of them as historical works because the prefatory materials in each work explicitly position them as such.[10] The captivity narratives thus assert a cultural authority to tell the truth about the wars they depict, and the veracity of the text, and thus its historical validity, derives from the images of embodied experiences. The displayed bodies described by the speaking/writing female captives are explicitly gendered markers, and gendered categories underwrite the images' instructive, indeed, ideological, force. The women's bodies, purportedly described by female speakers, function as historical evidence. But there is a risk involved in adopting rhetorical drag: ironically, these deeply feminized images undermine the texts' aspiration to assume the cultural authority to tell the truth and simultaneously to explain the meaning of that truth. As the male editors/impersonators note in their prefatory materials, the female speaking "I" as an interpreting voice in historiographical discourse was discrepant, rare, and, because rare, compelling. Indeed in Rowlandson's case, Ter Amicam famously exonerates Mary Rowlandson for "thrust[ing]" her account "into the Press" (Rowlandson 9) on the grounds that it represents her "particular knowledge" (10). This preface endorses a first-person account, because, as Ter Amicam states, it is the *experience* of the other that allows the reader to understand the historical (and here, theological, and indeed, personal) meaning of the events. The power of the experience is most forcefully and directly displayed by the "I" who experiences. By uniting the object—the female captive's body—with the grammatical subject—the woman's "I"—these texts produce a persuasive figure of faithfulness, an alleged reproduction of Rowlandson's experience.

Experience underwrites the effect that several captivity scholars such as William Scheick and Michelle Burnham have termed "authenticity." This "authentic experience," as expressed by the attacked and suffering captive, sanctions the woman's imputed authorship, and, by extension, her publication. As Jim Egan argues, however, contemporary scholars must not take experience as a self-evident "reliable form of knowledge"; rather, we must attend to the "writing that made experience an important category and a source of rhetorical as well as political authority" (12). These captivity narratives should be understood as extensions of the project Egan sees in earlier New England writing: to produce images and stories of experience as a credential of cultural authority. When experience speaks through "empirical" observations and personal narrative, it assumes a new form of cultural authority that may challenge the traditional forms, for example those of state and church. By impersonating captive women, male writers recognized and appropriated this experiential credential while retaining their own positions of patriarchal and often institutional privilege. These women's captivity narratives serve as extraordinary representations of the convergence of old and new epistemological forms and the ways in which those forms produce specific values of authority and authenticity within gendered figurations. Offering a certain model of historical information, a feminized "particular knowledge," the texts relayed to readers in both old and New England, and later, in the United States, the stories and meanings of cross-cultural conflict.

The representations of female experience, however, do not supersede the gender regimes that constrain female intrusion into the domain of historiography. The rhetorical construction of the female captive as both subject and object of her text is unstable, and the instability emerges from the category of experience itself: women's experiences conventionally did not include assuming roles of public authority. Moreover, the long tradition of viewing women's bodies as objects subverts or destabilizes the authority of the captive woman's expression, her voice of experience. That is, her subject position is always threatened by her object position. These first-person captivity narratives therefore simultaneously erected and deconstructed the foundations for their own authority. "Self" expression was mobilized for "self" display, and the tensions that emerge from the conflict between rhetorical subject and historical agent appear most spectacularly in moments of body viewing: when the purported speaker simultaneously sees herself (or, in many cases, sees herself with her infant as an extension of her maternalized body) and tells readers how to read her.

To circumvent the problem of competing conceptual and grammatical categories—the subject-object tension—the impersonators emphasize the captive woman's privileged position as survivor. As Susan Sontag notes, and as the recent Jessica Lynch episode demonstrates, images "of the suffering and martyrdom of a people are more than reminders of death, of failure, of victimization. They invoke the miracle of survival" (87). As survivors, the female captors become privileged *informants* for the men who write their stories because they survived to tell the tale. Moreover, Sontag's commentary on war photography helps to explain, by analogy, the work of the captive woman's voice in these impersonated narratives. Although it is anachronistic to posit such things as early American photographs, we may come to a broader understanding of the manifest cultural meanings of these texts—both for the texts' early American readers and for contemporary readers and scholars—if we read the images of (their "own") survival produced by the women's voices with a consideration of the multiple effects of photography, its capacity to illustrate and to instruct as well as to obscure the hand of the photographer. We might view female captives through the trope of the lens and consider how these female narrators are made to function, by the male authors/editors, on both sides of the "camera," as both composing subjects and composed objects of the narratives.

This doubled effect of the first-person voice as both subject and object is enhanced by the prefatory materials, which positioned readers to interpret the women's voices in specific ways. Thus a key concern of *Rhetorical Drag* is the dialogue, which articulates the captive woman's voice with the authoritative and interpretive apparatus of introductions and annotations. While constructing a woman's first-person voice, the male writer's practice of rhetorical drag also incorporates a variety of editorial methods and textual markers that seek to establish the categories of meaning—experience, and its concomitant values, the authentic and thus the authoritative—that support the claims and practices of historiography.

Each of the women in this study whose voice was "taken from her own mouth" was an actual person who experienced captivity, as far as the historical record can be trusted. Each lived in a sociopolitical relation to the Native (or European) people who held her captive, but each, as well, had a certain status within the culture from which she was taken and to which she returned. Being a woman and being a captive positioned her as a survivor and as a potential informant, as did her social status and her location on a frontier. Each of these subject positions, as well as her embodied experience of captivity, became the provenance, the space from which her voice might speak. Her speaking voice, her "self" expression, became part of a broader cultural landscape, one in which her specific experiences were subsumed into the gender impersonator's vision of colonial and early national history.

Using the Lens

Rhetorical Drag moves chronologically, historicizes each text, and recursively situates each narrative in relation to its predecessors. Not a genre study, but a study of how genre and a set of rhetorical practices converge to fashion history, *Rhetorical Drag* argues that historical voices—privileged, manipulated, purloined—force current readers constantly to reinterpret our own practices with an eye to the "tricky" texts we seek to interpret.

The first chapter examines "The Narrative of Hannah Swarton," the first-person woman's captivity narrative produced by Puritan culture following Rowlandson's *The Sovereignty and Goodness of God*. Rather than review the Rowlandson narrative, a text whose relatively recent canonical status has resulted in more commentary and interpretation than any other captivity narrative, this chapter briefly recurs to elements in *Sovereignty* to demonstrate the Swarton narrative's literal affiliation with it. Following early bibliographers, I argue that Swarton's text is actually the work of Cotton Mather, whose father, Increase Mather, is believed by many scholars to be the editor, or "sponsor," of the Rowlandson text.[11] The Swarton narrative demonstrates that Cotton Mather's act of gender impersonation both enacts a filiopietistic homage to his father and, indeed, does him one better by wholly inhabiting the "I" of Swarton's text.

To contextualize this reading of the narrative, I examine Mather's 1692 treatise on the conduct of women, *Ornaments for the Daughters of Zion*. The affiliations between that text and the narrative demonstrate that the Swarton text is a practical application of Mather's theories concerning women's social roles. A further comparison, derived from formal analysis of his sermon and its Appendix, reveals a direct correlation between Mather's lists of "humiliations" and the experiences that his Hannah Swarton describes in the narrative. Included in this formal analysis is a comparative reading of the figures of Hannah Swarton and another captive, Hannah Duston, whose story ends the sermon proper. Finally, the chapter considers Mather's selective republication of the Swarton account and argues that changes in political and social conditions, as well as in Mather's publication goals, eventually limited the utility of the text's gender imposture and thus ended Mather's career as a female (author) impersonator.

Chapter 2 extends the study of Hannah Duston that emerges at the end of chapter 1. Hannah Duston was in the audience on the day that *Humiliations Follow'd with Deliverances* was preached, and her story is printed as an "Improvement" that appears immediately at the end of the sermon, just before the Swarton appendix. This unusual account is a description of an escape from captivity during which Hannah Duston killed and scalped her captors, including several children. The text is enclosed within quotation marks in the sermon, and it is written in the third person. Chapter 2 traces Duston's reputation from this third-person account through later versions by Thomas Hutchinson (1764), Timothy Dwight (1816), John Greenleaf Whittier (1831), Benjamin Mirick (1832), Nathaniel Hawthorne (1836), and Henry David Thoreau (1849).

Each version of Duston's account grapples with the enormity of Duston's behavior, and each offers a remedy or apologia for the gender transgression of killing and scalping. While these revisions reveal the limitations to using the "I" of an author/captive whose reputation is impeached or suspect, I argue that the revisionists recognized these limitations in the Duston story and developed strategies to accommodate them, while using Duston's experiences in their own historiographical projects. The dominant strategy for policing Duston's gender transgression is to impute a proto-psychological motivation for her acts, thus circumventing the first-person voice by supplying a "voice" of conscience. Rather than impersonating the violent captive, the men impute "appropriate" gender characteristics by assigning thoughts, feelings, and responses to Duston. The shift from gender impersonation to gender imputation underscores my argument that rhetorical drag is crucial to understanding the performative aspect of gender in the captivity texts: the male authors fashion a Duston whose femaleness is utterly dependent upon the ways in which they think she should have acted. Their drag thus encompasses not just the body but their entire ontological reconstruction of the captive.

For each of the male writers following Cotton Mather, Hannah Duston's actions offer an entry into literary and historiographical *self*-expression that is directly tethered to gender formations at the time of their writing. This "Duston function," for example, permits Hawthorne to counterpose her savagery to her husband's fatherly devotion and provides Whittier with a model for a hysterical maternalism. The chapter culminates in Thoreau's appropriation not only of Duston's notional words but also of her body.

Chapter 3 examines *God's Mercy Surmounting Man's Cruelty,* the 1728 captivity narrative of Elizabeth Hanson, and demonstrates that rhetorical drag might be used to diminish female agency in contexts in which women actually had religiously sanctioned access to public expression. While the Society of Friends initially encouraged women's public speech to a much greater degree than Puritans did, my reading of the Hanson narrative argues that Quakers adopted gender impersonation to craft a model of female comportment that sought to redress earlier Quaker practices. Hanson's narrative can be traced to an unidentified "Transcriber" who, according to the title page of the first edition, took the relation from "her own mouth." However, as I demonstrate, strictly controlled Quaker publication practices make it probable that more than one hand was involved in shaping this text.

This example of a Quaker captivity narrative employs Hanson's voice to reproduce images and themes from the earlier Puritan narratives but with a noteworthy tenor of passivity. The passive tone offers a new model of female behavior that contrasts sharply with the tradition of Quaker women's outspoken public carriage, particularly in colonial New England, and as such it indicates that the Hanson narrative served a specifically gendered program of public relations for the Quaker men who published it.

In order to set the narrative in a larger religio-cultural frame, the Hanson chapter draws extensively on early Quaker history: its martyrology, radical gender egalitarianism, reports of persecution in New England, and most importantly, the Society's evolving censorship practices. As well, the chapter compares the Hanson text to an earlier Quaker captivity narrative, Jonathan Dickinson's *God's Protecting Providence* (1699). This comparison emphasizes the degree of gender differentiation the Society sought to impose by the early eighteenth-century publication of Hanson's narrative in order to rehabilitate gender roles from the early egalitarian models of public activity toward a more conventional, male-dominated public sphere.

Chapter 4 examines two texts, *The Narrative of the Captivity of Mrs. Johnson* (1796) and *A Genuine and Correct Account of the Captivity, Sufferings and Deliverance of Mrs. Jemima Howe* (1792). By the late eighteenth century, women's print publication was no longer an unusual phenomenon, and, accordingly, these texts offer different sets of rationales for the use of rhetorical drag. The Johnson and Howe texts draw on the richly developing discourses of sentiment to tell the stories of the captives. Unlike the earlier narratives, these texts were composed and published almost forty years after the captivities took place. Both accounts tell the tales of women initially captured by Indians, but whose captivities are spent for the most part among the French in Canada.

Unlike the earlier captivity narratives, the Johnson and Howe texts, by portraying events from the French and Indian War, assume a status as historical documents at the time of their publication. This characteristic is emphasized in the Howe text, which displays a persistent self-consciousness about its own historical standing, a self-consciousness that can be attributed to the Reverend Bunker Gay's fashioning of the text for use in Jeremy Belknap's history of New Hampshire. As well, both *The Narrative . . . of Mrs. Johnson* and the *Genuine and Correct Account . . . of Mrs. Howe* draw on the emerging cult of sensibility—in particular, female sensibility—that influenced many of the women's novels of the period. Both texts demonstrate that women's writing in this period, whether historical or literary, had to exhibit the gender traits associated with domesticity and sentiment. Moreover, these texts should be considered within the context of recent critical debates advanced by Michael Warner, Larzer Ziff, Jay Fliegelman, and Christopher Looby, among others, which argue for the cultural meanings of print versus performative, or "voiced," representations in the early Republic.

Additionally, the chapter offers data from archival research into the authorship of the Johnson narrative and reveals that, although current critical scholarship presumes that Johnson herself wrote the text, it is probable (and has been asserted by earlier bibliographers) that the actual author was a local man, John C. Chamberlain, a New Hampshire lawyer and participant in a circle of literati that included Joseph Dennie and Royall Tyler. Johnson's narrative offers a fine example of rhetorical drag, and the narrative therefore is a key text for a critical discussion of the cultural meanings of pseudonymity as a complex collaboration of voice and print extensively practiced in the early Republic.

As well, the Howe texts clearly demonstrate the value of a woman's voice for early American historiographers, especially as the narrative represents a revelatory example of the writing of local history. This kind of historical discourse, which the Duston chapter examines through nineteenth-century revisionists such as Timothy Dwight, Leverett Saltonstall, and Thoreau, constructs an American history based in the local and viewed through an antiquarian lens. Following the trajectory of various Howe versions, the chapter traces historiographical trends from the filiopietistic to Romantic antiquarianism, focusing on the ways in which the woman's voice and experiences are appropriated for the male writers' projects. Howe's language appears to be directly imported from contemporary seduction novels, and the various rhetorical interpolations—in particular, letters to, from, and about Howe—rely heavily on gendered constructs of sentiment and sensibility and on popular epistolary conventions to authenticate Howe's voice.

This book is, of course, deeply indebted to previous studies of captivity narratives. Without the groundbreaking rediscovery work of

Pearce, Vaughan and Clark, Slotkin, and, more recently, Derounian-Stodola and Levernier, the current explosion in critical work would not have been possible. Kathryn Z. Derounian-Stodola's earlier work on captivity narratives, especially her series of articles on the Rowlandson narrative, has made my study possible. Derounian-Stodola and James Levernier's *The Indian Captivity Narrative, 1550–1900* includes a section on authorship in which the scholars describe the tangled thickets of captivity narrative authorship, although they choose examples from the nineteenth century, bypassing the texts in my study. They argue that the "combined skills of historians, biographers, bibliographers, and textual critics" must be brought to bear on any inquiry into the historicity of the captivity narratives, and they maintain that "ultimately, inferences should not be determined or differentiated by the vehicle of their presentation unless a thorough study has been completed concerning the background of the narrative. Any investigation of the captivity narratives must, therefore, be text- and culture-based, not author-based, because authorship is so problematical" (13). *Rhetorical Drag* follows this advice in both spirit and method.

Of the recent critical studies, Christopher Castiglia's *Bound and Determined* offers a brilliant and carefully researched argument about the crucial role of women's captivity narratives in the formation of the notion of "white womanhood" and images of "culture-crossing." Michelle Burnham's *Captivity and Sentiment* as well as the incisive and invaluable introductory essays in several anthologies (see Sayre and Derounian-Stodola) have provided theoretical, historical, and intellectual background for this work. *Rhetorical Drag* extends these important studies and offers another "lens" on captivity, as Annette Kolodny famously characterized her early feminist intervention in the scholarship of captivity. In reexamining the conditions that produced these narratives—the impersonated "I," the attention to, and fashioning of, specifically gendered rhetorical forms and figures, and the historical and literary aims of the authors and publishers—*Rhetorical Drag* reads these "tricky" elements as crucial components in the formation of early American literary and cultural history.

CHAPTER I

~∞~

"Being Read with a Greedy Attention"

Mather in Drag

Indeed, there are more women than men in the Church and the more virtuous they prove, the more worthy will the Church be to be figured, by a woman that fears the Lord.
—Cotton Mather, *Ornaments for the Daughters of Zion*

Cotton Mather's 1692 treatise on "the character and happiness of a virtuous woman" reveals the moral power vested in representations of Puritan women.[1] For Mather, virtuous women not only constitute the majority of church membership, but they in fact *embody* the virtues he exhorts his entire congregation to practice. The preeminent value of God-fearing women in the church derives from their figuration: they are models to be observed and copied. As such, they have social value as exemplars but no personally vested power as historical agents because, as observed figures, they cannot, in Mather's formulation, interpret their own behaviors to others, to the observers. That interpretive power belongs to male writers like Mather who use the model of a virtuous woman for their political, social, and religious interests.

Virtuous or not, women could not be ministers, and only in rare cases had they access to publication.[2] They practice virtue but do not preach it. Anne Hutchinson's case is the most noteworthy evidence of this phenomenon among the Puritans, but the unseemly sight of a woman preaching informs the Puritan disapprobation of Quaker practices as well. Excluded from pulpit and press, the conventional conduits of moral instruction in Puritan New England, women were instructed to lead virtuous lives, which might then be rendered into a suitable *representation* of virtue, most often by male preachers and authors such as Cotton Mather.[3]

Mather predominates among male interpreters of female piety, but he is by no means the only one to recognize the didactic potential in the figure of the virtuous woman.[4] His *Ornaments for the Daughters of Zion* became a popular conduct book for later generations of pious women, and the text offers various roles for women to play within Puritan culture, including the role of author.[5] However, the focus of *Ornaments* is the goodwife figure, whose sphere is family and congregation, a woman laboring in the home and quietly proclaiming God's grace through her faith. This prevailing image of women as quintessentially familial and bound by church community recurs throughout Puritan literature, in texts both about women and supposedly written by them. Mather's concern in *Ornaments* is with the salvational possibilities in representations of women: how can he render their figures for the improvement of the entire church? Yet his use of the female image exceeds the purposes of religious instruction and demonstrates the broader social and political aims of Mather's historiographical project.

By producing a woman's figure in print, bringing her experiences and expression into the public realm, Mather mirrors the central act of Puritan life: public confession of the personal experience of justification in the church. When the circumstances of a Puritan's conversion experience were spectacular, purported transcriptions of those oral recountings were often published as appendixes to sermons. Mather's *Warnings from the Dead,* for example, was printed with "a pathetical *Instrument,* in Writing" "obtained" from Elizabeth Emerson shortly before her execution for infanticide.[6] Elizabeth Emerson's "writing" warranted publication because of her notorious reputation as the murderer of her own infants and because she apparently (according to the "Instrument") accepted the full weight of spiritual and civil retribution for the murders. Thus, the conventional Puritan proscription against a woman speaking in public was superseded by the powerful instructional potential of her recorded voice. The dispensation accorded Mary Rowlandson to publish her captivity narrative relied on this same exemplary function, although Rowlandson stood in good repute. The rarity of a publication by a woman enhanced the value of the lesson she proclaimed; Rowlandson became the unique case that demanded attention. However, representations of singular or unconventional women necessitated complex rhetorical constructions to refashion images of these women as both spiritually excellent yet socially transgressive. A woman presuming to teach or lead by invoking her own experiences became a woman out of bounds.

Female public expression embodied this tension between exceptionalism and transgression, and the notoriety attendant upon a woman's publication under her name imputed to authorship both conditions. Authorship of printed matter thrust at least the figure of the author into the public domain, to be considered as part of the text, the name on the title page. Michel Foucault's discussion of the role of the author's name in ascribing to "its" text a "certain mode" and a "certain status" suggests this linkage (107). Women's authorship not only classified the text as exceptional in seventeenth-century Puritan discourse, but it also affiliated the work with historical images of femaleness. "Obviously, one cannot turn a proper name into a pure and simple reference. It has other than indicative functions: more than an indication, a gesture, a finger pointed at someone, it is the equivalent of a description" (105). This descriptive attribute conferred on the female author an array of characteristics derived from cultural representations of women. Historical precedent—in the case of Puritan discourse this is often construed as biblical reference—and the personal reputation of the writing woman shaped the text's production *and* interpretation of gender roles. Specifically, in the culture of Puritan New England, the woman's reputation had to adhere to strict models derived from biblical types or emblems. The virtue of the female author manifested in her good reputation, and ministers molded her reputation, recasting it for the lessons at hand.

Texts attributed to female authors in this period often explicitly express anxiety concerning the tension between sanctioned publication and suspect personal exhibition occasioned by Puritan gender regimes. These texts repeatedly stage the problem of offering to the public a spiritually conducive text that simultaneously displays the female self. Yet this tension also provides the space for inscription, a compositional gap that can be filled with language that generates both the text itself and the figure of the woman writing it. Puritan texts ascribed to women, such as Anne Bradstreet's poetry or Mary Rowlandson's narrative, illustrate the social utility of that space for advancing Puritan beliefs and practices.[7] They draw on the exceptionalism/transgression of the first-person female voice, with its emphasis on the woman's reputation, and, in the case of captivity narratives, they invoke the singularity of the dislocated and spiritually stranded captive.

This singularity is grounded in the captive's experience. Again, Egan's point is crucial here: scholars must attend to the "writing that made experience an important category and a source of rhetorical as well as political authority" (Egan 12). When Increase and Cotton Mather produce women's captivity narratives, they do just that: by reproducing the women's captive experiences *in the women's first-person voices,* they mobilize a powerful rhetorical effect to underwrite, literally, their cultural and political authority as interpreters of providential history.

To understand the rhetorical potential of the captive woman's first-person voice, I examine Cotton Mather's long treatise on proper female conduct. In *Ornaments for the Daughters of Zion,* the most prolific writer of the period fashions a historical and religious overview of women's roles and the value of reputation. This consideration of women, especially women as authors, provides an insight into the provenance of one woman's captivity tale, "A Narrative of Hannah Swarton." In the Swarton text, Mather mobilizes seventeenth-century Puritan views of female public expression to serve some of his culture's dominant ideologies and to advance his own historiographical project. He accomplishes this by appropriating Swarton's voice as well as her experience. Elaborating on rhetorical elements found in the Rowlandson text, he produces the perfect captivity narrative, one that accords with his version of the Puritan errand in New England. Hannah Swarton's story begins, then, within Mather's vision of righteous women and goes on to develop tropes and figures found in the Rowlandson narrative. This combination presents us with a unique opportunity to interrogate the representation of female experience and its public expression in authorship within New England Puritan contexts. As well, by attending to the Swarton narrative's structure and figuration, we discover that, for Mather, not only the church, but also providential history, should be "figured . . . by a woman that fears the Lord."

"Wise unto Salvation"

Ornaments for the Daughters of Zion offers several roles for women in Puritan society, including authorship. Mather argues that "our God has employ'd many women to write for the Church, and inspir'd some of them for the writing of Scripture" (3). Considering European and North American women writers, he asserts, "for even the Books publish'd by that Sex were enough to make a library far from contemptible, nor has even the New English part of the American Strand been without Authoresses that would challenge a Room in such a Library" (3–4). Mather cites Anna Maria von Schurman, a Dutch pietist, and he implicitly refers to Anne Bradstreet, the most familiar "authoress" of Puritan New England.[8] In fact, at several points, *Ornaments* argues persuasively that women should write and presumably publish their compositions, and Mather admonishes those who would deny women the intellectual, but more importantly the moral, authority to write: "a Privilege not far from the second Advancement of that Sex may be Esteemed, that share which it has had in writing those Oracles which make us Wise unto Salvation. As one woman was the Mother of Him who is the Essential Word of God, so divers women have been the writers of his Declarative Word" (3).[9] For Mather, women's writing is analogous to motherhood, specifically to the divine motherhood represented by Mary. The simile that links maternity with the process of writing allows Mather to promote an identity of "female" with "mother" in order to illustrate the generative parallels. Women's experiences of maternity thus sanction their participation in cultural reproduction, permitting them to reproduce their experiences in their own voices.

Mather's identification of women writers as mothers is metaphorical in this instance, but contemporary seventeenth-century texts published with attributions of female authorship often emphasized the author's actual maternal role. In some cases, the texts were published specifically as artifacts for the spiritual consumption of the author's family. For example, Sarah Goodhue's 1681 letter, a publication allegedly composed in the Goodhue home and "found after her decease," is "directed to her husband and children with other near relations and friends,"[10] a small audience indeed.

Goodhue's text begins "Dear and loving Husband" then addresses the children for five of its twenty paragraphs. Following Anne Bradstreet's model, the text includes a poem that names each child in a couplet. The children are admonished to "be ruled by him [their father]" and to "Endeavour to learn to write your father's hand, that you may read over those precious sermons, that he hath taken pains to write and keep from the mouths of God's lively messengers" (521). Curiously, the charge is "to learn to write" that they may read, rather than to compose their own meditations or take notes on the lessons from the pulpit. For the children, writing therefore becomes a tool of secondary import, an instrument toward the greater end of reading their father's notes on homilies. Part of Sarah Goodhue's maternal concern is to reinforce the power of the father. Although the letter contains many passages advising the children on proper conduct, its central image is "a tender-hearted, affectionate and entire loving husband" (522). Sarah Goodhue's role as spiritual advisor to her children is everywhere surpassed by the representation of her husband as teacher. As the mother is to the children, so the husband is to the wife.[11] It is he who writes, she who reads and hears, the sermons she now misses due to illness: "Was it not to this end that the Lord was pleased to enable thee and give thee in heart to take (as an instrument) so much pains for his glory and my eternal good, and that it might be thy comfort: As all thy reading of scriptures and writing of sermons, and repeating of them over to me, that although I was necessarily often absent from the publick worship of God, yet by thy pains and care to the good of my soul, it was brought home unto me" (523). Joseph Goodhue thus carries the public word, "an instrument" for domestic dissemination of the ordinances, back to the privacy of his home for his wife and children to study.

Consistent with the figure of the writer as an instrument of God, Sarah Goodhue's husband is the conduit of spiritual teaching: his is the primary writing in the text. Thus the presumed author attributes her spiritual progress to the man who writes for her to read. The figure of Joseph Goodhue as father and teacher dominates the text: Sarah Goodhue's own writing acts as a testament to her husband's writing and to *its* value for her children. Within the house, Joseph Goodhue reports the teachings of the ministers and thereby reenacts the scene of public worship, with the gendered hierarchies intact.

Goodhue's letter displays some characteristics recurrent in the early Puritan texts attributed to female authors: the author's husband plays a prominent role in the text,[12] and it contains an apology justifying the writing.[13] Its title page, emphasizing that it is the dying testament of a wife and mother, presents the Puritan woman as a hinge figure within the home. Although subject to her husband's authority (even the apparently benign authoritarian practice of Joseph Goodhue), at the same time she represents an authority figure for her children. Moreover, by the sheer act of writing she assumes an authoritative position even while proclaiming her submissiveness. The textual representation of an eminently virtuous Sarah Goodhue, who writes about her familial and spiritual experience within her home, conforms to Cotton Mather's statement in *Ornaments for the Daughters of Zion* that the church is worthy to be "figured by" such a woman.

Sarah Goodhue's figure of piety and obedience thus grounds and makes possible the publication of this text. The letter attributed to her reinforces the public teachings about private familial relations, and, by portraying a Puritan family in which authority operates along properly hierarchical—and gendered—lines, the Goodhue text uses the wife/mother image to bring the private into the public, published realm as an intact representation of the orderly Puritan household. This articulating wife/mother figure illustrates power relations flowing through a single subject who both receives and delivers the homiletic instruction and interpretation that Harry S. Stout characterizes as "the central ritual of social order and control" (3), the nexus of Puritan cultural power.

Because she both learned from her husband (himself an instrument of the ministers) and taught her own children, Sarah Goodhue represented a proper example of a female writer. Her social value, even in death, derived from her good reputation as a dutiful wife and mother. Motherhood, however, was not a prerequisite for all women authors, as is evident in Mather's *Ornaments*. Exemplified by the unmarried Pietist Schurman, many of these were impossible models for religious and social practice in the daily conditions of New England society. Furthermore, in his second Conclusion, Mather provided a catalog of heroic women, from Thomyris, "that could lead an Army against the Persians, and Zenobia that could head an Army against the Romans," to Queen Elizabeth. These women, virtuous and wise public agents (warriors and rulers), join "the Daughter of Pythagoras who made Comments on her Father's Books," Hypatia, and "the Empress Eudocia, who composed Poetical Paraphrases on divers parts of the Bible" (36). Amazons and intellectuals, historical women represented courage, wisdom, and usefulness, either as military leaders or scholars, but these roles simply were not available to the goodwives of Boston. This array of notable and comparatively privileged women provided Mather with justifications for his argument that women could be virtuous, despite the legacy of Eve: "But, behold, how you may Recover your impaired Reputation! The Fear of God will soon make it evident, that you are among the Excellent of the Earth" (43).

"Those Public and Precious Privileges"

Reading across the Atlantic and back to antiquity for examples to remedy women's "impaired Reputation," Cotton Mather emphasized specifically female virtue in order to amplify his point that women are "rational" as well as "religious," that, in fact, the rational and the religious are mutually reflective.[14] Dismissing traditional representations of women as inherently irrational beings (but careful not to name the authors of the "scurrilous" texts), Mather championed virtuous and wise women, among whom were the "New English Part of the American Strand," the authoresses of Puritan New England.

By the 1692 publication date of *Ornaments,* the "New English" authoresses most familiar to a New England reading public were Anne Bradstreet and Mary Rowlandson. Both women required champions: Bradstreet's Boston edition was posthumously published, and the preface to Rowlandson's *Sovereignty* "To the Reader" famously displays the anxieties attending an act of female publication. Both Bradstreet's death and Rowlandson's "modesty" necessitated the common practice of including a preface by another hand, but beyond these considerations, the content of the prefaces spoke to the peculiarity of women's writing. They served as apologias for the authors and mitigated the extraordinary phenomenon of a woman's emergence into the public sphere.

But the prefaces also functioned as a version of the *nihil obstat,* absolving the female author from an imputation of unseemliness or lack of virtue. Ter Amicam warned the reader in his preface to Mary Rowlandson's narrative: "I hope by this time none will cast any reflection upon this Gentlewoman, on the score of this publication of her afflictive deliverances" (66). Reputation was a constant concern for the female author, and, as seen in the cases of Anne Hutchinson and Mary Dyer, and even the notorious Mistress Hopkins,[15] outspoken women were particularly at the mercy of those men who refigured them within institutional discourses such as court testimony and sermons as well as occasional publications. Rigorous gender segregation and the concomitant restraint on public roles mandated that women's writing be controlled by men's writing, compositions that bracketed and interpreted not only the primary text but also the public perceptions of the authoress.

Ter Amicam's preface directs a reading of Mary Rowlandson's narrative that focuses on its function as an example of divine intercession. The series of images, specifically the tribulations and privations she suffers, constructs a spiritual exemplum, full of "the many passages of working providence discovered therein" whereby "the Lord hath made this Gentlewoman a gainer by all this affliction" (67). The preface ends with a warning: "Read therefore, Peruse, Ponder, and from hence lay up something from the experience of another, against thine own turn comes" (67–68). Rowlandson's text is "a memorandum of God's dealing with her" (65), and Rowlandson, captive then author, functions as an aid to the imagination: "none can imagine" and "no serious spirit . . . can imagine" her captivity (67). In narrating her own experiences, Rowlandson gives the reader an image from which he or she can "lay up" the lessons of extreme suffering and deliverance.

Susan Sontag's formulation of the work of war photography offers a useful heuristic here, because the images produced in the Rowlandson text seek to unite what Sontag, reading Virginia Woolf, sees as the primary work of photographic representations of atrocity.[16] Sontag notes that contemporary cultural expectations tend to allow "photographs to be both objective record and personal testimony, both a faithful copy or transcription of an actual moment of reality and an interpretation of that reality—a feat literature has long aspired to, but could never attain in this literal sense" (26). What Sontag characterizes as an *unachieved* aspiration of literature in fact constitutes the fundamental claim of historiographical description; this linkage—conflation, even—of "objective record" and "personal testimony" in the verbal image of the historical informant asserts and confirms the faithfulness of the "transcription of an actual moment of reality."

Sontag's construction of literature's aspirations, this goal of uniting "objective record" and "personal testimony," aids us in understanding some of the meanings of the images produced in the Rowlandson narrative. Ter Amicam's preface requires readers to find in the text a conflation of the powerful categories of gender and of personal experience. Significantly, this goal is deeply embedded in the text as providential history. Ter Amicam asserts that, along with the biblical stories of Joseph, David, and Daniel, these stories "do represent us with the excellent textures of divine providence, curious pieces of divine work: And truly so doth this [the Rowlandson text]" (65). The preface therefore argues that the narrative will "truly" represent "divine work" in King Philip's War, and the veracity of the text—and its historical validity—derives from the images of Rowlandson's embodied experiences.

Rowlandson's body, as described by her voice, is an explicitly gendered marker, and gendered categories underwrite this image's power as an instructional, indeed ideological, artifact. Her embodied experience, "spoken" by Rowlandson through the text, functions as historical evidence, here, evidence of providential work. But, as Ter Amicam makes clear, this deeply feminized image undermines the texts' aspiration: to assume the cultural authority to tell the truth and to explain the meaning of that truth. The female speaking "I" may serve to bear witness but not necessarily to explain the meaning of its own experience.

However, the power of the experience is most forcefully and directly displayed by the "I" who experiences. By uniting the object—Rowlandson's body—with the subject—her "I"—the narrative produces a powerful figure of faithfulness, here, a putative reproduction of experience.

Those experiences are exceptional; as Ter Amicam notes, "so none can imagine what it is to be captivated . . . but those that have tryed it" (67). Captivity was a rare experience for New England settlers in 1682, in comparison to its frequency in the succeeding decades of warfare. With little precedent other than the biblical captivities, it was a condition wide open to interpretation and (mis)representation. For example, the preface alludes to the sexual vulnerability of the female captive unless divine intercession "curb[s] the lusts of the most filthy" (67), although rape was virtually unknown in the Indian cultures of northern New England. This physical threat to Rowlandson's chastity echoes the preface's concern for her reputation, her "modesty" (65). Indians might endanger her body, but both the actual experience of captivity and the narrative's publication threaten her standing as a Puritan goodwife.

The public representation of both her body and her voice requires explanation and exculpation; thus Ter Amicam preemptively defends Rowlandson's propriety: "And therefore though this Gentlewomans modesty would not thrust it into the Press, yet her gratitude unto God made her not hardly perswadable to let it pass, that God might have his due glory, and others benefit by it as well as her self" (65–66). He first emphasizes that captivity can only be thoroughly appreciated by those who have suffered it and then demands that the reader sympathetically identify with Rowlandson.[17] Finally, he interprets Rowlandson's experiences as evidence of divine dispensation. Through Ter Amicam's interpretation, the personal experience is transformed into a providential sign for all to read and understand. Here lies the justification for publication: because the text dramatizes God's mercy, specifically the spectacular form it takes in the New England forests, it warrants dissemination as example. This fact takes precedence over all others, including the threat to the woman's reputation. The dual definitions of dispensation, in its Puritan construction, allow for such flexibility. As both a system of divine ordering and a license for exceptional cases, dispensation provides a sense of God's plan, albeit not completely revealed, coupled with the concept that that plan is made visible through the unique experience of the individual, especially if the experience is itself unusual.[18] Thus, Rowlandson receives a dispensation to publish because her experience testifies to "God's glory." Yet the problem of the public woman lingers. Ter Amicam explicitly acknowledges Rowlandson's violation of boundaries when he commands the reader to "excuse her then if she come thus into publick, to pay those vows [to publish this manifestation of God's mercy], come and hear what she hath to say" (67).

As a woman assuming the public stance of author, Rowlandson requires preemptive forgiveness, and so the preface rhetorically grants absolution by its insistence on her exceptionalism: "Let such further know that this was a dispensation of publick note" (66). Another aspect of Rowlandson's special status derives from her husband.[19] As

"that worthy and precious Gentlewoman, the dear Consort of the said
Reverend Mr. Rowlandson" (65), Rowlandson reflects the glory of "that
faithfull Servant of God, whose capacity and employment was publick in the house of God" (66). His "publick" employment devolves
onto her, and she acts as her husband's proxy, privately, by attempting
to defend their children in the attack (Joseph Rowlandson was away
requesting more defensive aid for the garrison) and publicly, by publishing the narrative, which presents readers with "many passages of
working providence . . . worthy of public view" (65). This work replicates the mission of a Puritan minister. The Mary Rowlandson of the
preface is truly an instrument of the ministry as well as an example of
"the Soveraignty of God, who doth what he will with his own" (67).

The tension between proscribed behavior and the didactic potential in exceptional circumstances accounts for the preface's reiteration
of the words "publick" and "publication." Those repetitions and the
text's concern for Rowlandson's reputation indicate the difficulty Puritan discourse had in publicly representing the (embodied) voice of a
woman. Rhetorically, Ter Amicam recognizes and solves the problems
by alluding to the unique and socially transgressive image of the female author, only to recuperate it. Declaring that no one can know the
sufferings of captivity, save those who have endured it, Ter Amicam
precludes objections to a woman "coming into the Press" (65–66) because none would know the value of her story—except Ter Amicam,
who instructs readers in its correct interpretation. Rowlandson functions as God's instrument, exemplifying providential care of "his dear
ones" (65); just as she is the beneficiary of a divine dispensation, her
text should be received as a special emblem of that dispensation. By
aligning the exceptional condition of captivity with the unique event
of a speaking woman, Ter Amicam uses gender roles to demonstrate
the extent of divine favor granted believers, even, and especially, under
unusual conditions.[20]

Writing as Ter Amicam, Increase Mather seizes on the instructional
potential in the figure of the virtuous woman, especially the virtuous
woman cast in exceptional circumstances—as does his son. In this
respect, the captivity narratives of Mary Rowlandson and Hannah
Swarton shift away from the operations at work in a text such as the
Sarah Goodhue letter. Women's captivity narratives such as Rowlandson's manipulate the double exceptionalism of wilderness survival and

female first-person public voice to represent the possibilities for Puritan practice in any place, at any time, and by anyone adhering to Puritan principles of self-examination and public confession, even a woman.

The extraordinary divine favor that sustained Rowlandson in her captivity experience thus carries over to permit, indeed, mandate, the publication of her story. More temporal than divine, this obligation to publish recasts the woman as an instrument whose text testifies both to providential favor and to her own special status within Puritan society. As her captivity has demonstrated, she is God's chosen, and her story therefore enjoys a divine and ministerial imprimatur. The woman's captivity narrative is a twice-blessed text, first in its author and then in its content. Once the ministerial preface approves the publication, the female author's text gains cultural authority from the rare use of a woman's first-person voice describing her own embodied experiences, a use, as Ter Amicam makes clear, that requires a special dispensation in order to enter the public realm.

Mary Rowlandson's text, as the first of its kind in Puritan New England, set criteria for subsequent writings in the captivity genre, although it is impossible to prove that Increase Mather knew this at the time of publication. Ter Amicam certainly indicates in the preface that he understood the possibilities for instruction and persuasion in the story. Emphasizing both dispensation and reputation, the preface creates in Rowlandson a kind of Puritan celebrity: she is biblically typed with Joseph, David, and Daniel but also represents a unique New England experience.[21] "To the Reader" explicitly links Ter Amicam's instruction with his personal evaluation of Mary Rowlandson as "Gentlewoman" and wife of the minister Joseph Rowlandson. He thus confers on Rowlandson the requisite credentials that allow her to speak her experiences by focusing on her reputation as a minister's wife singled out by God to demonstrate divine mercy. That is, his endorsement, indeed, construction, of her reputation in print covers her body and legitimates her voice.

This combination of divine and ministerial authority, turning on the concepts of dispensation and reputation, can be found operating in subsequent captivity narratives attributed to women. When both God and a Mather interest themselves in a woman's text, there is certainly much at stake for Puritan culture. The doubled instrumentality of the female first-person narrator provides unique opportunities for lessons that exceed spiritual instruction and encompass larger issues of political and social import.[22] The figure of the female captive who returns to write her story demonstrates the means by which Puritan ideologues not only refashion geographical and political frontiers but also reshape the cultural frontiers demarcating private-public discourse.[23] In this way it reconfigures the scene of public witness: the customarily silent woman not only testifies to personal salvation, but also speaks her experience in the broadest possible manner, the printed text.

In the conjunction of images of captivity, gender, and authorship found in women's captivity narratives, representations of power, powerlessness, and social authority exist in a dynamic relationship to one another. For example, Ter Amicam endorses Rowlandson's publication to give evidence of divine dispensation and thereby asserts his prerogative as minister to grant legitimacy (his dispensation) to her unusual undertaking. However, it is Rowlandson herself, moving across the New England landscape and finally encountering King Philip, who earns the experiential authority to speak to the public in her voice—to publish—the particulars and the consequences of her captivity.[24] In this case, divine and ministerial authority present the singular female who recounts her exceptional tale to spread the news of Providence at work in the New England wilderness. The preface seeks to control the representation of Rowlandson's voice and experience under the rubric "dispensation" and to place her safely back within the fold.[25]

It is important to note that Rowlandson's journey begins and ends within the pale of Puritan practices. Although Lancaster was an outpost settlement, Rowlandson's husband was the minister for the community, and Rowlandson returned to Boston, where her story was published.[26] Thus, with all her removes, Mary Rowlandson's journey terminates in the heart of New England Puritan culture.[27] She spent her entire captivity among the Narragansetts in the wilderness, and the captivity had lasted approximately three months, an excruciatingly long time for her, but not nearly as long as other captivities. These particulars of the Rowlandson captivity differ extensively from subsequent narratives. We may view her text as the preeminent example of the genre not only because it is the first of its type and relatively long, but also because its dramatic rendering of physical hardship and mental anguish produces rich images of the conditions of captivity.

However, an examination of those captivity narratives published in the last years of the seventeenth century reveals that *The Sovereignty and Goodness of God* offers later writers not so much a model to emulate as a template against which to measure differences.

Stresses in Puritan culture reveal themselves in these differences. Reading for the ways that subsequent female captivity narratives vary from Rowlandson's (and on occasion echo it), we can recognize several cultural preoccupations. The texts address prescribed gender roles (and their corollary, the fashioning of a reputation) as well as fears concerning the vulnerability of northern borders to Indian and French attack. Variations in and circumstances of publication—including date of publication, accompanying or embedded texts, attributions of authorship, and contemporary contextualizing documents—demonstrate that the seventeenth-century women's captivity narratives address an array of issues: shrinking spheres of Puritan influence (and declension in the spheres purported to be properly constituted congregations), control of historiography (especially the writing of New England Providential history), and the wars against the French (with the implicit threats of papistry). This catalog of dread partially illustrates the broad context of the Puritan "errand into the wilderness" and the place (and utility) of women's voices and experiences in it.

Understanding the importance of gender in these narratives allows us to examine the errand, especially as its messengers attempted to construct a coherent society by instruction. Since instructional texts were crucial to shaping the culture, authorship represents a powerful instrument serving those, like the Mathers, who held positions of authority. Authorship poses a great burden—to display truthfully working Providence—and a great avenue to power as an agency of cultural formation. The circumscriptions governing female authorship, notably dispensation and reputation, permitted some spiritual and political leaders to reconfigure the female author, from *subject* of her narrative to *object* used for instructional purposes. Thus they could control the persuasive power of a personally exorbitant author, whose "particular" experiences make her an instrument in their hands.

The Hand-Maiden as Instrument

Properly an instrument is an efficient cause moved by the principal to an effect above its proper virtue.
— *Baxter's Catholic Theology* (1675)

Writing begins with an awareness of the person, not as an individual but rather as a social category.
— Jonathan Goldberg, *Writing Matter*

The cultural prominence of the Mathers throughout the seventeenth
and early eighteenth centuries arises from several factors that include
their longevity and their prolific publication. Both Increase and Cotton Mather wrote on a range of issues that extended beyond particular theological concerns; the topics of their publications vary from
printed execution sermons to treatises on comets or the efficacy of
inoculations against smallpox. Diary entries by Cotton Mather testify
to his almost obsessive concern with his own authorial practices and
with publication.[28] Like the description of Joseph Goodhue's sermon
notes as God's "instrument," Mather considered his writing a means
to further the work of Providence on earth.

Some of Mather's diary entries illustrate the collapse of distinctions
between "private" writing—for example, Joseph Goodhue's notes—
and "public" writing, here defined as the publication by printing
press of texts meant for wide circulation. Particularly, Mather's emphasis on the trope of instrumentality confounds a reading of strictly
bound realms of private and public. In the long entry for 20 August
1697, Mather records a day "sett apart, for the Exercises of a secret
THANKSGIVING before the Lord" (1: 226). Having first confessed
his "horrible Sinfulness," he writes: "I then solemnly declared unto
the Lord, that I made *Choice* of this, as my *chief Happiness,* to bee a
Servant of my Lord JESUS CHRIST, and an Instrument of His Glory"
(1: 227). He follows this declaration with a catalog of reasons for
thanksgiving. The "one special Article" is God's support for finishing
what will become the *Magnalia Christi Americana,* here called "my
church-history": "I will in this Place, transcribe a few Lines of my Introduction to that History" (1: 229).[29] Thus the private diary receives

a transcription of the (proposed) public document, and its introduction is embedded within the personal accounts of Mather's daily life, where he records his determination to act in God's behalf. Writing, both private and public, represents an essential instrumentality, an exalted endeavor in which Christ is coauthor and for which Mather acts as both author and publisher.[30]

Authorship, for Mather, is simultaneously the act of an instrument and the instrument itself.[31] For example, the public document signed at Mather's behest by the contentious members of the Watertown church represents both the means and the sign of reconciliation: "I did endeavour to do service, (especially, at miserable *Watertown,* bringing the People in the east part of that poor Town, to sign an Instrument, wherein they confessed the Errors of their late Actions, and promised by the Help of Christ, a regular Behaviour; and otherwise helping the Council that mett there)" (1: 235). This doubled function of the authorial instrument—both tool and testament—collapses the public and private realms. With divine guidance, Mather expresses his interior life to provide teachings and models for the public. Although all authors convert private thought into public expression, Mather's conception of instrumentality *conflates* his private thoughts with divine intention. The provenance of these expressions—his sermons, histories, biographies, and retellings of current events—explicitly appears as God, the First Author, with Mather as temporal author and instrument. Authorship therefore is the public rendering of a providential aim privately revealed to Mather as willing recipient of divine favor—"His favouring mee, with the *Liberty of the Press*" (1: 228).

Among the stratagems Mather chose in publishing his divinely inspired texts were anonymity and pseudonymity. In "To the People of New England," the opening address of *Decennium Luctuosum,* Mather argues for his own anonymity as the author of his history of the ten-year war with Northeast tribes. However, the text includes a sermon delivered by him the previous September. He then elaborates on the conceit of anonymity by aligning his hand with God's, effectively making himself the instrument of divine revelation: "I pray, Sirs, Ask no further; Let this Writing be, like that on the Wall to Belshazzar, where the Hand only was to be seen, and not who'se it was. The History is compiled with Incontestable Veracity; and since there is no Ingenuity in it, but less than what many Pens in the Land might Command, he

knows not why his Writing Anonymously may not Shelter him from
the Inconveniencies of having any Notice, one way or other, taken of
him" (181). The purposes of this (false) anonymity, couched in terms
of reticence and, especially, humility, are obscured by claims of "Incontestable Veracity," an assertion that "the Author pretends that the famous History of the Trojan War it self comes behind our little History
of the Indian War" and most directly by the invocation of the biblical
hand of God as a simile for the authorial hand. Thus the instrument
and the power that it serves become one, and given Mather's strongly
idiosyncratic style, the authorship could hardly be in question for most
who read this "anonymous" history, even had they been absent from
the original sermon.[32]

Mather's convoluted approach to authorship—his alternate claims,
denials, and demurrals—achieves its most peculiar form in the captivity narrative of Hannah Swarton. Appended to his 1697 printed
sermon *Humiliations Follow'd with Deliverances,* the Swarton narrative stands at the end of a work detailing the tribulations of captives
from the continuing skirmishes with the tribes along the frontiers. It
is textually distinct from the body of the sermon, literally designated
an appendix; like Rowlandson's, the Swarton narrative is written in
the first person. The story portrays a Hannah Swarton whose startling—and suspicious—capacity for theological debate indicates her
exceptional grasp of subtle doctrinal positions, noteworthy in a frontier woman. And the curious dialogue this narrative conducts with the
larger text that precedes it (and, to some extent, with Rowlandson's
narrative) demonstrates some uses of the first-person female narrator
both within the Mather canon and within the broader sphere of New
England Puritan literature. In these respects, the Swarton narrative
avoids the tensions resulting from what Tara Fitzpatrick calls the "dueling textual voices" of the narrator and "the established ministers,
who vied with the returned captives for authorial control of their narratives." As she convincingly argues, "the women captives' ministerial
sponsors sought, with decreasing success, to interpret the individual
experiences of the captives as lessons directed at the entire community,
regardless of the captives' own implicit resistance to such appropriation" (3). But Mather's complete authorial appropriation of Hannah
Swarton's "I" produces a new set of tensions, ambiguities, and images
that speak more to *representations* of female voice and the author's

reputation than to the exceptional status of the returned captive and her need to tell her own story.

Hannah Swarton left no personal records apart from the alleged narrative of her captivity. Her name appears in the list of redeemed captives presented by Mathew Cary to the Council of the Massachusetts Bay Province in October 1695.[33] There, she appears as "Johana Swarton" from the town of York. As Emma Coleman notes, there are several errors in the hometown ascriptions of the various captives, and from the narrative we know that Hannah Swarton resided in Casco (now Portland), Maine (Coleman 1: 74). Margaret Stilson, who was "in the same house with [Swarton]," was redeemed by Cary as well, although Colonel Tyng and Mr. Alden, mentioned as members of the captive English contingent in Quebec, were not on the list of those redeemed.[34]

The historical record of Hannah Swarton,[35] then, exists in the Cary list and in the appendix to Cotton Mather's 1697 text, "A Brief Discourse On the MATTER and METHOD, Of that HUMILIATION which would be an Hopeful Symptom of our DELIVERANCE from Calamity. Accompanied and Accommodated with A NARRATIVE, of a Notable DELIVERANCE lately Received by some ENGLISH CAPTIVES, From the Hands of Cruel INDIANS. And some Improvement of that Narrative. Whereto is added A Narrative of Hannah Swarton, containing a great many wonderful passages, relating to her *Captivity and Deliverance.*"[36] According to the testimony of the "Narrative," Hannah Swarton moved to the Casco settlement from Beverly, Massachusetts, and, as such, lived outside the public ordinances of Puritan polity. This lack of ministerial control differentiated most Maine settlers from other captives, who, exposed though they were in the frontier towns such as Haverhill and Lancaster, had the benefit of established congregations.[37] Indeed, the inhabitants of the Province of Maine historically had been a thorn in the side of the Massachusetts Bay Colony, not only aligning themselves with the Crown during the uprising of 1688 but then also petitioning King William for "assistance and protection" against the Massachusetts rebels.[38] Maine had a bad reputation as a region of outlaws, "ungospelized plantations,"[39] and, as a corollary to that, Catholic sympathizers—a thicket of renegade settlers requiring the firm hand of Congregationalist discipline. The settlements in Maine did not function as proper frontier buffers; instead, they represented the threat of a porous, exposed, and vulnerable array of backsliding or irreligious

English communities, established to trade with the Indians and French rather than congregated around an ordained minister. Both the political and religious concerns with these outlying settlements emerge in Mather's portrait of Hannah Swarton.

In his bibliography of Cotton Mather's works, Thomas Holmes notes that the Swarton narrative "printed for the first time in *Humiliations*, is told, unlike the [Hannah] Dustan account, in the first person. Evidently Cotton Mather was Hannah Swarton's 'ghost writer.' The narrative is printed entirely without quotation marks. The story is told with rich and intimate details of Swarton's experience, but the text of it in polished prose, embellished with Biblical references, allusions, and illustrations, with occasional moralizings in the true Matherian manner, is clearly Mather's."[40] Holmes notices the affiliation between the stories of the two Hannahs who appear in *Humiliations,* Duston (variously spelled "Dustin" and "Dustan") and Swarton. Although the Swarton text "was advertised in *Tulley's Almanack* for 1697 as a part of an intended publication entitled *Great Examples of Judgment and Mercy,* that work was probably not printed. . . . We know that the Swarton Narrative as it appears in *Humiliations* was printed with this work and does not consist of sheets printed with and transferred from any other work, for the Narrative begins on signature E2, while the leaf E1 contains the last two pages connected with the Hannah Dustan Narrative" (2:496n.6). Mather includes Duston's heroic escape from her captors in the primary text but appends Swarton's relation as a cautionary tale of the spiritual perils of frontier life in an ungospelized plantation. Whereas Duston's experiences emphasize her divine deliverance and Mather celebrates her heroism, Swarton is most clearly marked out for humiliations. As Mather's instrument for instruction, the Swarton narrative administers a warning to those choosing to live "outside the public ordinances," and, more significantly, it baldly reveals Mather's use of authorial prerogatives. By ghosting for Hannah Swarton, Mather could become her, simultaneously representing her experiences and projecting himself *as Hannah* into the northern wilderness and the parlors of the papists.[41]

Some captivity scholars, such as Ulrich, Ebersole, and Strong, maintain that Hannah Swarton wrote her own narrative, although their evidence for this position is arguable. Strong asserts that the text does not display the "typifying epithets characteristic of Mather's descriptions of Indians" that appear in his other writings (123–24). It is important to note that, if Mather were engaging in gender impersonation, as I will demonstrate, he would need to adopt the body and voice of Swarton, not inhabit his own distinctive voice.[42] Similarly, Ebersole argues, and Strong concurs, that the text resembles a conversion narrative, a genre open to all Puritans and encouraged by church practice. This resemblance in itself might just as easily be read, as I argue below, as Mather's manipulation of generic conventions for his own ends. Indeed, his production of Elizabeth Emerson's *Instrument,* although not strictly a conversion text, purported to express her spiritual state before her execution (see discussion of Emerson below). Ultimately both scholars' arguments seek to retain Swarton's authentic voice as the provenance of the text in order to construct and interpret her agency within the captive experiences.

These arguments demonstrate the crucial need for scholars to attend not only to the conditions of the publication of texts attributed to women but also to the rationales that drive our scholarship. When Ebersole rejects Vaughan and Clark's suggestion that the narrative's "abundant and precise biblical quotations suggest a clerical hand" (Ebersole 148), he seeks to emphasize the sophisticated scriptural awareness and religious practices of lay Puritans (78). Significantly, his advocacy of lay spiritual capacities leads Ebersole to an implicit moral condemnation of scholarly positions such as that of Vaughan and Clark (and, by extension, mine), because "the Vaughan-Clark position strips the ordinary men and women of their basic human dignity by denying that they, too, could be hermeneuts in their own right" (79). In the particular case of the Swarton narrative, and in each of the instances of gender impersonation considered in this study, I hope to demonstrate that rhetorical drag is not in itself a morally repugnant instance of fraud, nor does it represent a denial of any of the captive women's "basic human dignity." Rather than examine the phenomenon within this frame, we may read the purloined voices and experiences as carefully controlled representations that shape and are shaped by powerful discursive regimes, particularly gender regimes. Mather's Swarton, seen through this lens, is an *artfully* and *successfully* rendered rhetorical strategy, a woman's voice that simultaneously invokes the distinction of female experience and is circumscribed by the culture's expectations of gendered behaviors. This conflation drives Mather's performance.

We can glean something of Mather's profound understanding of rhetorical manipulation in his apparently intimate writing. Diary entries for the autumn of 1696 illuminate Mather's motives for publishing Swarton's story. His entry for 2 October describes a "secret Fast" practiced "Especially to obtain Mercy for this Land in its deplorable Circumstances, and a mighty Revolution upon the Kingdomes of Great Britain and upon the French Empire" (1: 205). Again, on 10 October he keeps a day of prayer for "Captives in the hands of cruel Enemies" with the resulting "Newes that came the Day following, of several Persons, escaped out of the Hands of the Indians" (1: 206). Mather's interest in the captives forms part of his larger political concerns. When he prays, his personal spiritual needs often align with the colony's more global interests: he "wrestled with the Lord" to obtain the knowledge that "a mighty Convulsion shall bee given to the *French* Empire; and that *England, Scotland,* and *Ireland,* shall bee speedily Illuminated, with glorious Anticipations of the *Kingdome of God*" (1: 207). For Mather, indeed, the personal (and, therefore, spiritual) is the political (and, therefore, historical).

The *Diary* notes as well Hannah Swarton's place in this expansive scheme. Eager to make use of "the terrible Disasters wherewith *some* are afflicted," Mather prepared for publication "a *Collection* of terrible and barbarous Things undergone by some of our *English Captives* in the Hands of the *Eastern Indians.* And I annexed hereunto, a memorable *Narrative* of a good Woman, who relates in a very Instructive Manner, the Story of her own *Captivity* and *Deliverance.* . . . Yea, I could not easily contrive, a more significant Way, to pursue these Ends; not only, in respect of the *Nature* of the Book itself, which is *historical* as well as *theological;* but also, in respect of its coming into all Corners of the Countrey, and being read with a greedy Attention" (1: 210). The "who relates" would seem to indicate that Swarton herself composed this text, but, as Holmes asserts and as an examination of the text's style and content demonstrates, the printed text is Mather's composition. The emphasis on the story's instructional use and on Mather's contrivance to publish something to be read with "greedy Attention" reveals the value of exceptionality in a woman's text, particularly as a magnet for public notice. "Historical" as well as "theological," and purportedly produced by a captive woman, this captivity narrative provided Mather with ample opportunity to pursue his "Ends," to "contrive a more significant Way."

His choice to impersonate Hannah Swarton rather than employ the third person depended for its success on the concepts of dispensation and reputation, apparent in the Rowlandson narrative, and here reconfigured to suit the circumstances of Swarton's 1690 Maine captivity. The dispensation is formal, inhering in the narrative's function as an appendix to the sermon; the text itself requires no apologia because its publication is literally contextualized. Reputation, however, is a more complicated matter, and this key concept enabled Mather to write in the first person as Swarton. Unlike Mary Rowlandson, "Gentlewoman" wife of a minister, Swarton lived in a free-floating frontier society, one relatively unconstrained by the rigid hierarchies within which reputation gains meaning. Indeed, as far as Boston was concerned, Hannah Swarton had no reputation—until Mather conferred one. In impersonating Swarton, Mather chose an outlier, a castaway from the Maine woods, a woman whose personal value in the Puritan hierarchy was insignificant. The text thus recognizes and manipulates the conventions of both gender and social status.

While Mary Rowlandson tried in her narrative to recuperate her social "credit" by publishing her sufferings, the Swarton text never addresses the anxieties Rowlandson displays, especially those concerned with reintegration into Puritan society. This is because Hannah Swarton's credit was identical to her text, both invented by Cotton Mather. He simultaneously constructed a reliable, reputable witness *and* her narrative, one "instrument" in the conflated Matherian sense of agent and document. The fiction of the first-person voice succeeds because the actual Hannah Swarton is a social nonentity and because her experiences produced a tale of humiliation and deliverance that dramatized the lessons of the sermon.[43] To that end, Mather employed the figure of Swarton to illustrate the individual points of his homily.

Humiliations begins appropriately with an image of Old Testament punishment, a scourging, and emphasizes the "Instrument, every stroke whereof gave *Three* Lashes to the Delinquent" (*Humiliations* 3). In the appendix, Hannah Swarton performs the dual role of delinquent and instrument for the readers of the printed sermon; she is both sinner and means of redemption because, in confessing her sins and properly suffering for them, she provides a completed figure of the redemptive process by which the reader can "lay by" the lesson. As Mather asks at the outset, "What signifies confession without reformation?" (*Humiliations* 14) and the re-formed Hannah embodies deliverance—after humiliation.

The sermon was "preached at the Boston Lecture on Thursday, May 6, 1697" and a "public fast was observed a week later" (Holmes 2: 488). As a jeremiad, it called for a fast to address the "Sad *Catalogue* of *Provocations*" (*Humiliations* 7) by which the population had angered the Lord and thereby drawn down his wrath. These provocations included twenty offenses, ranging from apostasy to "the woful Decay of good *Family Discipline*" (*Humiliations* 9). There is little attempt to classify the sins by degree of severity, so that the "multitudes" castigated for being unregenerate are listed along with the problems evinced by "a *Flood* of *Excessive Drinking*." *Humiliations* thereby stands as a compendium of ministerial anxieties and preoccupations that predictably encompasses both spiritual and social issues, personal salvation and cultural conformity.

For example, referring to the text of 2 Chronicles 12.7 ("When the Lord saw, that they humbleth themselves, the Word of the Lord came unto Shemajah, saying, They have humbled themselves, I will not destroy them, but I will grant them some deliverance"), the second lesson describes the necessity of regular fasting, a duty not practiced "often enough" by the church in New England: "Like Silly Children we know not when to *Feed,* and when to Forbear *Feeding.* But our Good God, in His Word ha's taught us!" (*Humiliations* 23). This theme is retrieved in the Swarton appendix with an ironic twist: "For the first Times while the Enemy feasted on our English Provisions, I might have had some with them: but then I was so filled with *Sorrow* and *Tears,* that I had little *Stomach* to Eat; and when my *Stomach* was come, our English Food was spent, and the Indians wanted themselves, and we more: So that then I was pined with want" (*Humiliations* 52). Swarton, "Like a Silly Child," represents not only the extreme of enforced fasting, but also the willful behavior of someone who succumbs to her emotions rather than attending to her needs. As well, Swarton's "want of Cloathing," so that she is "pinched with Cold," aggressively answers the sermon's call to put aside "Gay Cloaths" for "Sober, Modest, Proper, and very Humble" attire and symbolizes the chastisement due to *"Churches* [who] fall asleep till they are stript of their Garments" (*Humiliations* 26, 34). This congruence of the sermon's aims and Swarton's embodied experiences recurs to Mather's vision, in *Ornaments,* of the church "figured by a woman that fears the Lord."

The preeminent icon of *Humiliations* is the *Judea capta* motif. As Annette Kolodny notes, "New England divines were quick to seize upon the emblematic, *typick* features inherent in the increasing incidence of captivity."[44] Mather recalls a tradition of coins made in commemoration of the Roman conquest of Israel then contextualizes it with one of his favorite scriptural representations of womenhood, the Daughter of Zion: "She being Desolate, shall sit upon the Ground" (*Humiliations* 31). As in *Ornaments for the Daughters of Zion,* the church (here synonymous with "New-England") is again figured by a woman. Translated from Israel to the northern woods, Judea no longer leans against a palm tree: "Alas, If poor *New-England,* were to be shown upon her old Coin, we might show her *Leaning* against her Thunder-struck *Pine tree, Desolate, sitting upon the Ground.* Ah! *New England!* Upon how many Accounts, mayst thou say with her, in Ruth I. 13. *The Hand of the Lord is gone out against me!"* (*Humiliations* 31). Mather tropes the woman/tree figure in the appendix, creating the image of Hannah Swarton, "pined with want," "pined to Death with Famine," and exhausted to the point of utter resignation, "so that many times I thought I could go no further, but must ly down, and if they would kill me, let them kill me" (53).

Yet Swarton "held out with them," sturdily marching, outlasting poor John York, who, weakening under duress, was killed by the Indians. Significantly, the only people who die in this narrative are men; women prevail throughout. The absence of men in the Indian captivity section of the Swarton text echoes their absence from the sermon (excepting the brief allusion to Thomas Duston's escape from the Haverhill attack). Mather closes the theological section of the sermon with a question: "Now, who can tell, how far one *Humble Soul,* may prevail, that shall put in Suit, the *Sacrifice for the Congregation?"* (*Humiliations* 39). The answer sat in front of him at the lecture in the person of Hannah Duston. Her trials readily provide the conclusion to the sermon proper, and her actions and experiences, in many ways, determine the figuration of Hannah Swarton.

The relationship of the two Hannahs is crucial to an understanding of what is at stake in the publication of the Swarton narrative as a first-person text. In dialogue with the sermon, the Swarton text reconfigures the image of a woman—the heroic, yet murderous, Duston, who killed and scalped her captors—superseding her role. The entire "Appendix" immediately follows the Duston passage, which is itself part of the sermon but distinctly bound within quotation marks. As well as creating a passive counter to the active Duston, the first-person Swarton text purports to be Swarton's version of her own experiences, a simultaneous claim to authenticity and immediacy figured in her body and voice. The Duston story, however, is removed from this immediacy graphically, by the quotation marks (which reveal it to be someone else's version of the events), and grammatically, by its third-person narration.

Indeed, the title page of *Humiliations* refers to the Duston escape tale as "A Narrative, Of a Notable Deliverance lately Received by some English Captives, From the Hands of Cruel Indians, And some *Improvement* of that *Narrative*."[45] Hannah Duston may have initiated her own escape, but at the Boston lecture she heard her own exploits narrated back to her, recontextualized—"improved"—by Mather, her exceptional acts reconfigured for the purposes of the sermon. Hannah Swarton, captured, sold to the French, and ransomed back to Boston, represents not only the more common fate of the captive, but also the value of passivity. That is, Duston is transformed from an active subject to a passive object, while Swarton, the passive sufferer, becomes the narrator of her own story, the speaking subject. Female resistance, even in Duston's version, needed to be contained: Swarton is ascribed the unusual role of author precisely because she is a nonresisting woman, humiliated by her sins, one whose reputation is based on her experiences in captivity then manipulated for its instructional value. The image of the passive woman, even one writing her own story, provides rhetorical closure in the printed version of the sermon that contains her words.

The juxtaposition of Hannah Duston and Hannah Swarton speaks to the problem of redeeming the captive woman from her position out of bounds, again a question of dispensation and reputation. As I will discuss in the next chapter, Duston's dispensation for her lethal actions derives both from her extraordinary deliverance and from her position outside the law: "and being where she had not her *own Life* secured by any *Law* unto her, she thought she was not forbidden by any *Law*, to take away the *Life* of the *Murderers*, by whom her *Child* had been butchered" (46), and her reputation is made upon her return by the acclaim she receives.[46] The repetition of "Law" and the emphasis on her child's murder surely attempt to justify Duston's actions. But for those in the congregation who recall the trial of 1693, the line reverberates with the fate of Duston's sister, Elizabeth Emerson, who was executed for infanticide. As I indicated above, Mather had a personal connection to Emerson, which is noteworthy because he not only preached the sermon on her execution day, but he later published that sermon with "a pathetical *Instrument*" "obtained from the young Woman."[47] Although one was punished and the other praised, the significant characteristic shared by the sisters is a capacity for violence, indeed, for murder. In light of Elizabeth Emerson's story, Mather's transformation of Duston from active deliverer to passive listener becomes more urgent: Duston's killings require exculpation in order to divorce her (frighteningly similar) behavior from her sister's.

Symbolically, however, Hannah Duston's exorbitant actions are redeemed through the representation of Hannah Swarton. Referring to a biblical figure, the sermon asserts that Duston and her companion Mary Neff "do like another *Hannah*, in *pouring out their Souls before the Lord*" (45). The concatenation of Hannahs creates an affiliation, from the Old Testament to Duston to Swarton, with Duston set off by the figures who "pour out their souls." The Hannah of 1 Samuel supplicates the priest Eli, and Swarton asks forgiveness while recounting her wilderness experiences: they reach out to the elders for deliverance. Thus an implicit comparison is set up between the two New England Hannahs. The "improvement" following Duston's story, directed at Duston, Neff, and Lennardson, makes it clear that none of the escapees had publicly confessed the *spiritual* experience of redemption. So, Mather admonishes them, "You will seriously consider, *What you shall render to the Lord for all His Benefits?*" (49). Hannah Swarton's narrative, which contains her testimony of spiritual redemption, concludes with that same text. Swarton therefore recuperates the still unregenerate Duston by providing the image of a woman who undergoes conversion during her captivity, thus making her first-person narrative worthy of dispensation and producing her new reputation. That is, if Duston's experience is noteworthy because it represents divine intercession resulting in her physical redemption, Swarton's story displays the greater providence of a religious conversion. Thus, at least in Mather's hands, female captivity permits a broad range of behaviors as long as the woman ends up firmly ensconced in the ministerial text, recaptured for Puritan instruction.

In this respect, the Swarton text improves on previous captivity stories, particularly Mary Rowlandson's. Cotton Mather authorizes his own work by obviously alluding to the popular 1682 text introduced by "Ter Amicam" (Increase Mather). Cotton Mather improves on his father's text, however, not merely by writing a preface but by composing the entire narrative. And, in following the Rowlandson text, Cotton Mather concludes the Swarton narrative with the same scripture (Psalm 116.12) Ter Amicam uses in his preface: "To conclude: whatever any coy phantasies may deem, yet it highly concerns those that have so deeply tasted, how good the Lord is, to enquire with David, *What shall I render to the Lord for all his benefits to me.* Psal. 116.12" (Rowlandson 115–16). While Ter Amicam admonishes redeemed captives (and their readers) to "enquire with David," Cotton Mather literally puts those words in Swarton's mouth ("What shall *I* render . . . ?") after he has used them himself in his address to Duston.

In several ways, then, "A Narrative of Hannah Swarton" becomes a condensed version of *The Sovereignty and Goodness of God,* its language and images abbreviated, telescoped, and combined in a rush to get to the crucial encounter with French Catholics. For example, the sense of urgency and chaos depicted through Rowlandson's twenty "Removes" is condensed in Swarton's terse statement, "Thus I continued with them, hurried up and down the Wilderness, from *May* 20, till the middle of *February"* (*Humiliations* 52–53). Whereas Rowlandson remained in the wilderness with the Indians from February 1675/6 to May 1676, Swarton's captivity lasted five years, from May 1690 to November 1695, and was mostly spent in Canada. (She arrived "in sight of some French houses" in February 1690/91). Yet the Rowlandson narrative is a book-length text, running to seventy-three pages in its 1682 Cambridge edition, while the Swarton "Appendix" is only twenty-one pages long.

The popularity of Rowlandson's narrative may have been reason enough for Mather's translation of some of its elements into his own publication. In recalling many features of the Rowlandson text, Mather at once asserts the primacy of *The Sovereignty and Goodness of God* and establishes the female captivity narrative as a genre with standard images: privation in the woods, loss of kin, and spiritual conversion. Mather's reiteration of Ter Amicam's scriptural quotation both in the Duston section and the Swarton narrative signals another, less obvious but potent, component of the emerging form: whether the text is prefaced by a minister or actually written by one, the (purported) authors depend on the sponsoring ministers for the dispensation to publish. The Rowlandson text, with Ter Amicam's preface and Joseph Rowlandson's closing sermon, gives Cotton Mather a model for ministerial publication that he quite capably wholly inhabits for his "*historical* as well as *theological*" project.

Both indirectly and directly quoting Rowlandson's narrative, Mather provides a shorthand, recognizable digest of wilderness suffering en route to Quebec. But Indian captivity is not the focus of the Swarton narrative. Hannah Swarton's main adversaries are not her captors, the murderers of her husband and son, but the French, who imperil her immortal soul. The distinction between Swarton's relationships with the Indians and with the French can even be traced in the narrative's disposition of pronouns: at times "we" refers to the English captives, at times to Swarton and her Indian captors, but "we" never comprehends the French. Unlike Mary Rowlandson, who resented her Indian mistress, and Hannah Duston, who killed two men, two women, and six children, Hannah Swarton seems sometimes even to appreciate her captors. She is often left alone with her Indian mistress, and the two fend for themselves, subsisting on a maggoty moose liver or contacting a canoe of squaws who give Swarton a roasted eel. The spiritual bond she will later form in Quebec with Margaret Stilson is foreshadowed in this earlier connection with the Indian women who tend to her physical needs, what Swarton calls her "outward man."

The brevity of the Indian captivity section allows Mather to acknowledge the physical dangers of life on the frontier on his way to the real matter at hand: emphasizing the spiritual traps awaiting English settlers placed in proximity to French Catholics. As well, the narrative exposes failures of the English missionary project when Swarton's "Indian mistress" declares "that had the English been as careful to instruct her in our Religion, as the French were, to instruct her in theirs, she might have been of our Religion" (*Humiliations* 55). There is hardly a religious or, for that matter, political concern of Puritan culture not addressed in this text.

A passage near the end of the narrative reveals just how far Mather will stretch captivity conventions to suit his ends. He uses the narrative to address contemporary social and political concerns, whereas the Rowlandson text, in general, confines itself to spiritual and psychological matters as they arose in *Indian* captivity. Removed from the wilderness, safe from Indian captors, Swarton finds herself serving in a French household. A theological debate ensues between Swarton and her French masters. Surprisingly adept at arguing doctrinal subtleties, Hannah Swarton functions most obviously here as Mather's instrument to prove the superiority of Puritan doctrine and practices over Catholic. The text itself nods toward the improbability of an unconverted frontier woman triumphing in theological argument with "the Nuns, the Priests, Friars, and the rest" (*Humiliations* 62). After a breathtaking scholarly fusillade from both sides, during which the Catholics bombard Swarton with scriptural passages and she answers in kind, the narrator confesses, "But it is bootless for me, a poor Woman, to acquaint the World, with what Arguments I used, if I could now Remember them; and many of them are slipt out of my memory" (*Humiliations* 64). Hannah Swarton triumphs because she has God (and Cotton Mather) on her side. That she is "a poor Woman" only makes the victory more compelling because she excels in a man's realm, with the sanction, and considerable rhetorical skills, of a Puritan divine.[48]

However, the indictment of Hannah Swarton's memory after so sharp a demonstration of its facility—when she literally cites chapter and verse to counter the Catholics—subverts the debate's authenticity and, ultimately, the very authority for the text, her remembrances. The authorial voice falters here, perhaps retreating from that frightening Hutchinsonian image of the female preacher, and reveals the fiction of the historical Hannah Swarton's authorship. From the description of her arrival in Quebec, we know that Swarton could not speak French, yet her skills improve dramatically so that she can hold forth against her adversaries. This, and the relentless interpolations of Mather's interests, should give the game away for later commentators. Yet Fitzpatrick ascribes authorship to both Mather *and* Hannah Swarton, contending that, although "Swarton's narrative conveyed the most absolute submission to the will of God, . . . [it] again conflicted with Mather's interests in transcribing her story" (17).[49] It is difficult to see a conflict of interests, given that the narrative produces not only a redeemed soul but also representations of religious declension, missionary failure, French coercion, Indian brutality, and the dangers of life outside Puritan polity: all images and themes Mather consistently employed to critique the political and religious establishments in Boston for administrative laxity in Maine.[50]

A redemption occurring without benefit of the "public ordinances" might seem to certify the exceptionality of Hannah Swarton.[51] However, in captivity, Swarton does find a "congregation" among the other captives in Quebec. In the midst of spiritual despairs over her own regeneracy, the narrator states, "I had gotten an *English Bible,* and other Good Books, by the Help of my Fellow Captives" (*Humiliations* 66). By means of this Bible and meditation, she achieves an understanding of her own salvation and describes it in the conventional language of conversion, noting the "Ravishing Comfort" (67) that fills her, and harkening to her previous sinfulness.[52] The group of English captives provides an impromptu reconstruction of basic Puritan practice:

> *I* found much Comfort, while *I* was among the *French,* by the Opportunities *I* had sometimes to *Read* the Scriptures, and other Good Books, and *Pray* to the Lord in Secret; and the *Conference* that some of us Captives had together, about things of God, and *Prayer* together sometimes; especially, with one that was in the same House with me, *Margaret Stilson.* Then was the Word of God precious to us, and they that *feared the L O R D, spake one to another* of it, as we had Opportunity. And Colonel *Tyng,* and Mr. *Alden,* as they were permitted, did speak to us, to confirm and Strengthen us, in the wayes of the Lord. (*Humiliations* 68)

Although neither Tyng nor Alden is an ordained minister, they function as representatives of the ministry in their exhortations to spiritual strength. The women pray together at home, but in the public world of the captive congregation, men lead. When the French finally prohibit the gathering, Alden sends a message *"that this was one kind of Persecution, that we must suffer for Christ"* (*Humiliations* 68–69). Thus, as Fitzpatrick notes, captivity "relocat[es] the central experience of trial and redemption" (17), but this narrative does so by reconstituting Puritan community in the "wilderness" of French homes and churches: the text explicitly refers to Swarton's "Captivity, among the *Papists*" (*Humiliations* 69).

In Quebec she is treated well by the French woman from whom she begs provisions and is finally bought by the "Lady Intendant." The emphasis upon female community reinscribes proper gender roles, which in themselves render Swarton properly passive. The first part of the narrative depicts Swarton obeying her Indian master and mistress, as when she aids them by gathering berries. When she arrives in Canada, however, this replaying of the Puritan domestic gives way to the pressing concerns of spiritual contest; once she finds herself in a functioning household, the role changes. As Laurel Thatcher Ulrich notes, Boston ministers saw the threat of Catholicism as more deeply troubling than the Indian menace, especially where the captives were women, because "twice as many females as males remained with the [French] enemy." She attributes this behavior to "the primacy of marriage, the influence of religion, and the supportive power of female networks" (*Good Wives* 208). These networks, explicitly portrayed in the scenes with her Indian mistress and the squaws, disappear once Swarton's captivity with the French becomes the focus of the narrative. Her only female friend in Canada is the Puritan Margaret Stilson.[53]

Indeed, the relatively condensed account of Indian captivity comes to a remarkable conclusion with a spectacular image. When Swarton visits the first European home she has seen in nine months to beg for food, she is given beef, bread, and pork and is expected to return to her captors. "But the Snow being knee deep, and my Legs and Hams very sore, I found it very tedious to Travel; and my sores bled, so that as I Travelled, I might be Tracked by my Blood, that I left behind me on the Snow" (*Humiliations* 60). Immediately after this sentence, Swarton asks to spend the night at the French house, and she never returns to the Indians. Here, the transformation in circumstances, which the narrative characterizes as a "Change, as to my *Outward man*," opposed to the "*Inward man*," is marked in blood. In the forest, suffering from scant cover, Hannah bleeds; once in French hands, she is brought to the hospital, where she is "Physicked and Blooded" (*Humiliations* 62). The move from external to internal, registered in blood, signals the beginning of her greatest trial. Previously, Swarton's emblematic suffering resonated with other accounts of wilderness captivity. Her blood on the landscape writes the recognizable tale of survival as seen in Rowlandson; in this respect, blood provides a metaphor for female authorship, the marks on the page that construct her tale of suffering. The shift from outward to inward "man" actually represents a shift from passive female captive to active male debater; moreover, Swarton's blood also marks the end of her story and the initiation of Mather's theological tour de force.

With this shift, the Swarton narrative's value as an Indian captivity tale is superseded by the powerful image of Protestantism conquering Catholicism.[54] Textual evidence—the amount of text dedicated to French, as opposed to Indian, captivity, the reconstructed Puritan congregation in the heart of Canada, and the passive Indian captive turned aggressive theological warrior—indicates that this story, although initially echoing previous captivity narratives, has a different agenda. It is indeed a tale of suffering, conversion, and return. And as a conversion narrative, it reinforces the concept that the greatest battles occur internally, in the form of spiritual wrestling in the privacy of the soul. Yet this wrestling is then externalized in the theological debates. Thus the flow of Puritan instruction is channeled into Hannah, then out again to the French, via Hannah Swarton's fictive authorship, an instrument of Mather in the Canadian wilderness.

"The Wonderful Dispensations of Heaven"

When Mather turns to history to chronicle ten years of debilitating Indian warfare, he constructs thirty "articles" to illustrate the awful depredations endured by English settlers throughout New England. *Decennium Luctuosum* is a catalog of horrors graphically informing readers about scalpings, eviscerations, immolations, and hatchetings. A series of captivity stories appears in the text, including "Article XXV," "*A Notable Exploit; wherein Dux Faemina Facti,*" the tale of Hannah Duston. Published only two years after *Humiliations,* however, *Decennium* does not include the Swarton text. Mather used his own material from other sources to compose the book, and the opening articles recount early skirmishes on the eastern frontier. It would seem that Hannah Swarton's story, beginning with the attack on Casco, would fit naturally into this scheme. But *Decennium Luctuosum* emphasizes Indian brutality, not French religious coercion. In fact, the final pages of the book portray the fallacies of Quakerism rather than the importunities of French Catholicism. Therefore, although the "Narrative of Hannah Swarton" purports to be an Indian captivity narrative, a personal account of suffering in the hands of the natives, it is more accurately characterized as a French captivity narrative, a "*historical* as well as *theological*" exercise. As such, Mather rightly excludes it from his study of the "sorrowful decade," keeping his antipathies focused on the "Nations of Indians."

As self-denominated historiography, *Decennium Luctuosum* moves away from earlier homiletic tracts employing current events to demonstrate providential displeasure. The text's obsessive classicism, interpolating more Latin and Greek than scripture, secularizes the project, albeit within the scope of Puritan providential history. Here is no sermon to instruct readers in the path of salvation but rather a highly sensationalized register of relentless misery, and occasional relief.[55] As conventional historiography, it required the omniscient authority of third-person narration. In the self-effacing tone adopted at the outset of *Decennium*, Mather states: "In Truth, I had rather be called a Coward, than undertake my self to Determine the Truth in this matter; but having Armed my self with some good Authority for it, I will Transcribe Two or Three Reports of the matter, now in my Hands, and Leave it unto thy own Determination" (14–15). He includes accounts from "a Gentleman of Dover" and "a Gentleman of Casco," which indict not only the Indians but particularly Governor Andros for their roles in fomenting the hostilities. The language of both accounts replicates Mather's own perfervid prose in the introduction and the following text; when he appends a third account, "which was published in September, 1689," it is an excerpt from one of his own sermons, *Souldiers Counselled and Comforted.*[56] Significantly, the "Gentlemen" whose reports are embedded in this Mather text produce an entirely different discourse from the Swarton narrative. Theirs is literally named "Authority" and represents public witness to political events, not personal (and spiritual) experience. So although Mather "transcribes" male authors to support his history, this purloined authorship is contextualized as historical, public, and authoritative: an admitted transcription, not a fictionalized first-person relation.

The last printed version of the "Narrative of Hannah Swarton" to appear in Mather's lifetime is in his 1702 *Magnalia Christi Americana.*

Having begun its literary life intended for a text never printed, then appearing as an appendix to a sermon, the Swarton passage finally rests among some of Mather's stranger productions. Reprinted in chapter 2 of the sixth book of *Magnalia,* the narrative seems to come full circle. From the unpublished *Great Examples of Judgment and Mercy,* Swarton's story moves to the section designated "Illustrious Discoveries and Demonstrations of the Divine Providence in Remarkable Mercies and Judgments on Many Particular Persons."[57] There are minor variants between the two versions; for example, the word "them" is more often rendered "'em" in the *Magnalia,* approximating a frontier woman's conversation more than the formal discourse of the printed sermon.

Magnalia recontextualizes Hannah Swarton's story once more. Clearly not of historiographical value—or it would have been included in the voluminous *Decennium*—the narrative assumes the status of a curiosity, an "extraordinary salvation." *Magnalia*'s Swarton follows descriptions of miraculous rescues and "rare cures," where Mather recounts the tale of the dropsical Sarah Wilkinson: "When she was open'd, there were no bowels to be found in her, except her heart, which was exceeding small, and as it were perboil'd. . . . Other bowels, none could be found: yet in this condition she liv'd a long while, and retain'd her senses to the last. But we will content ourselves with annexing to these things a narrative of a woman celebrating the wonderful *dispensations* of Heaven" (356). Proceeding from the amazing hollow woman to Hannah Swarton, this segue seems quirky at best. Yet relegation of the narrative to a passage of "believe it or not" spectacle reveals its oddity even in Mather's estimation. By 1702, over thirty years of intermittent, sometimes acute, warfare had made captivity commonplace. Gory, horrific tales fill *Decennium Luctuosum,* and women constitute the majority of sufferers. Without fierce anti-Indian rhetoric, the Swarton narrative cannot perform the ideological work that a story like Duston's can. Nor can its highly stilted version of religious contest, which actually portrays the French as kind, if zealous, missionaries, suffice for the scathing criticisms that continuing warfare requires. As a conventional spiritual conversion account, the "Narrative of Hannah Swarton" provides insufficient propaganda to warrant reprinting as history. Subject of a text without social utility except as an exhibit in Mather's freak show of remarkables, Hannah Swarton, who never wrote her own story, is an appropriate emblem of his use of rhetorical drag: a hollow woman, filled in by Mather's (divinely directed) hand.

Ulrich describes Hannah Swarton as "the ideal captive" (*Good Wives* 180). Indeed, Swarton represents the *idealized* captive, Mather's extension into the theological thickets of Catholic Canada, whose "means of . . . Deliverance, were by reason of Letters" (*Humiliations* 71). In staging Hannah Swarton's conversion not in the wild forests of northern New England, but in the civilized venue of the French Lord Intendant's home, Cotton Mather literally domesticates the captivity narrative. Alluding to the familiar imagery of deprivation, he moves quickly to the more important business of conversion in the face, not of physical suffering, but of religious antagonism. This rush accounts for the narrative's structure, which is composed of eight lengthy paragraphs; by the third, Swarton is "very courteously provided for" in "M. Le Tonant's" household. Although she has suffered the grueling journey of winter travel through the northern Maine forests and lost her family in the attack, Swarton's gravest concern is arrival in Canada, "for fear lest I should be overcome by them, to yield to their Religion" (*Humiliations* 59). The horrors of Indian attack and near-starvation fade in comparison to the greater snare of Catholicism.

Mather cannily taps popular images of suffering, such as the *Judea capta* motif, to assemble his own version of captivity's humiliations. Adopting a woman's voice, he elaborates on the figure of the virtuous woman, extending the instrumental potential for this usually silent segment of the church. Mather's own complicated engagement with the vicissitudes of authorship allows him to invoke certain expectations about female authors in his readers while simultaneously creating a new use for woman's publication, as a variation on pseudonymity and anonymity. In this, he relies on what Foucault characterizes as the author's "classificatory function." "Such a name," here, the woman's name, "Hannah Swarton," "permits one to group together a certain number of texts, define them, differentiate them from and contrast them to others. In addition, it establishes a relationship among the texts" (Foucault 107). Although Hannah Swarton's name appears only once as putative author of "her" narrative, the scarcity of women's texts in the period affiliates her relation with Mary Rowlandson's and so claims credibility only from an extraordinary experience like captivity. This credibility derives from the first-person voice of the woman who narrates her experiences, and it is different from the cultural authority that inheres in the male accounts Mather interpolates into *Decennium;* female captives' voices are tied to embodied, particular experience; they achieve publication status only as informants. Within the social organization of gender in late seventeenth-century Boston, these voices could not function as interpretive, historiographical authorities, as do the men's texts. This distinction accounts for the Swarton narrative's absence from Mather's historical productions and its final home in a series of curiosities. "The Narrative of Hannah Swarton" had outlived its usefulness by 1702; as an instrument in the vast project of ecclesiastical and secular history, which *Magnalia* attempts to construct, the woman's story remains much too personal, even idiosyncratic, to serve as an entry into the public spectacle of Puritan progress. Appended to the tale of the hollowed-out woman, Hannah Swarton's narrative represents the limits of a female voice's utility for Mather. He never published as a woman again.

CHAPTER 2

❧

"Peculiar Efficacy and Authority"

Hannah Duston's Missing Voice

Words that are spoken in an Ordinance of the Lord Jesus Christ, carry with them a peculiar Efficacy and Authority.
—Cotton Mather, *Humiliations Follow'd with Deliverances*

Hannah Duston, captured in an Indian raid on Haverhill on 15 March 1697, escaped and returned home to tell her tale.[1] The simplicity of this statement belies its resonance, the richly rendered, culturally complex responses to the bare facts. By 1697, Indian attack was a commonplace for the frontier dwellers in the Massachusetts Bay Colony, yet Duston's tale was singular. While Rowlandson's famous narrative portrays a captive physically redeemed through the offices of a colonial agent, Duston's extraordinary self-deliverance posed a counter to Rowlandson's version of redemption. In its exorbitance, Duston's story transformed the possibilities of the experience of captivity, integrating a (violent) agency not previously portrayed in female captivity tales.[2] This transformation—later often rendered as gender transgression—drew many writers to the tale and to the figure of Hannah Duston herself. Not surprisingly, this seventeenth-century New England story begins with Cotton Mather.

Duston's tale is well known; the following is my brief retelling based on Mather's sermon, *Humiliations Follow'd with Deliverances*.

Commemorative 1973 Jim Beam whiskey bottle in the shape of Hannah Duston.

According to that text, Hannah Duston had given birth a week before the attack on her Haverhill home. Her husband, Thomas Duston, was working in the fields while Duston lay at home with their seven other children and the infant. She was attended by a neighbor, Mary Neff. In the midst of the attack, Thomas Duston managed to save the seven oldest children by shepherding them in front of him while he shot at the pursuing Indians from his horse. Thomas Duston and the children reached the garrison safely; Hannah Duston and Mary Neff were captured by the attackers. Roused from the house, Duston and Neff were told to march. Almost immediately, one of the attackers seized the infant and "dash'd out the Brains . . . against a Tree." Other captives were killed as they fell from fatigue.

To this point, the story adheres to the conventional plot of most seventeenth-century New England captivities. However, as the raiding party split up, Duston and Neff were assigned to a group of twelve Indians: two men, three women, and seven children.[3] Samuel Lennardson, a twelve-year-old taken from Worcester, was included in the group. During the trek from Haverhill to a camp on an island in the Contoocook River (a tributary of the Merrimack), the captives were told they would have to run the gauntlet when they reached the Indian settlement at Pennacook. Duston "heartened" Neff and Lennardson to make an escape. On the seventh day of their captivity, Duston arose, awakened the other two, and, taking the Indians' hatchets, killed the men, a woman, and six of the children (one woman escaped; one child she apparently spared to take with her). They scalped the corpses and returned to Haverhill. Duston, Neff, and Lennardson appeared in Boston and were present when Mather preached the sermon that would soon be printed as *Humiliations Follow'd with Deliverances,* which included a rendition of their story.

Hannah Duston's "I," unlike Hannah Swarton's, is absent from this first published account of her captivity experiences, and this absence encourages constant retelling. She is never granted the dispensation to write her tale, to explain her apparently outrageous actions; even a purloined authorship such as Hannah Swarton's cannot contain the excesses of a woman who kills and scalps. This lack of dispensation is evident in the portrait we have of her in Mather's *Humiliations Follow'd with Deliverances.* There she appears as the silent auditor, part of the congregation, listening to her own story presented to her by a leading minister of the church. She is rendered an instrument, already transformed from subject to object of the lesson, alienated from the right to tell her story. Indeed, the text of *Humiliations Follow'd with Deliverances* presents the section on Duston's experiences as graphically belated or removed, encased in quotation marks and written in the third person.[4] That is, the textual appearance of the story designates it as previously told by someone else, before Mather related it back to her. The quotation marks and third-person voice publicly remove the text from her provenance as the woman who experienced the events and therefore the one who has the authority to shape her experiences into a narrative. As well, the printed sermon follows the quoted text with an "improvement" by Mather, in which he "opens" the quotation as he would a passage from scripture to teach the lessons of the story. Duston's own relation of her experiences (spoken by her in Samuel Sewall's home and possibly in Cotton Mather's) disappears into the sermon, hidden behind the quotation marks. Transforming Duston from speaker to auditor, Mather forever prevents Duston from producing a first-person account, because he establishes himself as the authoritative teller of her tale.

I have discussed the reasons for this transformation of Duston, from active instigator of her own rescue to passive recipient of the narrative Mather preached, in contrast to the production of the Hannah Swarton narrative, which Mather did not preach but wrote. Gender conventions regulating women's speech and Swarton's status as a frontier woman with no real social position permitted Cotton Mather to confer a reputation on Swarton as he simultaneously granted "her" a dispensation to publish. With Duston in the audience, he establishes her reputation but transforms dispensation in its function as license because he has superseded her, already employed her for instructional purposes. The necessity for a first-person account is obviated because Cotton Mather, in preaching then printing the sermon, made sufficient use of it—made Duston his perfect ministerial instrument.

This prolepsis grounds all subsequent Duston narratives. As narrator, not only is Duston a supernumerary, but the unspeakable nature of her actions precludes her personal relation of them. The very immediacy presumed to characterize first-person narrative and the quality of authenticity derived from that immediacy forbid her own version from appearing: it is difficult to imagine a Puritan woman granted a dispensation to describe and explain the acts of murder and scalping. As well, the memory of Hannah Duston's sister Elizabeth Emerson, who was executed for infanticide (and also provided Mather with an "instrument"), compounded the perceived family tendency toward violent women who required explanation. Duston's reputation, made by Mather (and adumbrated by her sister's), is irretrievably bound by the killing and scalping; therefore, so is her instructional potential. That is, Mather could—and did—produce an explanation for Duston's brutality, but the rationale was his interpretation, not hers. Her brutal acts prohibited the kind of first-person narrative that the fictive Swarton published because her voice was compromised by her behavior from the moment Mather characterized it.

Therefore, the portrait of Hannah Duston as captive, victim, and heroine relies on Mather's rendering her *his* figure, whose significance derives precisely from his interpretation. Leigh Gilmore's analysis of Freud's Dora offers a useful framework for considering the interpretive prerogatives at stake in a woman's narrative shaped by an authoritative male. As Gilmore notes, instrumentality anchors the endeavor: "In his 'prefatory remarks,' Freud indicates that the development of a new narrative technique to reproduce the analytical scene of the talking cure will mark the founding of a new science. He writes that 'the presentation of *my* case histories remains a problem which is hard for me to solve.' The task, as he sees it, is representational. It involves the production of a narrative based on Dora's narrative that recasts her as a character in his narrative rather than as the speaking subject of her own" (Gilmore 56; emphasis mine).[5] Gilmore demonstrates that the woman's silence is necessary for the male authority figure to construct the "true" and "useful" narrative, especially when the woman's actions are so egregious within her social milieu that another truth must be constructed. Considering that Mather, in his position as minister, functions as a kind of protoanalyst (albeit trained in Calvinist conceptions of the soul, not Freudian constructions of the unconscious), we can see that Mather uses Duston, similarly to the way Freud uses Dora, as an instrument that opens a version of her "self" to view, that exposes her interiority. Her experiences may ground the lesson at hand ("peculiar Efficacy") but they must remain firmly in male interpretive control ("and Authority"). Especially when the woman's experience is too painful, too unacceptable, or too disruptive, it challenges, for example, prevailing gender norms, and a concerned male authority must intervene to police the narrative's potential exorbitance.

This captive model of female authorship, seen in Duston's silencing and refiguration, reveals both the instructional and the subversive potential of female authorship. As long as the female author can explain herself in terms that her culture can understand and condone—and can exemplify or illuminate a desired end, that is, function as an instrument—she is granted a public voice, even if it is, in Rowlandson's and Swarton's cases, the unusual dispensation to publish. If her character does not conform to contemporary standards of feminine behavior, she is silenced and refigured. Thus Mary Rowlandson's spiritual conversion, Hannah Swarton's victory over the French Catholics, and, as

I argue in chapter 3, Elizabeth Hanson's domestication in the wilderness comport with dominant ideological imperatives of their historical moments while relying on particular presumptions about female authorship operating at the time of publication. Duston is excluded from this publishing sorority because Mather's sermon eliminates the need for her personal account and because, as historical conditions change, the killings become the irreducible sign that female behavior cannot be fixed or controlled, only interpreted and reinterpreted. Duston's behavior thus constitutes, in Marjorie Garber's terms, a "category of crisis" that calls for a variant version of rhetorical drag.

As Hannah Duston sat listening to Cotton Mather's rendition of her captivity and escape during his sermon on Thursday, May 6, 1697, she could not know that his version of her experiences would generate many revisions throughout the eighteenth and nineteenth centuries. Scholars have commented on the persistence of Duston's story in American literature, and the continued emphasis, of course, upon her exceptional behavior.[6] Duston attracted several commentators and revisionists precisely because of her Amazonian conduct. The significance of the periodic Duston retellings lies in the images of women and their social spheres that the writers constructed for their contemporary readers; furthermore, they reveal some of the cultural constraints and structures shaping the figure of female voice/narration that held well into the nineteenth century, by which time women's publication had expanded enormously.

The accounts of Hannah Duston's captivity and escape, found in the work of Thomas Hutchinson (1764), Timothy Dwight (1821), John Greenleaf Whittier (1831), Benjamin Mirick (1832), Nathaniel Hawthorne (1836), and Henry David Thoreau (1849), conduct a dialogue with Cotton Mather's primary relations (1697, 1699, 1702), and complicate and transform the concepts of dispensation and reputation that governed female authorship in the seventeenth century. As we have seen, Ter Amicam literally conferred a dispensation on Mary Rowlandson's narrative, and Cotton Mather apparently granted Hannah Swarton access to publication by appending "her" narrative to his own printed sermon. Some of Cotton Mather's cultural concerns—notably, the authorization invoked for historiographic enterprise—resurface in the Hannah Duston corpus, and they alter the concept of dispensation itself. The reformulation is essential because no fully realized first-person account of her captivity by Hannah Duston has survived, if indeed one ever existed. This fact, even more than her outrageous behavior, predicates the recurrent publications, because each of the male writers relies on the absence of Duston's voice to authorize his representation of her, a representation that reflects his contemporary understanding and manipulation of female voice. This version of rhetorical drag performs gender as a particular consciousness, a set of interiorized enactments that demonstrate to readers how Hannah Duston *should have* behaved and thought about her acts.

Considerations of proper female behavior appear in each revision of Duston's story. Indeed, in the story of Hannah Duston, the men find a disturbing counter to prevailing modes of female propriety and then, in their own versions, seek to recuperate those modes. Hawthorne in particular manipulates the Duston legend to address his concern with the public woman as teller of her own tale. Others view Hannah Duston as a disruptive figure within the conventionally male enterprise of historiography. Her actions jarred uncomfortably with the hagiographic and filiopietistic histories produced in the new nation and provoked a spate of policing, explanatory texts. The spectacular image of Hannah Duston repeatedly calls to later authors who themselves echo Mather's use of Duston as a model for their own "peculiar Efficacy and Authority."

In her study of the Duston stories, Kathryn Whitford states, "from the beginning it appealed not only to the historical imagination of its readers but to the moral imagination as well" (304).[7] Hannah Duston thus represents an opportunity to reimagine female behavior in order to serve the personal and professional ends of the authors writing about her. This practice of using Hannah Duston begins with Mather's appropriation of her story first to illustrate his 1697 sermon, then to buttress his historiographical projects in *Decennium Luctuosum* (1699) and *Magnalia Christi Americana* (1702). An examination of his Duston texts shows that the uses of her story varied even within the Mather corpus.

In order to understand Mather's variant versions of Duston, we must consider the quite different authorial ends of the three texts in which they occurred. The appearance of the Duston story in *Humiliations Follow'd with Deliverances* (1697) and *Decennium Luctuosum* (1699), barely two years apart, requires an explanation of its role in those texts as envisioned by Mather. How does her tale serve to illuminate both a sermon on the religious declension of Puritan congregations and a history of the "sorrowful decade" of wars with native tribes? Unsurprisingly, in the Mather texts, Duston's experiences suit both spiritual and political goals. Mather's original version of Duston initiates a series of reconsiderations. Each implicates her story in contemporary historiographic and political narratives; each demonstrates the generative potential of Duston's missing voice.

"Subservient unto the Main Intention Thereof"

Like the "Narrative of Hannah Swarton," the narrative of Hannah Duston's captivity and escape maintains a dialogue with the main text of *Humiliations Follow'd with Deliverances*. However, Duston's story is not a printed coda attached at the time of publication. The language preceding the Duston passage indicates that these words were read out at the sermon: "And, I suppose, there happens to be at this very Time, in this Assembly, an Example, full of Encouragement unto those HUMILIATIONS, which have been thus called for" (*Humiliations* 40). Therefore, the Duston story achieves the status of explicit and physically present exemplum, while the Swarton narrative appears only textually, as the appendix to the printed sermon.

   Mather's use of Duston's story, like his impersonation of Swarton, relies on a consonance of imagery shared by his sermon and her tale to make his point that the sufferings of the colonists are deserved. The three judges in the opening passage who attend an Old Testament scourging are echoed in Hannah Duston, Mary Neff, and Samuel Lennardson, themselves acting as judges and executioners in the case of their Indian captors. The juridical images serve to exculpate Hannah Duston's actions, and therefore, the language draws parallels between Old Testament judges and colonial captives: "When the Punishment of Scourging was used upon a Criminal in Israel, it was the Order and Usage, that while the Executioner was Laying on his Thirteen (and therein Forty save one) Blowes, with an Instrument, every stroke whereof gave Three Lashes to the Delinquent, there were still present Three Judges, whereof, while one did Number the Blowes, and another kept crying out, Smite him! a Third Read Three Scriptures, during the Time of the

Scourging: and the Scourging Ended with the Reading of them" (*Humiliations* 3–4). The "Blowes" recur in the crucial moment of Hannah Duston's tale, when "they struck such Home Blowes, upon the Heads of their Sleeping Oppressors, that e're they could any of them struggle into any effectual Resistance, at the Feet of those poor Prisoners, They bowed, they fell, they lay down; at their feet they bowed, they fell; where they bowed, there they fell down Dead" (*Humiliations* 46–47). Moreover, the triplets of the opening section here return in this later passage—"bowed" and "fell"—and linguistically link the judges and captives-turned-judges (and executioners). Duston's "Home Blowes" are utterly justifiable—in specifically legal terms—because "she was not forbidden by any Law, to take away the Life, of the Murderers, by whom her Child had been butchered" (*Humiliations* 46). Thus Duston acts as both judge and "instrument" by deciding the fate of the Indians and carrying out the execution. As we shall see, this legalism, which exonerates Duston in Mather's text, fails to persuade later writers. Not bound by Mather's typological approach to history, subsequent revisionists rewrite the critical terms of exculpation by applying their contemporary criteria for female behavior.

For Mather, however, Duston provides a doubled instrumentality. Killing and scalping, she functions as a providential avenger, one chosen to administer justice to the "Raging Dragons." Simultaneously, Duston remains a victim, a captive whose infant was murdered before her eyes and who endured a long trek through the northern forest only to be threatened with the gauntlet. Like the Old Testament criminals of the sermon's opening passage, she is to be stripped and scourged. As a victim, she exemplifies the humiliations destined for the unregenerate and lapsing congregations; as an avenger, she embodies the triumphant role of Calvinist Christianity in the wilderness.

Particularly, Hannah Duston's actions align her with the "Wicked and Hurtful men [who] have been called the hand of God" (*Humiliations* 30). For Mather, Nero presages the contemporary "French Nero," who so torments Puritan settlements that he can be seen himself as an instrument in a divine plan to teach the lessons of humility and conformity to English settlers: "But indeed, there is the Mighty Hand of God, in all Afflictive Dispensations of His Providence; and now, O Let us Humble our selves, by Considering, how much the Dispensations of His Mighty Hand, have Humbled us" (*Humiliations*

30). Mather preaches that, as a congregation, "we" are "brought Low through Affliction," "brought very Low," to "make us feel and own our own wretchedness" (*Humiliations* 30). The congregation, therefore, is to assume the same position under the "Mighty Hand of God" as the Indians whom Hannah Duston kills: "They bowed, they fell, they lay down; at their feet they bowed, they fell; where they bowed, there they fell down. Dead" (*Humiliations* 46–47). Yet Duston and her accomplices are instructed, in the "improvement": "You are now rescued from Captivity, and must not think, That they are greater Sinners, who are Left behind in the most barbarous Hands imaginable. No, you, that have been under the Mighty Hand of God, are to Humble your selves, under that Hand" (*Humiliations* 48–49).

Recognizing this doubled role, we see how Hannah Duston's instrumentality is doubly effective. Both judge and criminal, she derives her utility from the unconventionally active role she took in her own escape, coupled with the submission she must demonstrate "under the Mighty Hand of God." The utility is specifically tied to gender because the church in New England "is figured by a woman"—in this sermon, *Judea capta*—and because Hannah Duston's acts were those of a man. That is, her gender trespass makes her an object that requires a disciplining interpretation, one that both castigates and extends that castigation to the congregation as an instructional exemplum. Duston's image therefore serves both as a valuable agent in New England providential historiography and as a negative example in light of the prescriptive literature defining proper female behavior, such as Mather's own *Ornaments for the Daughters of Zion*.

Thus, Hannah Duston is a complicated and troubling heroine not only because her image serves as both Old Testament judge and Old Testament victim but also because she is as well a wife, a mother, and a neighbor. While Mather delivers her to the congregation as an Old Testament type (including Jael, who is herself a judge in the case of Sisera), he must also consider that she sits among the assembled as a real woman whose physical presence may resist easy transformation into exemplar. In the sermon, Mather employs strategies to address the actuality of Hannah Duston, the real person. First, he subtly castigates her for the very endurance that saved her. Using asides—in the printed sermon these comments appear within brackets[8]—Mather interrupts the dramatic flow of the description of the attack by asserting that Duston did not react the way a good neighbor would on seeing the death and destruction around her:

> About Nineteen or Twenty *Indians,* now led these away, with about Half a score other, English *Captives:* but e'er they had gone many Steps, they dash'd out the Brains of the *Infant,* against a Tree, and several of the other *Captives,* as they begun to Tire in their sad Journey, were soon sent unto their long Home, but the Salvages would presently bury their Hatchets in their Brains, and leave their Carcases on the ground, for Birds & Beasts, to feed upon. [Christians, A *Joshua* would have *Rent his Clothes, and fallen to the Earth on his Face,* and have *Humbled* himself Exceedingly upon the falling out of such doleful Ruines upon his Neighbours!]" (*Humiliations* 43)

Immediately following this last aside, a quick "however" contrasts Hannah Duston's reaction to Joshua's prostrate response by describing her almost preternatural perseverance. So Hannah Duston persists, through her infant's murder and the destruction of the community, to become a Jael, an avenging angel. In the process, "however," she loses credibility as a good neighbor and affectionate mother; she becomes a woman already exhibiting quite unwomanly characteristics.[9]

What Hannah Duston lacks in maternal and neighborly feeling is amply compensated by Thomas Duston's efforts to save his children. Again, like the legal question of her right to kill, this point is considered in Mather's text, but it is elaborated by the later authors. Here, strict gender propriety prevails in the description of paternal care and courage. While the story opens with Hannah Duston lying in, it switches in the second sentence to Thomas Duston's activities during the attack. Discovering the raid in progress, Thomas Duston rushes to relieve his family and to warn Hannah:

> E're she could get up, the fierce *Indians* were got so near, that utterly despairing to do her any Service, he ran out after his Children; Resolving, that on the Horse, which he had with him, he would Ride away, with *That,* which he should in this Extremity find his Affections to pitch most upon, and leave the Rest, unto the care of the Divine Providence. He overtook his children, about Forty Rod,

from his Door; but *then,* such as was the *Agony* of his Parental
Affections, that he found it Impossible for him, to Distinguish any
one of them, from the Rest; wherefore he took up a Courageous
Resolution, to Live & Dy with them All. (*Humiliations* 41–42)

The "*Agony* of his Parental Affections" contrasts sharply with Hannah Duston's ability to get up and walk through the forest after witnessing her infant's murder and to survive the journey to Contoocook
Island, and—more disturbingly—to take up hatchets to kill six Indian
children. Indeed, the deliverance of Thomas Duston's seven children
mirrors the destruction of the six Indian children Hannah kills (and
the one she spares). The Duston children are safe with their father; the
infant who remained with their mother is murdered: he can protect
them; she cannot. Even within Cotton Mather's formulation of Hannah Duston as a heroine, made explicit in the title of the episode as
it appears in *Decennium Luctuosum,* there are clear inadequacies in
Hannah Duston as mother and neighbor. The actual Hannah Duston
in the congregation destabilizes his representation of her in the sermon
as a providential agent and therefore necessitates his "improvement"
of her story.

Thus, *Humiliations Follow'd with Deliverances,* excluding the appendix published as Hannah Swarton's narrative, ends with "An Improvement of the foregoing Narrative." Here, Mather opens the door
for the further "improvements" by subsequent revisionists and provides the authoritative tone and license to psychologize adopted by
these later writers. In the "improvement," Mather emphasizes that his
words, "spoken in an *Ordinance* of the Lord Jesus Christ, carry with
them a peculiar Efficacy and Authority." Directly addressing Duston,
Neff, and Lennardson, he tells them exactly what they should take
from their experiences: "The *Use,* which you are to make of it, is, To
Humble your selves before the Lord Exceedingly" (*Humiliations* 48).
The second-person address thereby embeds them into the sermon; they
are no longer the "Subjects of such a Wonderful *Deliverance,*" but the
objects of the lesson. Much of the passage employs the imperative,
rhetorically abolishing any first-person "I" and emphasizing what the
listeners—here, "you"—must understand from their experiences.[10] The
"improvement" not only signals Mather's appropriation of the story
for his own use—and in his own voice—but also indicates that the very

agency Duston demonstrated is now recontextualized and transformed utterly into the submissive acceptance of his explanation.

Thus, with the final text of the sermon proper, Mather produces an "instrument" like Elizabeth Emerson's statement "taken down" before her execution, and he interprets it for the congregation. The imperative mode and the second person return the story to the level of personal experience while simultaneously directing a reading of those experiences. Emphasizing the "Right Use" of Hannah Duston's story, Mather initially sees it as an instrument for his exegetical and homiletic ends. However, his subsequent disposition of the tale in his later works expands its "Right Use" from theological exemplum—a vehicle for religious exhortation—to an incident in the providential history of the Massachusetts Bay Colony. This shift to the historiographical puts Hannah Duston within a broader field of inquiry for the later commentators, especially for historians such as Hutchinson, Dwight, and Mirick. But the religious origins remain in the residue of moral policing that all later revisionists employ to tell the Duston story.

In 1699, two years after *Humiliations Follow'd with Deliverances* appeared, Cotton Mather published *Decennium Luctuosum* to document the ten years of warfare between the English colonists and the French, including the various peoples who allied themselves with the French. *Decennium* recapitulates Hannah Duston's story from *Humiliations* but with some variations.[11] Removed from the homiletic context, Hannah Duston is no longer compared to Old Testament judges, no longer figured by *Judea capta*. In the absence of these resonances, mitigations for Duston's behavior disappear, and the story becomes an example of moral triumph in Mather's clearly defined war between good and evil, between the English and the "Formidable Savages." Entitled "*A Notable Exploit; wherein,* Dux Faemina Facti," the passage is article 25 in a list of thirty incidents assembled from various sources to demonize the natives while gaining sympathy for the colonists who suffered most at their hands. This is most likely the source of the story for the later commentators, since *Decennium Luctuosum* was the original text for the seventh book of *Magnalia Christi Americana,* in which these episodes were recorded, and the *Magnalia,* in turn, became the best known of Mather's works. Robert Arner places Hannah Duston within Mather's larger historiographical enterprise: "His Biblical allusions simultaneously provide him with a moral framework to justify Hannah's deed and a means of placing her exploits in an epic context related to the national destiny of the Puritan people" (19).[12]

The epic nature of Mather's project is visible in the variants he uses in "A Notable Exploit" to reframe the focus of Hannah Duston's tale from humiliation to triumph. As Holmes notes, Mather received information after the 1697 sermon to augment his initial published relation (Holmes 490); considering that the three captives only reached Haverhill "some five or six days before their public appearance at the Boston Lecture on Thursday, May 6, 1697" (Holmes 491), Mather may not have had sufficient opportunity to thoroughly revise a received statement into a text more closely to his own style or ends. But the two-year interim between publication of *Humiliations* and *Decennium* allowed him to revise and enlarge the narrative to suit the purposes of his new history.

The first variant occurs in the opening paragraph. *Humiliations* begins: "On the fifteenth day, of the Last *March, Hannah Dustan,* of *Haverhill,* having Lain in about a Week, attended with her Nurse, *Mary Neff,* a Widow, a Body of Terrible *Indians,* drew near unto the House where she lay, with Designs to carry on the bloody Devastations, which they had begun upon the Neighbourhood" (*Humiliations* 41). Hannah Duston is the subject of the sentence grammatically, and she appears as the first character in the drama. Two years later, in *Decennium,* the subject of the sentence changes and the focus shifts: "On March 15. 1697. the Salvages made a Descent upon the Skirts of *Haverhill,* Murdering and Captiving about Thirty Nine Persons, and Burning about Half a Dozen Houses. In this Broil, one *Hannah Dustan,* having lain in about a Week, attended with her Nurse, *Mary Neff,* a Widow, a Body of Terrible *Indians* drew near unto the House, where she lay, with Designs to carry on their Bloody Devastations" (*Decennium* 138). Thus, by 1699, the obvious subjects of the narrative are "the Salvages," although the suggestive metonymy in the noun "Skirts" feminizes the setting. The Indians do indeed descend on the women (and men); but the complicated syntax of both the first sentence in *Humiliations* and the second sentence in *Decennium* makes clear that the narrator cannot decide whom to emphasize. There follows, then, the quick shift to the episode of Thomas Duston, an unambiguous hero. As the *Decennium* version continues, it eliminates the bracketed asides from the text of *Humiliations,* which address the congregation, and which, as demonstrated above, implicitly blame Hannah Duston for not succumbing in the attack as she watched her child and neighbors die. "A Notable Exploit," like "A Narrative of a Notable Deliverance from Captivity," emphasizes the Indian captors' Catholicism. But where *Humiliations* states, "and for the shame of many a *Prayerless Family* among our *English*" (44), the *Decennium* passage reads, "and for the Shame of many an English Family, that has the Character of Prayerless upon it" (141). The change signals that Englishness rather than piety is the salient characteristic of *Decennium*'s audience; the appeal switches from common religion to common national heritage. This switch is consonant with the aim of *Decennium:* to unite colonists in their enmity toward the French and their Indian allies while constructing a history of the English community.

In both versions of this passage one phrase remains constant: "I must now publish what these poor women assure me." Thus the testimony of Duston and Neff grounds either discourse: no matter what the final project—homily or history—the women's experiences authenticate it, but it is Mather who relates the tale and makes their private communication a public artifact.

The most extensive variant appears in the final paragraphs of the two works. Confusing diction results in a strange collapse of heroes and scalps: "But cutting off the Scalps of the *Ten Wretches,* who had Enslav'd 'em, they are come off" (*Humiliations* 47) and "But cutting off the Scalps of the Ten Wretches, they came off, and Received Fifty Pounds from the General Assembly of the Province, as a Recompence of their Action" (*Decennium* 143). The verb "come off" literally means the captives escaped, but its proximity to the "scalps" muddies the meaning. The garbled syntax betrays the anxiety raised by the acts of "an aggressive and opportunistic woman" (Ulrich, *Good Wives* 172). Yet the concluding paragraph of "A Notable Exploit" foregrounds the congratulations and rewards received by the three captives from a grateful community. This contrasts sharply with the final comment in the "improvement" in *Humiliations,* where they are warned repeatedly to humble themselves.

The use of Hannah Duston in Mather's corpus thus charts his fashioning of her reputation for quite different ends. Relying on her personal experience as an exception to the rule of women's normally submissive behavior, Mather nonetheless refigures her experience to assure its correct interpretation in published discourse. Her exorbitant behavior warns the congregation against lapsing standards of piety (in *Humiliations*) and represents the personal qualities required to survive in an English community still struggling on its wilderness frontiers (in *Decennium*).

Mather's authority invests the story of Hannah Duston with whatever exemplifying value he chooses to emphasize: "notable deliverance" or "notable exploit." Duston's female figure provides him with an object to manipulate, to "improve" upon, and to depict as a historical agent, albeit an agent in his firm control. Her exploit may have been notable, but she returns/is returned to the status of a Puritan goodwife, sitting silently in the congregation. The third-person captivity narrative, which lacks the immediacy and personal expression (voice) of Rowlandson's or the fictive Swarton's first-person accounts, relies upon the notoriety of Duston's exploits yet excludes her from the presentation of them. That exclusion, and Mather's concomitant "improvement," or commentary, gave her little scope in which to produce any meaning from her own experiences.

Duston's own characterization of the captivity and escape appeared much later, in a 1724 testament for church admission in which she stated, "I am Thankful for my Captivity, twas the Comfortablest time that ever I had: In my Affliction God made his Word Comfortable to me"[13] (Derounian-Stodola 56). But *her* written testimony never contributed to the accounts by her later revisers, because most of them base their versions of her story on the one they found in Mather. Manipulating the gendered distinctions of private and public discourse in a culture in which women were forbidden to speak in church, Mather fashions Duston's experiences in different texts for different aims. In so doing, Mather signals that the irreducible fact of her killing and scalping must be explained and that the very act of explanation (even justification, in his case) provides a fruitful avenue for (re-)interpretation. His appropriation of the public role Duston played, his construction of her first as religious exemplar, then as historical agent, preempts the need or, indeed, a desire for Hannah Duston to reassert her public role by publishing her own first-person account. Duston's meaning was, from the moment she set foot back in Boston, no longer hers, because her experiences became the intellectual property of Mather to wield as he saw fit. Thus "figured," Hannah Duston offered the paradox of a violent yet silent woman whose acts invited repeated reinterpretation and whose voice was appropriated through interiorized, psychologized characterizations, another form of rhetorical drag.

"A Compleater Composure"

Apart from arguing for the author's anonymity, Mather's "To the People of New England," the preface to *Decennium Luctuosum,* offers the work as a "Collection of Matters" (Mather's?), which in themselves constitute a "Considerable" history (8). Unlike Homer's *Iliad,* whose history of the Trojan War, Mather writes, "seems, all made of Poets Paper," Mather's history, in which he claims "the Fault of an Untruth can't be found," is legitimate and compelling (*Decennium* 7–8). As the first history of the decade's wars, *Decennium Luctuosum* claims to be authoritative but not exhaustive. The "Author," Mather writes, "now he hath done, he hath not pull'd up the Ladder after him; others may go on as they please with a compleater Composure" (*Decennium* 8).

In following Cotton Mather up the ladder, historian Thomas Hutchinson relied on his precursor's work to inform and authorize his own project. Although Hutchinson's preface to his *The History of Massachusetts . . .* echoes Mather's truth claims in the preface to *Decennium,* Hutchinson admits, "I have found some difficulty in guarding against every degree of prejudice, in writing the history of my own country. I hope, by shunning one extreme, I have not run upon the other" (Hutchinson 1: vii). This difficulty derives in great part from Hutchinson's conception of history, similar in practice to Mather's filiopietism, as a public expansion on the genealogical. The preface acknowledges that Hutchinson's historical material comes "from my ancestors, who, for four successive generations, had been principal actors in public affairs" and includes some papers from Samuel Mather, Cotton Mather's son and Hutchinson's brother-in-law (Hutchinson 1: v). Hutchinson asserts that "in general, we are fond of knowing the minutiae which relate to our own ancestors" and regards the Massachusetts colony "as the parent of all the other colonies of New-England" (1: vii).

Mather's *Magnalia* serves as a "parent" to Hutchinson's history, and therein we find a further familial—and gendered—affiliation that characterizes Hutchinson's portrait of Hannah Duston. According to

Hutchinson, Duston's actions are "ordinarily . . . not to be expected" from women (2: 102). In Massachusetts history, the preeminent example of a woman who behaved in an extraordinary and unacceptable manner was Hutchinson's great-great-grandmother, Anne Hutchinson. By relying on Mather, and to a lesser degree, on historian Daniel Neal, Hutchinson could find explicit parallels drawn between Anne Hutchinson and Hannah Duston in both sources. Indeed, Hutchinson's rendering of Hannah Duston can be seen as a rehabilitation of his ancestor, a means of transferring Anne Hutchinson's egregious dissent into a heroic deed whose "fame" "soon spread through the continent" (2: 102).

Anne Hutchinson's infamy arose from her role in the Antinomian crisis that culminated in her expulsion from the Massachusetts Bay Colony in 1638. Because Anne Hutchinson publicly espoused a radically personalized relationship with God and questioned the purview and teachings of some ministers, she was viewed by her minister-prosecutors as a heretic and a threat to the stability of the community. Turning to the *Magnalia*'s passage on the Antinomian crisis, "Hydra Decapitata," Hutchinson must have been struck by Mather's title for the section, "Dux Faemina Facta," which Mather translates as "Women made leaders" but is more accurately translated in the singular, "a woman made leader." This title resonates linguistically with Mather's subtitle for the Duston article in *Decennium*, "Dux Faemina Facti" (a woman leader in the deed). Of course, the linguistic echo does not undermine the constructions' differences: one signifies a heretic, the other a heroine. Yet an examination of Thomas Hutchinson's other cited source, Daniel Neal's *The History of New England*, reveals that Neal, too, pairs the two women linguistically. He describes Anne Hutchinson as "a *Lincolnshire* Gentlewoman, of a bold and masculine Spirit." Then, in his passage on Hannah Duston, which is quoted almost verbatim from Mather's *Decennium*, Neal editorializes on Duston's character (and diverges from the Mather text) by describing her as "a Woman of a masculine Spirit" (2: 182). Thus, the link between Anne Hutchinson and Hannah Duston was forged even before Hutchinson began his own history.

Not only do Hutchinson's sources link the two women, but the issues of documentation, public versus private speech, and control of reputation inform the stories of both women. Anne Hutchinson's words are rigorously documented (Hutchinson includes a transcript of her famous "examination" in an appendix) and one of Anne Hutchinson's complaints to the court is that words she spoke in private discourse to the examining elders at a previous meeting—words that she assumed would remain private—were brought against her at trial. Winthrop replies that "though things were spoken in private yet now coming to us we are to deal with them as public" (Hutchinson 2: 428). The boundaries between private and public discourse are thus adjudicated by the male authorities. Indeed, the entire controversy pushed those boundaries of personal conscience versus communal interest, and as Amy Schrager Lang argues, it is no coincidence that the historical personage most associated with (and most harmed by) the debate is a woman.[14] As Cotton Mather's "improvement" of Hannah Duston demonstrated, women's private experiences required the intervention and interpretation of male authorities: men fashioned the reputations and granted (or withheld, in Anne Hutchinson's case) dispensation for their private actions.

Thomas Hutchinson, too, needed to reinterpret Anne Hutchinson because he was both a historian and her descendant. That is, her reputation directly impinged on his, and the kind of rehabilitation he effects through Hannah Duston, another woman whose family was suspect (because of Elizabeth Emerson's execution), rebounds onto him as Anne's great-great-grandson. Initially, Hutchinson takes pains to criticize his forebear. She appears to be supported by many leading citizens, and "so much respect seems to have increased her natural vanity." She "thought fit to set up a meeting of the sisters also, where she repeated the sermons preached the Lord's day before, adding her remarks and expositions" (1: 57). For Thomas Hutchinson, Anne Hutchinson's greatest crime lies not in the particulars of religious heresy but in the more troubling implications of her individualist stance against prevailing order: "The fear of God and love of our neighbour seemed to be laid by and out of the question" (1: 59). Anne Hutchinson placed herself outside the law, a position literalized by Mather's Duston, who "had not her own Life secured by any Law unto her" (*Magnalia Christi Americana* 7: 91). But Duston is carried to that place by Indians; she finds herself in an extraordinary position, while Anne Hutchinson claims that exorbitance for herself. Additionally, to avoid the charge of prejudice, Thomas Hutchinson cites most of Anne Hutchinson's accusers—William Hubbard, Thomas Hooker, and the temporizing John Cotton—and postulates that "she considered herself divinely commissioned for some great purpose, to obtain which, she might think those windings, subtleties and insinuations lawful, which will hardly consist with the rules of morality. No wonder she was immoderately vain, when she found magistrates and ministers embracing the novelties advanced by her" (1: 71). Hutchinson intersperses his retelling of the Antinomian dispute with a discussion of the hostilities between the colonists and the Pequots. In this linkage, then, his Anne Hutchinson threatens the community's cohesion while it is struggling with grievous dangers from without: fomenting internal division, she risks the colony's existence. He contrasts this with Duston's actions, which not only result in her fame, as opposed to Anne Hutchinson's infamy, but also with the narrative's emphasis on social cohesion. Immediately following his final sentence on Duston's rewards and the gifts she received from neighbors and dignitaries, the next paragraph notes that Lieutenant Governor Stoughton "had kept free from controversy with other branches of the legislature. . . . Internal disputes and controversies in states, are, ordinarily, most effectually avoided or suspended by imminent external dangers" (2: 102).

This inversion of Anne Hutchinson and Hannah Duston proceeds, then, along several registers. From the linkage in his sources, Thomas Hutchinson crafts a pairing of his own. Naming Anne Hutchinson an "enthusiast," he cannot rehabilitate her, because her outspokenness and challenge to the law conflict with his own deeply held belief in the status quo, those Tory sympathies that ultimately cost him home and wealth during the American Revolution. However, in the figure of Hannah Duston, Hutchinson finds a woman whose words are never documented, whose actions, already outside the law, threaten no one but her captors and indeed reinforce the concept of English superiority over the natives. Duston kills Indians; Anne Hutchinson is, first, banished, then killed by them (murdered in an attack on her homestead in New York after her exile). In calling Duston a heroine, he finds a counter to his troublesome female ancestor.

The culturally authoritative version of history practiced by Mather, Neal, and Hutchinson uses the exorbitances of these female figures to raise and then dispose of the problem of personal, individualized experiences that might subvert social hierarchies. Anne Hutchinson posed a greater threat to Puritan polity than did some of her better-placed male colleagues such as John Wheelwright because she transgressed gender as well as theological proscriptions. Similarly, Duston's gender trespass forms the crucial element in her story.

Hutchinson's interpretation of Duston, like Mather's and Neal's, links Anne Hutchinson and Duston, an affiliation taken up by later writers, notably Hawthorne. While Duston's silence contrasts with Anne Hutchinson's volubility, both women function as historical markers, emblems of personal, private, and morally suspect eruptions that invite the "Mighty Hand" of male authority to control their effects. Exceptional behavior—here, acts that threaten the regulating models of religion and gender—is figured as female, and then rhetorically recaptured and reformed for insertion and instruction into the male writers' historiographical projects, projects that themselves subtend dominant regimes.

The Hutchinson Duston, although closely following Mather, varies in some important respects and contains at least one notable stylistic oddity. He begins the passage: "There was a woman (Hannah Dustan) a heroine, made prisoner at this time whose story although repeatedly published, we cannot well omit" (2: 101). He gives no reason for the importance of the story, but because he names her a heroine from the outset, the reader faces no moral dilemma in understanding her actions. Even as Duston is immediately cast as a famous and valued historical personage, by placing her name in parentheses, Hutchinson foregrounds the fact that she is a woman and emphasizes her gender rather than her name. Unlike Mather and later commentators, Hutchinson does not dwell on the scene of Thomas Duston's escape with his children. The sentences are short, so the narrative in Hutchinson's hands assumes a flat, factual tone in great contrast to the editorializing and interpolation of the other authors: "The terror of the Indian gantlet seems to have inspired Dustan with resolution, and she prevailed upon the nurse and the English boy to join with her in the destruction of the Indian family. The Indians kept no watch. The boy [Samuel Lennardson] had been with them so long, as to be considered as one of their own children" (2: 102). He does, however, note that "from women, ordinarily, attempts of this sort are not to be expected." And with that, he delivers the crux of the story in the passage's longest sentence:

> In the morning, a little before day, Dustan arose, and, finding the whole company in a sound sleep, calls upon her confederates to join with her, and with the Indian hatchets they silenced such as they began with, and yet took care not to make so much noise as

to awaken the rest; and in this manner they dispatched the whole family, except a favorite boy, whom they designedly left, and an old woman they supposed they had killed, but who jumped up, and with the boy make their escape. (2: 102)

This shift to the present tense in "calls" signifies the dramatic tensions inhering in the killings and imparts an immediacy to the piece in its most compelling moment. Duston is clearly the leader, rousing the others to the deed and deciding to spare the "favorite boy." The passage ends on a dispassionate note: "They took off the scalps from the ten, to bring them home with them," and he names the scalps "trophies."

In rewriting Mather, Hutchinson eschews Mather's fiery language and assumes for the most part a temperate, almost detached style, relying on the facts of the incidents to carry the narrative. The thrust of the passage is that Hannah Duston, although behaving in an extraordinary fashion for a woman, justifiably acts in self-defense, avoiding the gauntlet and making her escape. Indeed, Thomas Hutchinson, unlike all the other revisionists, seems unwilling to engage in any discussion of the morally troubling nature of the deeds. His Duston is most clearly a heroine, much appreciated by her community. There are no lessons to be gleaned; rather, Duston, although exceeding her female role, performs an unambiguous act of civic heroism, dispatching the society's enemies while saving herself. Her needs and those of the colony are congruent. And there is no room for further interpretation or moral quibbling. As such, Hutchinson's portrait is the least explicitly problematic version of Hannah Duston, quickly acknowledging her abnormal behavior while retrieving it for posterity as the characterization of a completely justified foremother, one whom Hutchinson might wish his readers to find in Hutchinson's own family.

"Some Very Singular Circumstances"

Thomas Hutchinson begat Leverett Saltonstall, who cites Hutchinson's history in his "Sketch of Haverhill, Massachusetts" (1816). If Hutchinson could not "well omit" Duston's story, Saltonstall reinforces the sense that by the early nineteenth century, Hannah Duston was at least a regional legend, a bit of local color: "In this descent [by the Indians in March 1687] the famous Hannah Duston was made prisoner, whose heroic exploit, though well known, deserves a place in the history of Haverhill" (128). In his account, she "prevailed upon the nurse and the boy to assist her in their [the Indians'] destruction" (129) and appears to be the trio's leader. Saltonstall's very short piece is valuable insofar as it indicates the direction Duston's story will take in the new century, and it continues the practice of male authorities who are compelled to tell her tale, which, by Saltonstall's time, had achieved the status of a legend. He de-emphasizes the scalpings, crucial determinants of Duston's moral nature for other nineteenth-century writers, and he thereby refrains from apologizing for her behavior in terms of existing constructs of female propriety. Still a heroine, Duston becomes for Saltonstall, and then Timothy Dwight after him, a marker in the regional history that, at least for Dwight, serves as a blueprint for the young Republic.

The regionalist cast to Duston's story is, of course, part of a larger nineteenth-century trend toward antiquarianism and nostalgia for the roots of the new United States. Timothy Dwight's rendition of Duston, like Mather's and Hutchinson's, depends in part on his position as descendant of a renowned family. Dwight's conception of New England as the cradle of the nation is intimately tied to his family's part in its colonial history. Duston, as a local heroine, represents an item in this larger genealogical/historical project.

According to Dwight's editor, Barbara Miller Solomon, *Travels in New England and New York* is, like Mather's *Magnalia,* a compendium of "geography, history, and biography, as well as aspects of economic growth, religion, politics, education, architecture, and whatever else he found relevant to the current state of New England" (Dwight 1: ix). A grandson of Jonathan Edwards and great-great-grandson of Solomon Stoddard, Dwight, who was also a Congregationalist minister, produced a version of historiography that is at least as genealogical as Hutchinson's or Mather's. As well, Solomon calls Dwight a "first generation federalist" because "the last pages of the *Travels* reflect his anxiety lest division of the states prevail" (Dwight 1: xxiii). So Dwight's stake in his major work (which was posthumously published in 1821–1822) is that it should demonstrate the cohesion and homogeneity in the country's origins and the lesson to be learned and progress achieved in the "transformation of the wilderness to civilized society" (Solomon,

in Dwight 1: x). The violent wilderness deeds of Hannah Duston challenge these goals; as a counter to the rational, pious founders, Hannah
Duston is both deviant and exemplar, an excessive woman yet a model
of frontier heroism. In this paradoxical role, Duston can represent both
the savagery of colonial life and the distance the American Republic
has put between itself and its brutal origins.

This distance is measured in terms of the *translatio studii,* the progression of human learning and improvement that moves west across
the globe. For Dwight, New England culture is the true American culture, and he stresses that its origins were homogeneous and characterized by the Puritan, whose social institutions valued, in Dwight's
words, "the state of manners and that of the mind" (1: xxxiv). Even if
the early settlers did not always meet their own standards of piety and
polity, they nevertheless display admirable strengths of character and
endurance, traits that descend through the bloodlines: "No sober New
Englander can read the history of his country without rejoicing that
God has caused him to spring from the loins of such ancestors, and
given him his birth in a country whose public concerns were entrusted
to their management. . . . The same enterprising character . . . has been
exhibited by their descendants" (1: 121).

Dwight constructed his *Travels* as an exercise in historical continuity, with New England as the font of American culture, and New Eng-
landers as the real Americans to whom others should look for models.
But in considering Hannah Duston's legend while traveling through
Haverhill, Dwight must reconcile his belief that the early settlers set the
moral tone for contemporary culture with the fact of her apparently
uncivilized acts. Duston's behavior was outrageous and incomprehen-
sible within nineteenth-century American models of gender roles; her
actions belied the representations of an essentialized passivity, so often an attribute of bourgeois womanhood. In Dwight's preoccupation
with the march of civilization, however, he necessarily views Indians
as revenants and impediments to progress.[15] Therefore the brutality of
Duston's deeds is somewhat mitigated by the savagery of her captors,
and Dwight attempts to see her acting legitimately in self-defense.

However, Dwight betrays a deep ambivalence towards Duston: she
is not quite an exemplary, heroically moral frontierswoman. Robert
Arner argues that Dwight's account is "written in straightforward, un-

adorned prose and [is], for the most part, consonant with Mather" (20). Yet Dwight's version is full of adornments not found in the Mather text, and these embellishments speak to his own attempts to domesticate and sentimentalize Duston for his contemporary audience.

Dwight's Hannah Duston appears in letter 39 in his "Journey to Berwick." He arrives in Haverhill and presents, as in his descriptions of previous venues, a brief history of the town, which begins with its settlement in 1637. From the outset, Haverhill "suffered often, and greatly, by savage depredations" (1: 295). The facts of Haverhill's history are "dispersed," however, and difficult to obtain. Here, Dwight underscores the danger of losing a legacy:

> This kind of knowledge is daily becoming less, and will soon be lost. It is much to be wished that inquisitive men throughout this country would glean and preserve the little which is left. It is a serious and unfortunate error of men in general to suppose that events familiarized to themselves by fireside repetition will be uninteresting to others, and that efforts to preserve them will be considered as either trifling or arrogant. In no country, probably, are the inhabitants more inquisitive than in New England. But their inquiries terminate, or have until lately terminated chiefly in things remote in time or place, and have been very little occupied by subjects pertaining to their own country. It is perhaps natural to man to feel that his own concerns, or any concerns, which are familiar to him, will be little regarded by those who come after him. Few parents are solicitous to have their own portraits taken; yet, after their decease, scarcely any legacy is thought more valuable by their children. (1: 296–97)

This long passage immediately precedes the description of the attack that resulted in Hannah Duston's captivity. For Dwight the loss of historical information is a metaphor for a family's loss, specifically the loss of a parent's portrait. The subsequent paragraph's focus on Hannah Duston—and, more importantly, on her husband Thomas—redresses the problem of historical ignorance. In fact, the paragraph on legacy ends with an asterisk that directs the reader to a note thanking the Massachusetts Historical Society for its efforts at retrieving and storing rapidly vanishing information.

So, as the letter proceeds to the Duston tale, the text's concerns are literally historiographical and metaphorically familial. Again, Hannah Duston provokes a discussion of the historical, as if her individual experiences as mother and captive both emblematize those of all early settlers and simultaneously distinguish her from them. Characterizing her captors as "unfeeling, insolent, and revengeful," Dwight wonders about Hannah Duston's maternal reactions: "What were then the feelings of the mother?" (1: 298). And, apostrophizing to invoke immediacy and sympathy, he describes the threat of the gauntlet: "This information, you will believe, made a deep impression on the minds of the captive women, and led them, irresistibly, to devise all the possible means of escape" (1: 298). The subsequent three sentences end a long paragraph on the captives' sufferings by succinctly stating the facts of the murders and scalpings, followed by the "handsome reward" (1: 298).

After relating the facts, Dwight indirectly addresses the reader in order to open the discussion of Hannah Duston's conduct of "this slaughter": "Precedents innumerable of high authority may indeed be urged in behalf of these captives, but the moralist will equally question the rectitude of these." He assures the reader "that she herself approved of the conduct which was applauded by the magistrates and divines of the day, in the cool hours of deliberation cannot be doubted" (1: 298). He thereby removes the possibility that Duston might have felt remorse, guilt, or even ambivalence for the killings because she had been directed to interpret her actions by the "divines of the day." Yet, in ascribing this certainty to Duston, Dwight cannot cite authority and engages in what is to become a hallmark of the nineteenth-century Duston stories: attributions of psychological motivation followed by an assessment of the justification based on that motivation. Where Cotton Mather "improved" Hannah Duston's experiences for religious and political lessons (and preached them directly to her), the nineteenth-century authors continue to expand the possibilities for her meaning in both historiographical and ideological discourse. Moreover, Hannah Duston's gender is of even greater concern for later writers, and contemporary ideologies of female domestication and submission demanded that her wild behavior be refigured and explained.

Dwight's emphasis on Thomas Duston, as Arner notes, sets the tone for later writers to evaluate Duston's actions in light of her husband's, an extended comparison missing from the Mather and Hutchinson accounts. Personal stories "familiarized . . . by fireside repetition" form the basis for Dwight's history, and, given Hannah Duston's behavior, Dwight chooses to valorize Thomas Duston's familial role. Arner marks a division in Dwight's rendition between Hannah's and Thomas's stories, and he locates the break at a revelatory sentence that "betrays [Dwight's] lingering ambivalence" (Arner 20). In turning to the escape of Thomas Duston and the children, Dwight begins, "But, whatever may be thought of the rectitude of *her* conduct, that of her husband is in every view honorable" (Dwight 1: 299). Certainly, Thomas Duston's careful shepherding of the children is above criticism, and, because he appears completely heroic, he is the more apt subject for illustration, more compelling, less bloody than an image of Hannah killing and scalping. As Arner notes, "Dwight seems to have been responsible for the attractiveness of the legend to illustrators. Imagining the scene as an artist would sketch it, he writes, 'this husband, and father, flying to rescue his wife, her infant, and her nurse, from the approaching horde of savages; attempting on his horse to select from his flying family the child, which he was the least able to spare, and unable to make the selection; facing, and fronting the enemy again; receiving, and returning their fire'" (22).

The breathless description of Thomas Duston's efforts is relayed in a long series of parallel clauses, all beginning with present participles: "flying to rescue," "attempting . . . to select," "facing," "retreating," "fronting the enemy," "receiving, and returning their fire," and "presenting himself . . . as a barrier." The immediacy is explicitly pictorial; any one of these acts can (and will) be rendered into an engraving. Dwight even describes potential compositions: "In the background of some or other of these pictures might be exhibited, with powerful impression, the kindled dwelling, the sickly mother, the terrified nurse with the newborn infant in her arms, and the furious natives, surrounding them, driving them forward, and displaying the trophies of savage victory and the insolence of savage triumph" (1: 299). This sentence ends the Duston episode in *Travels* and fulfills Dwight's call for parental portraits, which preceded the passage. By shifting focus to Thomas and literally assigning Hannah to the background, Dwight gives the reader an out: we no longer dwell on the morally problematic—"sickly"—Hannah but can comfortably view in painterly detail the male heroism of a forefather saving his descendants. Hannah

Duston's deeds, as fashioned by Mather and Hutchinson, are thus sub-
ordinated to the more acceptable, physically vigorous achievements of
her husband. Her "sickliness" here not only contrasts sharply with
Thomas's hearty heroism, but it also contradicts the endurance attributed to her by Mather and demonstrated by her perseverance during
the trek following her capture. For Dwight, this persistence in the face
of suffering is due to "intense distress" and "anxiety," not to heroism
or health, and he nowhere refers to Hannah Duston as a heroine, as
did Mather and Hutchinson. As well, he oddly exonerates the Indian
attackers by stating that "the slaughter [of the lagging captives] was
not an act of revenge, nor of cruelty. It was a mere convenience: an
effort so familiar as not even to excite an emotion" (1: 298). The Indians' "convenient" slaughter thus contrasts with Duston's own slaughter of her captors that later provokes a discussion of its justification.

Dwight engages the legend because it persists in local history and
his antiquarian practice is to include this kind of historical information
in all his descriptions. But in telling the tale, he must tame its particulars, and he accomplishes this through a gendered comparison. Hannah Duston represents a deeply troubling figure; recasting the legend in
terms of Thomas Duston, Dwight produces the good parent's portrait
and relegates Hannah Duston to scenery and stage prop, a more appropriate model of nineteenth-century female submission, even passivity.
Yet even Dwight cannot reconcile this portrait of Hannah Duston with
the facts, and his characterization of her resists rehabilitation: "Few
persons, however, agonizing as Mrs. Dustin did, under the evils which
she had already suffered and in the full apprehension of those which
she was destined to suffer, would have been able to act the part of nice
casuists; and fewer still, perhaps, would have exercised her intrepidity"
(1: 298–99). In Dwight's vision of the Republic, history demonstrates
that in previous "efforts" against enemies, be they Pequot, Canadian
French, or the British forces at Lexington, "not one was undertaken
for purposes of revenge, plunder, or victory, but merely from necessity
and self-defense" (1: 121). Hannah Duston's murder of children and
women, retrieval of the scalp "trophies," and victorious homecoming to
Boston subvert Dwight's rather glorified—and inaccurate—notions of
colonial history. Her gender makes it imperative that she be refashioned
into an acceptable, if resistant, model of female propriety and relegated
to the background of the new American illustrated histories.[16]

Dwight's portrayal of Duston initiates nineteenth-century attempts to modify her indelible acts, to cover them with so many quibblings, psychological attributions, and moral fulminations that characterization becomes caricature. These retellings constitute a specifically nineteenth-century version of rhetorical drag. Whereas Mather justified Duston's actions by stating that she was "not forbidden by any law" from killing and scalping her captors, he refrains from characterizing her mental state, preferring, clearly, to speak *to* her spiritual state after the events. Dwight's (and subsequent authors') representations of Hannah Duston resonate with the contemporary turn to interiority, the emergence of the proto-psychological model of Romantic sensibility, such as those found in Brockden Brown's novels and even the gothic fiction of Mrs. Radcliffe. That is, in these specimens of rhetorical drag, from Dwight onward, readers encounter Hannah Duston as both historical agent and fictional character, whose voice is always psychologized and internal, yet externalized through quotation. The facts of Duston's experiences *and her responses to them* become a field of elements to be imaginatively transformed and reorganized by Duston's revisers so that they may write history while righting a gross violation of their own conceptions of gender propriety. The broader implications of the Duston revisions indicate that the category crisis marked by these particular rhetorical drag formations emerges from nineteenth-century attempts to narrate a heroic American past that included brutal and morally repugnant actions by early Americans. Ineluctably linked to this historiographical crisis, contemporary conflicts between Euro-Americans and Native Americans retained the violent and indefensible character of the past.

"To Make a Right Use of the Deliverance"

Regional histories such as Saltonstall's and Dwight's provided source material for Whittier, Hawthorne,[17] and Thoreau, the three major figures who consider the Duston story in the nineteenth century. The critical difference between these three Duston pieces and the previous texts is that the later works are not avowedly historiographical; indeed, all rely on Romantic aesthetics rather than a rationalist historicism to interpret the significance of Hannah Duston.[18] As well, each of these authors explicitly develops a personal connection to Duston that far supersedes the historian's supposedly objective relationship to his subject. The authorial distance pretended by Hutchinson, Saltonstall, and, to a less successful extent, Dwight shrinks for their successors. Hannah Duston's morality and propriety, with which the earlier historians concerned themselves briefly, become the central issues of the short pieces by Whittier (1831), Hawthorne (1836), and, to a lesser extent, Thoreau (1849). In this respect, these three, with varying emphases, bring the appropriation of Hannah Duston full circle, back to the moment of Mather's "improvement."

The story therefore leaves the realm of the avowedly historical to enter the emergent field of historical romance. Because she really lived and killed and scalped, Hannah Duston remains vexingly, simultaneously, factive and fictive.[19] This oscillation is what Whittier and, more pointedly, Hawthorne attempt to stabilize and refashion into a discursive conduct figure of "do" (Whittier) or "don't" (Hawthorne) female behavior. While fashioning Hannah Duston's experiences into their accounts of old New England, they simultaneously display their broader concerns about gender transgression. As in the earlier instances of rhetorical drag, whoever produces the picture of the woman's life correspondingly interprets and judges it. This element of adjudication, directly traced to Mather, recurs—literally with a vengeance—in the accounts of the 1830s. Only Thoreau's odd, dreamlike impersonation of Duston eschews judgment and, in its rendition of her experiences, crafts a uniquely personalized and, intriguingly, highly feminized model of historical authority.

"An Apology Is in Even Worse Taste than a Preface"

Duston's vengeance represents the central issue in Whittier's story, "The Mother's Revenge." John Pickard describes the collection in which it appeared as "a narrow sheaf of eighteen poems and stories which revealed Whittier's conception of New England romance. It was a concept clasped to the notion that the most fertile area for romance and tradition lay in the past," and he notes that Whittier modeled himself on Scott and Burns (*Memorabilia* 48). However, in composing a tale based on Hannah Duston's story, Whittier found material resistant to easy refiguration in terms of romance. Because Hannah Duston's acts belied his conception of female character, his strategies in retelling Duston's story illuminate some of the problems nineteenth-century male authors had with Duston, and they indicate, too, that these men exhibited ambivalence and, occasionally, anxiety in the face of women telling their own stories.

The opening paragraph of "The Mother's Revenge" delineates contemporary gender roles and describes the "maddening" results if they are ignored:

> Woman's attributes are generally considered of a milder and purer character than those of man. The virtues of meek affection, of fervent piety, of winning sympathy and of that "charity which forgiveth often," are more peculiarly her own. Her sphere of action is generally limited to the endearments of home—the quiet communion with her friends, and the angelic exercise of the kindly charities of existence. Yet, there have been astonishing manifestations of female fortitude and power in the ruder and sterner trials of humanity; manifestations of a courage rising almost to sublimity; the revelation of all those dark and terrible passions, which madden and distract the heart of manhood. (*Legends* 125)

Beginning with the singular "woman" as a metonymy for all women, and ending with the universal "manhood," Whittier distinguishes not only domains of the sexes but also their interpretive value. Women are "generally limited," and they are "milder" and "purer" than men. Because her "sphere of action" is so utterly circumscribed, she can only engage in "quiet communion with her friends." For Whittier, then, Hannah Duston represents a woman outside his definition of "woman." As such she embodies a version of transcendence, "sublimity," which demands containment, lest "the revelation of all those dark and terrible passions . . . madden and distract the heart of manhood." Initiating his Duston retelling with a discussion of appropriate gender characteristics, Whittier sets the stage for his own performance of rhetorical drag.

As he reiterates in the second paragraph the dangers the early settlers encountered, Whittier again refers to conventional gender roles—the "forefathers" and "woman herself"—to clarify his meaning. Reduction of women to the image of "woman" allows him to tame Duston:

if she is an aberration, then "woman" safely represents the quiescent private angel, a creature who neither needs nor seeks access to public discourse.[20] However, within this restrictive model of female behavior, Whittier acknowledges that some women had stories to tell. Like Ter Amicam, Whittier grants a dispensation to these women, who "have left behind them a record of their sufferings and trials in the great wilderness." The records "are full of wonderful and romantic incidents, related, however, without ostentation, plainly and simply, as if the authors felt assured that they had only performed a task which Providence had set before them, and for which they could ask no tribute of admiration" (*Legends* 126). Obviously, Hannah Duston is not one of these authors, and, as we know, most of the foremothers did not leave written records.[21] Whittier's dispensation recurs to the one accorded to Mary Rowlandson by Ter Amicam, a defense based on providential will and the woman's "modesty": "they could ask no tribute of admiration." So the dispensation is problematic, as is the description of the plain and simple style attributed to the suffering women. Rather, this passage signals Whittier's entry into the league of male authors telling Hannah Duston's story, using it for its "wonderful and romantic incidents," and retooling Hannah Duston herself by means of his own supposedly feminized style.

Although Whittier's efforts at folk narrative can be traced to Scott's and Burns's romantic aesthetic as well as to Irving's *Sketch Book*, his prose pieces often display the sentimentalism found in early women's periodicals (in which some of his own works were published). While employing ballad and sketch, he drew on regional material as well as prevailing styles associated with female authors. "The Rattlesnake Hunter" and "The Human Sacrifice" display the Gothic horrors and uncanny images found in Mrs. Radcliffe's works. His didactic tone echoes domestic education texts such as Lydia H. Sigourney's *Letters to Young Ladies*. Throughout his life, Whittier fully encouraged and admired female authors.[22] His support of the Lowell factory worker Lucy Larcom was instrumental in her move from factory to parlor. He appended his sister's poems to his own *In Hazel-Blossoms* (1874) and wrote the introductory memorial to *Letters of Lydia Maria Child* (1883), noting that although "comparatively young, [Child] had placed herself in the front rank of American authorship."[23] However, his critical evaluation of women's works depended not only on aesthetic worth but, more importantly, on their moral didacticism.

In Whittier's later published writings, then, he maintained that women authors were capable and deserving of success at publication. Yet for Whittier, a Quaker whose religious beliefs included equal access to Inner Light, the gender differences remained clearly defined.[24] The same ideologies that delineated "women's sphere" shaped his conception of authorship: for Whittier, the practices of authorship divided along gender lines. Thus women authors should concern themselves with morality and feeling, while male authors must demonstrate a vigorous manliness. This explicitly gendered, yet vague, criterion recurs in his reviews and informs his drag version of Hannah Duston.

For example, in 1828, Whittier praised Susannah Rowson's *Charlotte's Daughter* because Rowson's characters are "described with pathos and sensibility." And although Rowson had been "censured for her uniform simplicity of style and scrupulous adherence to the realities of life," her writings contained "a truth—a moral beauty . . . which harmonizes with our purest feelings—a language which appeals to the heart, not in the studied pomp of affectation, but in the simple eloquence of Nature."[25] In the same period, he appreciated Milton's "strength and boldness" (Cady and Clark 18), and, to him, Burns's works appeared "entirely destitute of affectation, and seem to have flowed from the heart of their author without any effort on his part; yet they are full of originality—bold—vigorous, and occasionally eloquent and powerful. Throughout the whole, there breathes a tone of manly independence" (Cady and Clark 19). Whittier hedges with "yet," allowing for Burns's heartfelt sentiments, while recuperating his male strengths as "bold" and "vigorous," qualities that differentiate it from the merely sentimental. Whittier assails Scott for "the moral tendency of his writings," which does not sufficiently castigate "the drunken exploits of profane and licentious cavaliers" whose "darker and more repulsive" traits are "softened with the too charitable light of romance" (Cady and Clark 22–23). American literature, however, suffers from a lack of "manly and vigorous exertion": "We are becoming effeminate in everything—in our habits as well as our literature, and there is no one fearless enough to investigate the causes of our weakness and apply the requisite remedies" (Cady and Clark 25–26).[26]

This conception of women's and men's differentiated authorial prerogatives informs Whittier's Hannah Duston, because he represents her as an author, one of the "many [who] have left behind them a record"—despite the lack of an authentic personal account—and because Whittier confers on his Duston the morality and sensibility she seemed, at least in some lights, to have so evidently lacked. Duston's bold and vigorous behavior, her "manly independence," sets her on the wrong side of the gender divide, and Whittier applies the "requisite remedies" to her situation by instilling in Duston a maternal madness born of her infant's murder.

In order to stage this apologia, Whittier shifts from the opening paragraphs' generalities concerning woman's nature and the records of captivity to the specifics of the Duston tale. The crucial act of Indian brutality anchors the story: "The savage held [the baby] before him for a moment, contemplating, with a smile of grim fierceness the terrors of its mother, and then dashed it from him with all his powerful strength. Its head smote heavily on the trunk of an adjacent tree, and the dried leaves around were sprinkled with brains and blood" (*Legends* 127–28). Following the murder, Whittier writes, "She has often said, that at this moment, all was darkness and horror" (128), using rhetorical sleight of hand to attribute words—a "record"—where none existed. From indirect discourse to omniscient narration, he completes the psychological justification: "a new and terrible feeling came over her. It was the thirst of revenge; and from that moment her purpose was fixed" (128). In the event that the reader does not understand the radical transformation caused by the infanticide, Whittier deploys metaphors familiar to both women's literature (the angel of the house) and frontier adventures (the Indian demon): "an instantaneous change had been wrought in her very nature; the angel had become a demon,—and she followed her captors, with a stern determination to embrace the earliest opportunity for a bloody retribution" (128). Thus Hannah Duston, initially a "heroic woman" (126), metamorphosizes into the very image of her captors. Whittier uses rhetorical drag to preempt, or at least mitigate, the crisis that arises from Duston's later actions. Asserting her voice in the present tense ("she has often said . . ."), Whittier justifies the transformation that his prose inevitably must produce, "angel" to "demon."

To rescue Duston from this image, Whittier selectively omits information on the actual killings. He never states that she killed women and children. The murders are accomplished methodically, "Blow followed blow," until she comes to "the last—a small boy." Here Duston hesitates—"'It is a poor boy,' she said, mentally, 'a poor child, and perhaps he has a mother!'"—and spares him (130). Quoting Duston "mentally," Whittier exonerates her in the name of motherhood. He accounts for the scalping by describing Duston "suddenly reflecting that the people of her settlement would not credit her story, unsupported by any proof save her own assertion." Thus "she deliberately scalped her ten victims" (130).[27]

"The Mother's Revenge," the only piece in *Legends of New England* based on an actual person, ends with an appeal to the future when "the simple and unvarnished story of a New-England woman," like many traditions, will be "treasured up as a sacred legacy" (30). This emphasis on legacy, similar to Dwight's concerns, also affiliates Whittier's version of the events with the "record" rendered "plainly and simply" by the women in his opening paragraphs. Whittier thus offers his collection as a foundational text in the "sacred legacy," and his impersonation of Hannah Duston, accomplished through indirect discourse, psychological quotation, and manipulation of familiar metaphors, recaptures her for a coming generation. In his portrait, she is rehabilitated through temporary insanity, an aberrant episode that ceases the moment she remembers her own maternal role while looking down on the last Indian child. Duston's record is Whittier's record, with contemporary notions of gender propriety restored and Duston's maternal nature intact. Her voice impersonated, her feelings and actions are shaped by his authorial imperative. Hannah Duston represents Whittier's entry into the "wonderful history of the past," her historicity morphing into legend, like "The Spectre Warriors" and "Aerial Omens" who fill the poems in *Legends of New England*.[28]

"The Bloody Old Hag"

Just as Hannah Swarton's trek is marked by her blood in the snow, the bloody murders of both settlers and Indians signal Hannah Duston's trajectory through the nineteenth-century texts. For Whittier, the essential element of her madness is triggered by the infant's death, figured in the gruesome image of "the dried leaves . . . sprinkled with brains and blood" (*Legends* 128). Hawthorne, however, emphasizes the blood of Duston's victims in his vilifying 1836 story, "The Duston Family." Revising and interpreting Duston for his readers, Hawthorne leaves no doubt that she is a colonial monster run amok in peaceful Indian forests. Here too, Hannah Duston's behavior places her literally and figuratively outside the bounds of female propriety: in the woods, committing murder.[29]

For Hawthorne, as for Whittier, Hannah Duston challenges his writerly attempts to control her meaning because she resists, at the least, the contemporary aesthetic roles assigned to women. Mary Poovey's discussion of the discourses of political philosophy provides a useful lens through which to interpret Hawthorne's dilemma, the category crisis at the heart of his version of Duston. Poovey argues, first, that the discourses of early eighteenth-century political philosophy divided by the end of the century into the apparently discrete vocabularies of aesthetics and economics. She then goes on to demonstrate that women are objectified in both discourses, as aesthetic objects of contemplation and/or commodities for exchange, and that this objectification marks the limits of the division of the earlier discourse. Each consideration—aesthetic or economic—requires that women be domesticated, kept within the private sphere for men's use. The domestic, therefore, is a function of the public—male—worlds of business and politics. That is, gazing at women from their positions in the public sphere, men construct a model of private and domestic familial virtue against which they measure a more public version of civic virtue. Thus the popular figure of the Republican mother in the early national period is a public figure of private virtue trotted out as a model for the civic man's political use. Hannah Duston problematizes this model because her actions disqualify her as a model of Republican motherhood (indeed, as Hawthorne emphasizes, she failed to protect her children in the attack). Therefore, her utility as an emblem of the domestic is hopelessly flawed, and Hawthorne seizes on this flaw to construct his improved model of the Republican mother and the Jacksonian father. Personified (anachronistically) by Thomas Duston, whose sex protects him from objectification, this (fore)father's appropriately vigorous feats provide a model of both civic and domestic virtue. Contemporary gender regimes permit Hawthorne to rewrite the Duston story as a fable of patriarchal ascendancy.[30]

With this problematic femininity at its base, the story becomes a site for reconfiguring gender roles. Hawthorne feminizes Thomas Duston, and, following Neal and Hutchinson, he accords to Hannah Duston a masculine, indeed, brutal, character. But the story offers more than simple role reversal. "The Duston Family" supports contemporary categories of gendered conduct and simultaneously vexes the categories by assigning them to inappropriate models. In so doing, the story uses Hannah Duston as the foil for an amplified and dominating masculinity that assumes into itself the traditional female role as repository of domestic virtue and sensibility. Because Thomas Duston functions as both father and mother, Hawthorne easily relegates Hannah Duston to superfluity; she becomes a childless mother detached from hearth and home, wandering and withering in the forest. This reconstitution of the Duston family, with an expanded father figure, rewrites familial gender roles while emphasizing the primacy, indeed, indispensability, of the patriarch.[31]

In order to depict Thomas as the sole and sufficient parent, Hawthorne must first refashion Hannah. Dwight's concern for her morally questionable behavior and Whittier's psychological defense of it evince an ambivalence about Duston not apparent in Mather's heroic portrait. However, Hawthorne's hostility toward Mather, vigorously asserted in "The Duston Family," surely influenced his estimation of a Mather heroine. In vilifying Duston, Hawthorne not only repudiates Mather; he reopens the colonial record for a reevaluation of women's roles from his own historical vantage as well.

"The Duston Family" was not Hawthorne's first foray into a historical study based on an exceptional woman. Like Neal and Hutchinson, Hawthorne considered Anne Hutchinson a major figure in colonial history; unlike them, he did not explicitly link Hutchinson and Duston as notorious women. However, his mordant character sketch, "Mrs. Hutchinson," published in 1830, warns readers of the consequences when a woman emerges conspicuously into the public realm. In the story, Hawthorne decries the "impropriety in the display of woman's naked mind to the gaze of the world" (15). "Mrs. Hutchinson" precedes the infamous "d——d mob of scribbling women" letter by twenty-five years, but, as Amy Schrager Lang notes, Hawthorne's anxieties about public women are apparent in the piece. Lang attributes Hawthorne's condemnation of Hutchinson to his conception of her crime as "social rather than theological." Hers is a "failure of domesticity that Hawthorne associates with the eloquence of 'the Woman,' because he regards it as a violation of the law that governs her nature" (13). Hutchinson's unseemly notoriety and public bearing combine with his anxiety about nineteenth-century female writers in this passage, and Hawthorne articulates the ominous roles played in the past—as well as the present and future dangers posed—by exorbitant, public women:

> But here are portentous indications, changes gradually taking place in the habits and feelings of the gentle sex, which seem to threaten our posterity with many of those public women, whereof one was a burthen too grievous for our fathers. The press, however, is now the medium through which feminine ambition chiefly manifests itself, and we will not anticipate the period, (trusting to be gone hence ere it arrive,) when fair orators shall be as numerous as the fair authors of our own day. . . . Woman's intellect should never give the tone to that of man, and even her morality is not exactly the material for masculine virtue. ("Hutchinson" 14)

Recurring to colonial history once more in his Duston sketch, Hawthorne finds a more egregious woman, one whose crime represents not merely an instance of "feminine ambition" but a murderous attack on the (Indian) family itself. Hannah Duston's acts place her beyond any recognizable—and gendered—moral scheme; therefore her historical meaning invites his reinterpretation. Because Hawthorne does not view Duston as a heroine, his image of her does not comport with the Duston found in Mather's *Decennium*. Thus he turns to an alternative source, Benjamin Mirick's 1832 study of Haverhill.[32]

Mirick's *The History of Haverhill, Massachusetts* offers itself as an authoritative version that corrects previous histories: "Many accounts have been published of the heroic deed of Mrs. Hannah Dustin; but the most of them which I have examined are very imperfect, and some of them inconsistent."[33] Mirick depends on additional information from Sewall's diary and local legend to extend and modify Mather's story, and he notes that Hannah Duston's reputation is already problematic for some readers. As did Dwight, Mirick appeals to the "strict moralizer" and addresses the moral ambiguity of Duston's actions:

> Various opinions are afloat concerning the justness of this certainly heroic deed. Perhaps the strict moralizer would say that, the fear of the gauntlet, which, perhaps appeared worse to them than torture or death, or of suffering their danger anew, would not justify the act. And it surely seems that she had lost a great portion of that sensibility, that fear of blood, that sympathy for another's wo, which is at once the delight and ornament of her sex; and which we have been taught to believe is an inmate [*sic*] and constant virtue of her bosom. But a prisoner among the savages—a wife who has seen her dwelling in flames, her infant cruelly slaughtered, and who expects that her husband and the rest of her children have been butchered, who is herself threatened with immediate torture, and with disgrace worse than death—a wife in such a situation would not be apt to critically analyze the morality of the deed. (92)

Fearing torture, death, or—a new twist in the story—rape ("disgrace worse than death"), Duston behaves insensibly, and her behavior contradicts the images that Mirick's readers are taught to believe are essential, "innate," to women. To rationalize her deviance, Mirick emphasizes that Duston is a *wife* who thinks she has lost the preeminent relationship that defines her: she presumes that her husband has been "butchered." No longer anchored by her identity as wife, she becomes disoriented and veers into masculine modes, losing her "fear of blood" and "sympathy for another's wo." Mirick's Duston is emotionally gutted by her experiences, and that lack masculinizes her. By appealing to supposedly "innate" characteristics, Mirick implies that any woman unrestrained by affective connections to men—indeed, any woman not a wife—may career into male realms of action, including violence. Hannah Duston's aggression marks the dangerous instability of unattached women who have no male protector "to critically analyze the morality" of their deeds for them: murder and mayhem ensue.

Mirick closely paraphrases Dwight immediately following this passage to recall Hannah Duston's missing protector: "But let what will be said of her conduct, there is something in the actions of the father and husband, disinterested perhaps, beyond comparison, and noble beyond example" (92). Thomas Duston's "deep, chaste and uncontaminated love for his wife and children . . . prompted his actions" (92). These considerations of sexuality, implicit in the rape threat, become explicit in Thomas Duston's "chaste and uncontaminated love." The sexual leitmotif provides a powerful undertone for sentimentalization, not, as one would expect, emphasizing the trials of Hannah the suffering captive, but focusing on Thomas, the triumphant savior of his children. Whittier accentuates the psychologically deforming experiences that led to Hannah Duston's acts, but Mirick and, to a much greater degree, Hawthorne proffer the image of the tender father over that of the rampaging mother.

Recurring to Mather's emphasis on the "*Agony* of his Parental Affections*," Hawthorne offers Thomas Duston's experiences as the crux of the tale. The first words of the sketch are "Goodman Duston," and the description of the attack begins with a view of Duston as he "had gone forth about his ordinary business" before the "event, which had nearly left him a childless man, and a widower besides" (229). Hawthorne's Thomas Duston, like Dwight's, acts decisively, in sharp contrast to his wife's "helpless state" (230). Although the children had already fled from the house, Thomas Duston opts to rescue them and to leave Hannah to her fate because "the thought of his children's danger rushed so powerfully upon his heart" (230). A pitiable scene ensues, in which Mather's assertion that Duston initially meant to save only one child is echoed, as all seven reach for him as he rides up: "Here is our father! Now we are safe!" (231). In an "anguish of spirit," Thomas's "heart" responds to the seven children, each described with excessive sentimentality. He then repels "the red devils," "the skulking foe" (232), until the family reaches safety within the garrison.

But, the narrative reminds us, "we must not forget Mrs. Duston, in her distress" (233). Amid the breathless description of Thomas Duston's heroic decision to save the children, an explanatory—and highly ironic, even grimly humorous—note slips in. Thomas Duston chooses the children because "he had such knowledge of the good lady's character as afforded him a comfortable hope that she would hold her own, even in a contest with a whole tribe of Indians" (230). As the narrative turns to Hannah Duston's experiences, the pace and tone shift. From the immediacy and desperation of Thomas's heroics, the prose switches to a slower, more deliberative assessment of Hannah's behavior. She rises from her bed, as did so many other captive women scarcely recovered from childbirth, to endure the march. As the captives depart, the baby is killed, her "little corpse" thrown at Hannah's feet. Here, the explanation for Hannah Duston's subsequent actions, advanced by Dwight and Whittier, seems to hold for Hawthorne: "Perhaps it was the remembrance of that moment that hardened Hannah Duston's heart, when her time of vengeance came" (234).

Hawthorne's use of the heart as a trope for "innate" qualities of tenderness and sympathy—that is, as a conventional synecdoche for female sentiment—reveals the profound complications of gender roles he offers in the contrasting images of Thomas and Hannah Duston. Thomas responds to his heart's prompting to save his children, but, in witnessing the infant's murder, Hannah loses her essentialized identity. The death defeminizes Hannah Duston by canceling the characteristic that defines her, her maternal (and conjugal) sympathy. Later, Duston is unable to respond emotionally to the Indian children of her captors because her heart is "hardened." Accordingly, Hawthorne explicitly aligns her—through the heart trope—with the execrable Mather, himself "an old hard-hearted pedantic bigot" (235) who hates the Indians because they are Catholic. Mather's vehement Indian-hating metaphorically transfers to Hannah Duston: she becomes a figure of violent Puritan intolerance, on whose authority Mather gleefully contrives his story. Through Hannah Duston, Mather's cruelty is literalized in the murders of the "touching" Indians.

If Thomas Duston dealt handily with a brutal "skulking foe," Hannah Duston finds herself within a family group who, despite "their loneliness and their wanderings, wherever they went among the dark, mysterious woods, still [kept] up domestic worship, with all the regularity of a household at its peaceful fireside" (235). The Indian family of "two stout warriors" and "three squaws, and seven children" mirrors the familial makeup of the Duston clan before the attack.[34] In the second half of "The Duston Family," this band recuperates the figure of the home destroyed in the first part of the story, and, in a profound reversal, Duston assumes the role of barbaric, ungrateful interloper. Domesticity reconstitutes itself in the woods: "The barbarians sat down to what scanty food Providence had sent them, and shared it with their prisoners, as if they had all been the children of one wigwam, and had grown up together on the margin of the same river within the shadow of the forest" (236). The Indians pray together as a family, but Duston, Neff, and Lennardson "prayed apart" (236).

This peaceful fireside scene leads directly to the dramatic climax of the story, the killings and scalpings. Here, the victims and murderers trade faces; Duston literally assumes the features of those who captured her and murdered her child. In the initial attack, her "chamber was thronged with the horrible visages of the wild Indians, bedaubed with paint and besmeared with blood, brandishing their tomahawks in her face" (233). When Duston awakens Neff and Lennardson to make their escape, "all three stood up, with the doubtful gleam of the decaying fire hovering upon their ghastly visages, as they stared round at the fated slumberers. The next instant each of the three captives held a tomahawk" (237). At this crucial moment, the narrative offers a curious internal apostrophe, a voice of rationality (and sentimentality) appealing to Hannah Duston's lost maternal instincts: "But, O, the children! Their skins are red; yet spare them, Hannah Duston, spare those seven little ones, for the sake of the seven that have fed at your own breast" (237). The authorial voice enters the text just in time to assume Hannah Duston's voice. Hawthorne's practice of rhetorical drag is a complex negotiation, assuming multiple positions—as omniscient narrator, as intensely engaged observer ("spare those seven little ones"), and then, finally, as intimate auditor, privy to Duston's thoughts.

As in Whittier's account, the text quotes Hannah Duston to reflect her own tortured psyche: "'Seven,' quoth Mrs. Duston to herself. 'Eight children have I borne—and where are the seven, where is the eighth!' The thought nerved her arm; and the copper-colored babes slept the same dead sleep with their Indian mothers. . . . There was little safety for a redskin, when Hannah Duston's blood was up" (237). Although the passage begins sympathetically, offering Duston's painful memories of her children and of the infant's murder, it ends with a damning hyperbole. No Indians are safe from the inhuman, utterly transformed "raging tigress" (237).

Significantly, Hawthorne omits the information, recorded by Mather and all subsequent Duston revisionists, that the captives were threatened with the gauntlet upon arrival in the next Indian town. As well, the one sentence describing the Duston baby's death bears no authorial comment on the brutality of the Indian who slew her, yet the deaths caused by Duston, Neff, and Lennardson are described with astonishment and disgust. There is no exculpation for Duston: Hawthorne portrays her scalping almost as a matter of course: "The work being finished, Mrs. Duston laid hold of the long black hair of the warriors, and the women, and the children, and took all their ten scalps, and left the island, which bears her name to this very day" (237–38). The murders, the scalping, the island, and her historical status thus conflate in one sentence. This omission of the traditional rationale for the scalping, that Duston took the scalps to substantiate the story of her escape, not only exaggerates Hannah Duston's abandoned femininity but also imputes to her an unseemly, unwomanly "feminine ambition," a spurious replacement for her lost femaleness. The scalps symbolize this perverse ambition: she takes grisly trophies to ensure that her public role will never be forgotten. For Hawthorne, Duston is a superb example of the public woman, untethered to the domestic, uncontrolled by a rational, yet emotionally astute, husband. She deserves nothing less than the horrific fate he envisions for her: "Would that the bloody old hag had been drowned in crossing Contoocook River, or that she had sunk over head and ears in a swamp, and been there buried, till summoned forth to confront her victims at the Day of Judgment; or that she had gone astray and been starved to death in the forest, and nothing ever seen of her again, save her skeleton, with the ten scalps twisted round it for a girdle!" (238).

Hawthorne's antipathy to Puritan intolerance is a critical commonplace, and the harsh descriptions of Cotton Mather within the story surely follow suit, but this last passage is a zealot's prosecution, a damning portrait of a cold-blooded killer, and a call for grisly revenge. Hawthorne's famous argument with Puritanism cannot account for the excessive brutality, the almost sadistic tone, of his conclusion. His final paragraph indicates that the obliteration of Hannah Duston, which he would have preferred to be literal—"that she had sunk over head and ears in a swamp, and been there buried"—is impossible. Her legend persists, but Hawthorne shifts the focus to certify the true hero/heroine: "This awful woman, and that tender-hearted yet valiant man, her husband, will be remembered as long as the deeds of old times are told round a New England fireside. But how different is her renown from his!" (238). "Tender-hearted yet valiant," Thomas Duston embodies an array of morally superior characteristics notably deficient in his wife. His feminized sensibilities, metaphorically represented by his *tender* heart, never overwhelm his masculine valor: he is the very model of a nineteenth-century husband, pursuing "his ordinary business" and saving his family when the outer world threatens. As a man, he moves both within and outside the domestic circle with equal facility, with equal propriety. In contrast, Hannah Duston, separated from her husband and family, abandons her female role and aggressively pursues a new performance as a "raging tigress." For Hawthorne, Hannah Duston represents an emotionally eviscerated, therefore unwomanly, woman, the antithesis of her manly, yet feminized, therefore fully human, husband. Rejecting passivity, sensibility, and sentiment to save herself, she symbolizes the dangers of a public woman who assumes personal authority, thinks for herself, and, worse, acts on her decisions. The story's closing line starkly reveals the cultural values at stake in revising a New England legend: Hawthorne replaces the heroine with a hero to erase the "bloody old hag" whose "renown" so threatens male prerogative in his version of the domestic.

"Every Withered Leaf"

While Hawthorne vilifies Hannah Duston and imputes a frenzied, murderous tone to her purloined and psychologized voice, Thoreau finds in Duston the perfect instrument for composing a new model of history. Absent from Thoreau's meditative and rhetorically complex rendering of the Duston legend are the erstwhile apologias explaining how a woman could act like a man; the question never arises in the brief Duston passage in *A Week on the Concord and Merrimack Rivers*. Rather, Thoreau's Duston provides him with an entry into an alternative version of history, one he has been constructing throughout *A Week* and pursues through *Walden* and the late *Journal*.[35] This personalized history derives from a peculiar relationship between narrator and subject, which renegotiates contemporary gender representations through the historical figure of Hannah Duston.

"The wildest scenes have an air of domesticity and homeliness even to the citizen," Thoreau writes shortly before the Duston episode appears in "Thursday" (*Week* 316). This interpenetration of the wild and the domestic replicates precisely the antinomies in Hannah Duston that so troubled earlier commentators. The apparent contradiction between the two concepts, implied in Thoreau's statement, collapses, however, in the gendered rhetoric that conventionally figures *both* nature and the home as feminized entities. The metaphorical congruence between the feminized figures of wilderness and home, or in Thoreau's terms, between "nature" and "the cultivated life" (328), informs Thoreau's singular use of Duston. As both Sharon Cameron and Perry Miller have noted, Thoreau's writing seems obsessively "sexist" in that there is scant attention paid either to women in general or to particular women within the corpus. Miller asserts that "what for long especially outraged commentators was the supposition that Thoreau flouted the highest, the most sacred, duty of masculinity: he was not interested in women!"[36] The few instances where Thoreau did refer to women therefore require scrutiny because they are so rare and because they offer insights into Thoreau's engagement with the gender regimes of his time. Thoreau's use of Duston's silence functions as an index, a way of understanding popular nineteenth-century American representations of female submission and domestication. Yet Thoreau's manipulation of these gender traits yields a representation of the historical as an intensely personal, feminized construct. This manifests in Thoreau's particular practice of rhetorical drag, in which Duston is neither an instrument nor an object that necessitates explanation or policing; in *A Week*, Hannah Duston becomes, for Thoreau, a site of identification.

The lines converging in the Duston section in *A Week* have several provenances. Contemporary social and philosophical discourses ascribed civil life to men and domestic life to women, a model Hawthorne assumes in his version of family values. As discussed above, Poovey argues that women in this bourgeois model become, ultimately, objects of aesthetic contemplation: the busy businessman requires relief from the relentless competition of the marketplace and demands of civic life, and he looks to the private as an antidote from the oppressive public domain. "At the heart of this semiotic system of discriminations is the difference upon which Burke anchored aesthetics: women are 'the sex'; men discriminate among women and so found civilization. Beyond this we have all the other discriminations that actually tie women to their bodies but do so simply as effects of a system that infuses differentiation with social meaning while claiming to reflect universal beauty and desire" (Poovey 96). This "fetishization of sexual difference" underscores Thoreau's account of Duston, but Thoreau's own differentiation of himself from the world of civic men—especially his alignment with a wilderness outside both the private and public worlds of society—complicates the gendered opposition. Thoreau uses the conventional social organization of sexual difference in order to reconsider public life as a function, even degradation, of the personal, the private, and the "natural."[37] Thus his composition of the Duston section requires the recognition of gendered roles so he can destabilize them and insert himself as immediate observer. Thoreau's particular enactment of rhetorical drag provides him with a space— here the space of Hannah Duston's historicity—both to perform and to observe. As well, by aligning himself with an exceptional woman, Thoreau finds an alternative to both the marketplace and the parlor, a position from which to stage a new story of human experience.

That story differs from traditional history in its reevaluation of the historical narrator as objective informant. The much-noted problem of the self in Thoreau's work originates in the *Journal* but extends through *A Week* as well. Although Linck C. Johnson demonstrates that Thoreau uses only a few sentences from his *Journal* account in "Thursday," Johnson also notes that this chapter is "where he charts a movement away from other men to primitive nature" (24). Verbatim passages of the *Journal* may not appear here, but sections of that work adumbrate "Thursday" as surely as the more obvious transcriptions appear in other sections of *A Week*. In particular, Thoreau's meditations on the relationships between history and biography and between biography and autobiography form an undercurrent in the boat trip down the Merrimack.

In the gap left by Hannah Duston's missing voice, Thoreau finds a space for a reworking of both historiography and autobiography, two practices whose generic differences he refutes. Similar to Emerson's famous dictum, "there is no History, only Biography," Thoreau writes in the *Journal:* "Strictly speaking the societies have not recovered one fact from oblivion, but they themselves are instead of the fact that is lost. The researcher is more memorable than the researched. . . . And it is the province of the historian to find out not what was but what is" (*Journal 1,* 414). Privileging present experience over "dead institutions," Thoreau presses the distinction between the culturally specific, authoritative "*annals* of the country" and transcendent "natural facts, or *perennials,* which are ever without date" (*Week* 219). Historiographic material is properly not only biographical but autobiographical, an effect of the living present: "Biography is liable to the same objection—it should be autobiography. Let us not leave ourselves empty that so vexing our bowels we may go abroad and be somebody else to explain him. If I am not I who will I be?" (*Journal 1,* 416). One answer to that question, for the Thoreau of *A Week,* is Hannah Duston.

The Duston passage in *A Week* offers several transformations; the most startling is Thoreau's shift from narrator to historical agent, that is, from the traveler, sailing up the Merrimack with his companion, to Hannah Duston, furiously paddling away from the scene of carnage on Contoocook Island. The metamorphosis requires a radical restructuring of time, accomplished through a prefatory syncopation: "The river has done its stint, and appears not to flow" (320). Having created this interstice in the present-tense narrative, the prose shifts to the past while sustaining a tether to the present[38]: "On the thirty-first day of March, one hundred and forty-two years before this, probably about this time in the afternoon, there were hurriedly paddling down this part of the river, between the pine woods which then fringed these banks, two white women and a boy" (320).

Thoreau initially twists temporality by setting the historical past in the immediacy of the narrative's present with "probably about this time." After a dramatic rendering of the scene, in which the scalps are described as "still bleeding" at the bottom of the canoe, he names Hannah Duston, Mary Neff, and Samuel Lennardson and produces the briefest rendition of the legend by far. Whereas the previous commentators followed Mather's attribution of heroism to Thomas Duston, Thoreau barely mentions him. The attack on her Haverhill homestead is viewed through Hannah Duston's eyes: "She had seen" her children "flee with their father," and "she had seen" her infant murdered. These were her observations, perfect in the grammatical sense, completed in the past by Thoreau, using Duston's eyes if not her "I." But once the story reaches the captivity and killings, it switches to the simple past, the narrator's view. The passage remains in the simple past until the crucial scalping scene: "But after having proceeded a short distance, fearing that her story would not be believed if she should escape to tell it, they returned to the silent wigwam, and taking off the scalps of the dead, put them into a bag as proofs of what they had done, and then retracing their steps to the shore in the twilight, recommenced their voyage" (322). The series of past and present participles retrieves the immediacy of the opening passage and provides the segue into the temporal dissonance of the next sentence: "Early this morning this deed was performed, and now perchance, these tired women and this boy, their clothes stained with blood, and their minds racked with alternate resolution and fear, are making a hasty meal of parched corn and moose meat, while their canoe glides under these pine roots whose stumps are still standing on the bank" (322). Where is this narrative situated in time? "This morning" might indicate a late summer day in 1839, the day when Henry Thoreau and his brother John sailed this portion of the Merrimack. Or is it sometime between 1847, when Thoreau began drafting "Thursday," and the 1849 publication of *A Week*? But the narrator writes from the spring of 1697, accomplishing a stupendous feat of synchronicity through the manipulation of tenses. If there had not been such a variety of verb tenses leading to this point, the passage might be considered only an instance of poetic license, heightening the dramatic value of a well-known New England tale. But subsequent paragraphs continue the temporal careening between the colonial era and Thoreau's own doubled present, 1839/1849. A sustained present-tense passage allows Thoreau to inhabit Hannah Duston's canoe: "their nerves cannot bear the tapping of a woodpecker," "they do not stop to cook . . . ," "the fish-hawk sails and screams overhead . . . but they do not observe these things, or they speedily forget them. They do not smile or chat all day" (322–23). *His* observations are *hers*, and he registers the natural phenomena—the fish hawk, the geese flying over-head—which the preoccupied Duston never notices. Inserting himself into the story of Hannah Duston, Thoreau uses her historical locus as a position from which to rerecord the events of the day, thus including the natural world previously missing from the Duston accounts. These phenomena are as integral to his version as the escape and scalpings considered by earlier writers, because Thoreau's history recognizes the entirety of the scene, including the nonhuman agents who "tell" her tale: "Every withered leaf . . . seems to know their story, and in its rustling to repeat it and betray them" (322).

Rhetorically, Thoreau's tense shifts relocate his narrator from the *Week*'s narrative present—as disjointed as it may be—into the seventeenth century. He turns again to a complex temporal manipulation in order to extricate himself from Duston's canoe. A paragraph-long sentence juxtaposes his "we" against the Duston company's "they." "We" are subjects in the present tense, while Duston, Neff, and Lennardson "have already glided out of sight," into the historical, if imperfect, past (323).

Yet Thoreau's historiographical refashioning does not deviate entirely from the conventional practices of contemporaries such as Mirick. In his final comment on Duston, Thoreau invokes the legitimacy of an unnamed scholar: "According to the historian, they escaped as by a miracle all roving bands of Indians, and reached their homes in safety, with their trophies, for which the General Court paid them fifty pounds" (*Week* 323). This sentence might be found in any Duston account, especially in the dry renditions of Saltonstall or Mirick. However, Thoreau recovers a tone of traditional authority only to subvert it with this startling turn to the literally familiar: "The family of Hannah Dustan all assembled alive once more, except the infant whose brains were dashed out against the apple-tree, and there have been many who in later times have lived to say that they had eaten of the fruit of that apple-tree" (324).[39]

The gruesome image of the blood-spattered tree and leaves, so sensational in Whittier, is transformed by Thoreau into a symbol of historicity. Duston's descendants partake of her experiences with every bite of the apple, enjoying a literal communion with the past. Thus the sentimental portrait of the family gathered around the apple tree is troubled by the faintly disturbing view of self-conscious eaters of the historically tainted fruit, although, in his evenhanded fashion, Thoreau appears to be nonjudgmental about the seemliness of the act. The scene invokes, of course, the original bad apple (eater), Eve. Reinforcing this correlation, the next paragraph immediately reinterprets the distance between the narrative present and Duston's time: "This seems a long while ago, and yet it happened since Milton wrote his Paradise Lost" (324).

With Milton—and the felt presence of *his* Eve—the narrative initiates a disquisition on the nature and writing of history. There is much evidence in *A Week*'s earlier passages and in the *Journal* to account for the ease with which the narrator slips into the canoe, into the past, and rewrites Duston's experiences. Yet "Thursday"'s engagement with gender and history does not conclude with this familiar—albeit oddly executed—tale from the colonial past. The pages following the Duston account reconsider the precise nature of history and its informants. In a startling revision of the "*annals* of the country," Thoreau's historical model produces a radically different form of authority.

Beginning with Milton, the passage continues with an argument that all history is culturally relative: "This seems a long while ago, and yet it happened since Milton wrote his Paradise Lost. But its antiquity is not the less great for that, for we do not regulate our historical time by the English standard, nor did the English by the Roman, nor the Roman by the Greek" (324). Thoreau contends as well that American Indian concerns, the activities of "the Pennacooks and Pawtuckets," necessitate inclusion in a complete historical accounting of the Merrimack. Then, telescoping and juxtaposing several Western and Eastern sources, the text refers to Mosaic, Hindu, Greek, and Roman narratives, all issuing in a solidus that graphically points to America (325). These familiar, authoritative narratives thus textually produce a political and social entity, the United States. But the next image quickly displaces these traditional sources by substituting figures invisible or marginal in conventional historical documents: "It is a wearisome while.—And yet the lives of but sixty old women, such as live under the hill, say of a century each, strung together, are sufficient to reach over the whole ground. Taking hold of hands they would span the interval from Eve to my own mother. A respectable tea-party merely,—whose gossip would be Universal History" (325). Here, Milton's Eve becomes Thoreau's Eve, indeed Thoreau's foremother. The march of the centuries is a family affair measured in women's lives, and the written documents disappear; history is gossip, a particularized, private medium, ephemeral, deferring record. Instead of the state as the ultimate product of history, the text offers the narrator as the final issue, the end of the chain concatenating "from Eve to my own mother." The shift in a model of history from written to spoken, from authoritative male discourse to a much maligned female-identified discourse, permits Thoreau to make himself the apotheosis of the present moment.[40] One reason Thoreau can so easily insert himself in this feminized chain is that he has just aligned himself with a woman, assumed her experiences: he "became" Hannah Duston.

Later in "Thursday," Thoreau meditates on poetic expression, particularly the unconscious "perfection in accident." Authentic personal expression cannot be found in writing: "The talent of composition is very dangerous,—the striking out the heart of life at a blow, as the

Indian takes off a scalp. I feel as if my life had grown more outward when I can express it" (329). The curious reinvocation of scalping here as the image of the deliberate, the compositional, talent contrasts negatively with the "tea-party" metaphor. That figure privileges speech over writing, female gossip over male historiography. But it is a *woman* who scalps in "Thursday," who methodically returns to scalp, "fearing that her story would not be believed" (322). This is yet another facet of Thoreau's identification with Duston. When she most transgresses her gender role, when she acts like a man by deliberately scalping, she ensures the composition of her legend. Moreover, this strangely elliptical statement questions the meaning of "expression" itself for Thoreau. Is he more "outward" when he is "other"—that is, when he is Duston? Her historical act of scalping thus does not escape his censure, as this passage indicates. But Thoreau maintains his identity with her even when she is most morally compromised on his terms, just as his own writing compromises his authentic expression.

Thoreau's gender switch itself derives from a long-standing narrative strategy that Sharon Cameron finds in Thoreau's journal writing, the primary source for all his published works. She notes that his composition method depended on a "self-cancelled state" wherein the self resists a reading as a coherent entity: "the self ventriloquizes the idea of a discourse so that as far as possible it is its own first and second person" (Cameron 93). That is, in the *Journal,* the first-person narrator invents another narrative self who in turn interprets natural phenomena for the first narrator. In the Duston episode, this second narrator becomes Duston, observing the events of the passage downriver. We are already familiar with several versions of ventriloquism and impersonation involving Hannah Duston, and it would have been easy for Thoreau to speak (more properly, to write) over her silence. The instrumentality of this model, supplemented by Thoreau's sporadic references to women, links his Duston to the previous versions while furthering his historiographical purposes. Just as Mather uses Duston as an exemplum and Hawthorne represents her as a perversion of the angel in the house, Thoreau shapes Duston into a vessel for his own complicated project by elaborating her instrumentality into a locus of identification. In so doing, he produces a revised understanding of history.

Thoreau's feminization of historical discourse emerges earlier, in an 1837 obituary of one Anna Jones that he wrote when he was twenty

years old: "After a youth passed amid scenes of turmoil and war, she
has lingered thus long amongst us a bright sample of the Revolutionary woman. She was as it were, a connecting link between the past and
the present—a precious relic of days which man and patriot would
not willingly forget."[41] As in *A Week,* a woman serves as the link in
the chain, the historical informant both inside and outside—"amid"—
public events. The intersection of a feminized figure and Thoreau's historical narrator produces a gendered model of observation, one based
on a belief that empirical experience constitutes the basis for a truly
inclusive historiography. That is, the sensibility necessary for this kind
of minute, particularized, personalized observation is characteristically
feminine. As Thoreau writes, "a man of fine perceptions is more truly
feminine than a merely sentimental woman" ("Love" 270).

This feminized sensibility, along with Thoreau's ability to reimagine himself as a woman, are attested to in journal fragments from
1849 and 1850. Perry Miller cites notes found in F. B. Sanborn's papers indicating that the 1849 fragment is "a response to the death of
[Thoreau's] sister Helen" (Miller 101). The passage begins "A Sister"
(graphically set apart from the surrounding paragraphs, as if a title)
and continues:

> One in whom you have—unbounded faith—whom you can—
> purely love . . . An enlargement of your being. Level to yourself
> . . . The stream of whose being unites with your own without a
> ripple or a murmur. & they spread into a sea.
>
>   I still think of you as my sister. I presume to know you. Others
> are of my kindred by blood or of my acquaintance but you are
> mine. you are of me & I of you I cannot tell where I leave off and
> you begin. (*Journal 3,* 17)

Continuing in this physically transcendent mode, the text finally dis-
misses bodies altogether: "I can more heartily meet her when our bodies
are away. I see her without the veil of the body. When I commune with
her I forget to speak." Finally, an apotheosis of brother and sister ab-
sorbs the universe: "When I love you I feel as if I were annexing another
world to mine. We splice the heavens." This overwrought prose (Miller
calls them "strangulated pages") could be attributed to Thoreau's heart-

felt loss of his sister, to whom it seems he was indeed quite close. However, other passages in the journal, as well as the Duston episode in *A Week*, combine with this journal entry to present a constellation of feminized images, simultaneously figures of authentic experience and of historical revelation. Later, in 1850, the journal produces yet another passage on women, history, and Thoreau:

> I cannot imagine a woman no older than I. The feminine is the mother of the masculine . . . The oracular nature of woman still in some sense broods over the masculine. Man's wisdom compared with womans fertile & dewy instinct (affection) is like the lightning which issues from the bosom of the cloud—except that *at last man becomes woman & woman man.* (*Journal 3*, 44; emphasis mine)

"At last" at the end of history, the genders reverse places but, interestingly, do not dissolve into unity. As we saw in "Thursday," the narrator places himself at the end of the chain of women whose "gossip would be Universal History," in the narrative present. He arrives there via Duston's canoe, transforming himself into Duston. Together the narrator and Duston reconfigure history, so that "at last" "it will not take a very great grand-daughter of [Eve's] to be in at the death of time" (*Week* 325).

Thoreau's revision of the Duston legend, like the previous versions, uses Hannah Duston to produce a vision of a kind of history; but Thoreau's Duston is more akin to Cotton Mather's Hannah Swarton than the Duston we find in Hutchinson and the others. Just as Mather impersonated Swarton to establish his authority as historian and to invoke the authenticity of Swarton's experiences, Thoreau becomes Duston to make himself a historical informant. Mather's history is providential, Thoreau's natural, and there is a huge disparity between their ends and means. But both find in captive women instruments through which to construct their personal versions of history. Mather's Swarton and Thoreau's Duston proceed from historiographical models of representative men. However, these biographical models treat women's experiences as more authentically transhistorical than men's. That is, women, as emblems of the personal, the private, and the nonauthoritative, provide the *matter* of history, while authoritative historians such as Mather and Thoreau interpret the women's lives for historical comprehension—for the record.

Hannah Duston, silent and silenced, offers the perfect instrument for all the authors keen to tell her story. Her own statement surfaced many years after these revisions were published and remains the only authentic record of her captivity and escape. As I noted in chapter 1, Duston used contemporary (1724) language to describe her experience as "the Comfortablest time that ever I had." That is, the captivity was an opportunity for her to strengthen her faith. This expression appears in an application for admission to her church. The statement seems to define the captivity as "the central experience of her life," and the letter "wisely emphasized its private aspect . . . rather than its public aspect. For her public role had led to notoriety and material gain, hardly model qualifications for one of the Elect" (Derounian-Stodola, *Women's Indian Captivity Narratives* 135–37).

The attempts to control the public understanding of Duston's behavior produced remarkable varieties of rhetorical drag. In part because Duston's voice was missing from the originative account, replaced by Mather's authoritative words, it could not easily be impersonated directly by subsequent revisers: they were forced to deal with the looming figure of Mather first. So they improved Mather, by offering justification, motivation, exculpation, and, indeed, vilification as they saw fit. Hutchinson, and the antiquarians as well as the nineteenth-century revisers, opened Hannah Duston's interior life to view; they impersonated her by describing and often supplying for their readers Duston's mental voice, her responses and reflections while in captivity. These enactments of rhetorical drag generate a range of functions, including instrumentality as well as identification. Each Duston reviser/impersonator interpreted Duston's captivity for his own historical project, and each struggled to reframe and contain her actions within contemporary gender regimes. Silent, Duston's figure continues to escape.

CHAPTER 3

✺

"The Original Copy and the Mistake of the Transcriber"

Elizabeth Hanson's Relation

I was concerned to stir up Friends to keep a faithful Record of all
their Sufferings, to be made use of as Occasion might require.
— Samuel Bownas, *Journals of the Lives and Travels of Samuel
Bownas and John Richardson*

Samuel Bownas's posthumously published *Journals* describe his experiences as a "Public Friend," a Quaker preacher certified by the London Yearly Meeting to travel as a missionary for the Society of Friends. During a 1727 visit to the colonies, he met with Elizabeth Hanson, a Friend who had been captured by Indians and carried to Canada in 1724–1725 and whose first-person story, *God's Mercy Surmounting Man's Cruelty,* was published in 1728.[1] Although the only extant first edition of Hanson's text lacks a title page, an advertisement in the *Pennsylvania Gazette* of 24 December 1728 provides the narrative's full title, which includes the guarantee that "the substance" of the narrative "was taken from her own mouth, and [is] now published for general service." We can assume then, at the least, that the narrative was not written by Hanson but was composed by an anonymous amanuensis. Yet later English editions of *God's Mercy* attribute authorship not to Hanson or any named transcriber but to Bownas himself. However, as both R. W. G. Vail and Richard VanDerBeets note,

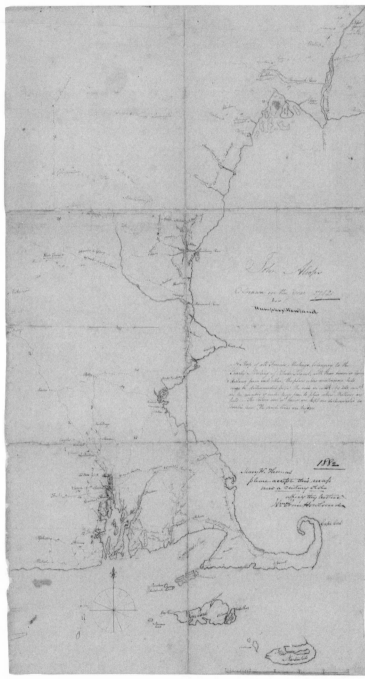

Map of 1782 showing Friends meetings in New England, drawn by Henry J. Cadbury. Courtesy of the John Carter Brown Library at Brown University.

Bownas's statement, placed at the end of the description of his visit with Hanson in his *Journals,* casts doubt on his authorship: "After my return to Europe [he was in Ireland in 1740] I saw at Dublin a relation of this extraordinary affair in a printed narrative, which was brought over by a friend from America."[2] The statement does not completely eliminate Bownas as author, especially if we consider the likelihood of an original manuscript transcribed at the time of the encounter, but it certainly gives cause to question the attributions of those English editions that were published after Bownas's death.[3] Significantly, the American editions of 1728 and 1754 do not list Bownas as author, and their last pages contain the initials "E. H." after the final sentence.[4]

The confusion concerning the authorship of *God's Mercy Surmounting Man's Cruelty* indicates that Hanson's text, like Mary Rowlandson's and Hannah Swarton's, was published with some measure of male intervention, whether it was the work of Bownas or the product of another hand. The extent of that intervention can be traced in the narrative's rhetorical disruptions; in shifting tones, parenthetical commentary, and proto-ethnographic discourse, and most notably in the figure of Hanson herself. An examination of these linguistic effects reveals that, the title page's claims notwithstanding, Hanson's imputed authorship serves purposes beyond the mere description of the redemptive value of captivity. By naming Hanson as author, the actual author or authors of *God's Mercy,* along with the men who sponsored its publication, elicit a woman's voice to achieve several goals: in addition to representing a conventional exemplum for religious instruction, Hanson's voice serves a broader agenda that includes a radical reformulation of the public role of Quaker women. To understand fully the work of this text's rhetorical drag, we must consider the dialogue between Hanson's imputed authorship/her first-person voice and the published testimonies of earlier Quaker women, especially the prophetic texts of female missionaries and visionaries.

As a captivity narrative, *God's Mercy* also conducts a dialogue with previous narratives, such as those attributed to the Puritan women Rowlandson and Swarton. All these female "authors" achieved public notice because of their captivities; indeed, captivity conferred on Elizabeth Hanson—and by extension, on her narrative—a specific status as instrument and exemplum in some measure because Rowlandson and Swarton achieved that status upon publication of their narratives.

Yet there are distinctions among the texts as well. Hanson's narrative was published in Philadelphia, not Boston, although she lived in New Hampshire and her captivity was spent traveling from Dover, New Hampshire, through northern Maine to Canada. Whereas Rowlandson and Swarton "figured" the Congregationalist errand into the wilderness for Calvinist historiographers such as the Mathers, Hanson's authorial "I" contributed to an emerging Quaker historical narrative, one that sought to compete with Puritan providential history while importing images and themes from those same Calvinist texts. We cannot identify the hand of the male ghostwriter in the Hanson narrative as we could Cotton Mather's in the Swarton text, but we can trace the utility of the text for a committee of unnamed Quaker men who sanctioned publication of the narrative. The Mathers may have invented the American captive heroine, through their own enactments of rhetorical drag, but the Quakers performed their own version as well.

Hanson's religious affiliation is often noted in studies of the narrative. However, these studies attribute Hanson's famous passivity to her Quaker beliefs without fully interrogating that passivity, especially as a gendered construct, in the cultural contexts of early eighteenth-century Quakerism.[5] My reading of *God's Mercy Surmounting Man's Cruelty,* however, began with the questions of why and how this rather obscure woman from the backwoods of Nock's Marsh in Cocheco (spelled "Knoxmarsh" and "Kecheachey" in the text), New Hampshire, was able to publish her captivity narrative with the approval of an intensively discerning Quaker publication establishment.[6] Accordingly, a fuller understanding of the Hanson narrative places it within the context of the Quakers' strict policies regulating publication, especially those policies regarding the documentation of Friends' "sufferings" during the early religious persecutions. Read within this highly controlled publication enterprise, Hanson's text marks an important shift in the Society's construction of the public act of testimony, and it represents Friends' shrewd use of a female voice to invent a secularized version of suffering.

As an illuminating complement to this reading, I trace the Hanson text's affiliation with an earlier Quaker captivity narrative, Jonathan Dickinson's *God's Protecting Providence* (1699). Just as Rowlandson's narrative served as the Puritan ur-captivity text, Dickinson's appears to be the first Quaker Indian captivity narrative set in America. *God's Protecting Providence* offers the novelty of an Indian captivity set in the Caribbean and Florida, and many of its elements affiliate the narrative with the growing literature of "sufferings." A comparison of the Dickinson and the Hanson texts reveals that the Hanson narrative emphasizes Hanson's conduct as specifically gender appropriate: she represented a reconstructed version of Quaker womanhood that supported the Friends' project of rehabilitating the Society in its own view and that of others. In the case of *God's Mercy*, this rehabilitation necessitated a performance of rhetorical drag.

Indeed, the Society's decision to transform its public image from that of a radical sect to an established church manifests throughout the Hanson narrative; it is particularly evident in the text's abandonment of earlier Quaker practices of disruption and intervention. To this end, the passive Hanson represents a conventional female figure against the earlier Quaker women preachers. She speaks as a more constrained and controlled woman, and in this figuration, Hanson signals the eighteenth-century Quaker retreat from confrontation with New England clergy. Thus *God's Mercy Surmounting Man's Cruelty* employs a woman's voice to counter Congregationalist images of hysterical and outlandish Quakers—especially female Quakers—as the Society moved to legitimate itself as a social and religious institution. The narrative thus became another element in the project through which Quakers carefully constructed and reinterpreted their own history. By the second decade of the eighteenth century, the Society of Friends had also disengaged from the long pamphlet battle with Congregationalists. Quaker polemicists turned to fashioning a public image of credibility and stability for their community as the Society entered more secular and more political terrain. The narrative therefore serves various Quaker agendas while employing the Puritan practice, most evident in the Mathers' writing, of treating the public appearance of a woman's voice as an exceptional, and therefore noteworthy, event, despite the Society's long-standing tradition of women speaking in public.

"There Was No Resistance"

As related in the narrative, Elizabeth Hanson's captivity experiences seem not to have differed significantly from those of other female captives. In a raid on 27 August 1724, a party of thirteen Indians captured

Elizabeth Hanson, her children, and a female servant at their remote farmhouse in Cocheco, Dover Township, New Hampshire. The attackers immediately killed one child in the house. Two sons, who had been in the orchards playing, appeared at the door, and one was killed because his screaming threatened the secrecy of the attack. Of her six children, then, Hanson set out with two daughters, one son, and her two-week-old infant. The Indians and their captives traveled through the northern New England forests for several days then divided into separate groups. Hanson's eldest daughter Sarah was taken away first, then her second daughter and a servant were assigned to another group. Hanson was left, along with her infant and six-year-old son, as the property of the raiding party's "captain." This master proved to be moody, initially helping Hanson over rough terrain and carrying her infant, but later tormenting her by threatening to eat the baby and by beating her son. By January, they had made their way to the French settlement of Port Royal in Canada. There, after some haggling and hesitation on the part of her master, Hanson and her two children were bought by a Frenchman. Hanson's husband came to redeem them after they had spent about one month with the French; he was able to secure Elizabeth and the two children with her as well as their younger daughter and the servant. However, Sarah's owner would not sell her back, and they had to leave her behind. They returned home on 1 September 1725. In April 1727, John Hanson attempted to redeem Sarah once more, but he died en route to Canada. The relatives with whom he was traveling located Sarah and tried to ransom her but were unsuccessful. Sarah married a Frenchman in order to escape her Indian captivity and settled among the French.[7]

These facts reveal that Hanson's captivity was comparatively brief (only six months long to Swarton's five years), although it took the family several months to travel back to their home. Moreover, her specific trials—the children's murders, the threat to her infant (her milk nearly dried up in the early days of the trek), her master's abuse—do not substantially differentiate Hanson's experiences from those of most captive women. For example, both Duston and Rowlandson lost children, and Duston's infant was killed in front of her eyes as well.[8] Derounian-Stodola and Levernier note the high number of pregnant and postpartum captives in the colonial period and indicate that, in the narratives, these conditions "draw attention to the woman's increased physical and emotional vulnerability" (146). Reproducing this motif, the narrative announces Hanson's vulnerability at the outset: "It must be considered that I having lain-in but Fourteen Days, and being but very tender and weakly, being removed now out of a good Room well accommodated with Fire, Bedding, and other Things suiting a Person in my Condition, made these Hardships to me greater than if I had been in a strong and healthy Frame; yet for all This, I must go or die. There was no Resistance" (5). As this passage demonstrates, *God's Mercy Surmounting Man's Cruelty* invokes the same tone of dependency found by Derounian-Stodola and Levernier in other captivity narratives. Yet this text is notable not merely for Hanson's similarities to the earlier Puritan captives, but also—and most intriguingly—for the differences it exhibits in the degree to which her vulnerability and passivity are emphasized. Whereas even the "ideal captive" Hannah Swarton disputed with her French captors, displaying a kind of spirited agency (albeit an agency constructed by Cotton Mather), Hanson disputes no one, offers no resistance, and spends a good part of her captivity accommodating an unpredictable and brutal master. As Ulrich notes, "In comparison with Mary Rowlandson, Elizabeth Hanson is a bland and almost passive heroine, perhaps because her narrative is shorter and less colorful, but also because she embodied qualities so often associated with an insipid and confining femininity" (*Good Wives* 230).

The characteristics Ulrich sees embodied by Hanson contrast sharply with those of earlier Quaker women as portrayed in both Quaker and Puritan documents. Elizabeth Hanson's Quaker foremothers enacted radically nontraditional roles as preachers and visionaries within the early Quaker movement. Because Quakers believed in continuing revelation derived from a divine light within, they were not bound, as Calvinists were, to the Pauline proscription against women speaking in church.[9] Margaret Fell's tract, *Womens Speaking Justified, Proved and Allowed of by the Scriptures* (1666), in fact reinterprets Paul and castigates ministers who censure women for preaching: "God hath put no such difference between the Male and Female as men would make. . . . all this opposing and gainsaying of Womens Speaking, hath risen out of the bottomless Pit, and Spirit of Darkness. . . . that Spirit hath limited and bound up all within its bond and compass, and so would suffer none to speak, but such as that spirit of Darkness approved of" (quoted in Bacon 16). Fell's statement explicitly validates the public proselytizing work of women. These visionary and proselytizing modes imputed to the Quaker preachers a public authority heretofore denied women. Fell, a wealthy aristocrat, spoke from a presumption that she was entitled to preach and write. However, many of the early female preachers were poor women from the rural areas north of London where the movement began. Without the class background of Fell, these women nevertheless claimed a right to teach, preach, and, notably, dispute with clerical authorities, practices that outrageously transgressed prevailing gender and class boundaries.

However, in her studies of seventeenth-century female Quaker prophets, Phyllis Mack cautions against reading the women's charismatic preaching as a direct exercise of a liberated personal authority. As Mack notes, questions of female agency and power were not so easily reconfigured: "Women as prophets enjoyed virtually the only taste of public authority they would ever know. Some of them used that authority to write and publish their own works, to organize separate women's meetings, or to challenge the greater authority of the male leaders. Yet the assumption that visionary women were pursuing a covert strategy of self-assertion ignores the very real problem of agency for seventeenth-century religious actors" (Mack 5). While Mack's focus is the subjective experience of prophecy, her argument that there is "a very real problem of agency" for the proselytizing women alerts us to the basis of that problem in the organization of gender within the Society. Whether their public appearances were made possible through an exercise in "self-transcendence," as Mack argues, or through a "covert-strategy of self-assertion," Quaker women's actions were interpreted by people outside the Society as, among other things, disturbing forms of gender transgression. In particular, Puritan responses to female Quaker preachers in their midst ranged from mild disapproval to lethal persecution. Yet the Society's own understanding of the role of women in the first years of proselytizing displayed a remarkable disposition toward gender roles. Mack states that these early Quakers "perceived the attributes of men and women to be fluid and interchangeable. The letters and visionary texts written by the first female prophets are often indistinguishable from those written by men" (9–10). This egalitarian view changed in the second generation of Quaker leaders, and the Hanson narrative illustrates the Quaker turn from at least nominally fluid gender roles to more conventional, and more constrained, conceptions of proper female behavior. Thus the history of female public authority in the Society of Friends informs Hanson's voice in *God's Mercy* and determines that voice just as Calvinist gender regimes dictated the delineaments of the Puritan women's captivity narratives. Fell's justification for "Womens Speaking" adumbrates Hanson's narrative, notwithstanding the more than sixty years and geographic distance between them, because the female religious activism she both legitimated and encouraged extended to the colonies and was practiced through to the end of the century.

Quaker women preachers visited Hanson's hometown of Dover, New Hampshire, as early as 1662 and were, according to one Quaker historian, "'the first publishers' of the Quaker message in what later came to be a great Quaker centre, namely, the Piscataqua region—particularly the country about Dover and Portsmouth, New Hampshire" (Jones 103). These women, Anne Coleman, Alice Ambrose, and Mary Tomkins, were convicted and sentenced under the antidissenter "Cart and Whip Act" of 1662 and as such were, late in winter, "stripped to the waist and tied to the cart to trudge under the lash through these eleven towns" (Jones 105). According to one account, when asked her name by a magistrate, Alice Ambrose replied, "My name is written in the Lamb's book of Life." Her retort demonstrates the defiance, zeal, and confrontational tactics of the early missionaries. As well, the notable missionary Elizabeth Hooten, reportedly George Fox's first convert, was whipped at the tail of a cart through several northern settlements, including Dover. Elizabeth Hanson and her unnamed amanuensis were probably familiar with the stories of these activist heroines not only because the events occurred in the area, but also because, as I shall discuss below, these kinds of "sufferings" were documented for retelling by the London Yearly Meeting, the official governing body of the Society in the early days of the movement.[10]

Although the source of Hanson's sufferings is Indian captivity and not religious persecution, her narrative should be examined within this model of female agency and activism, not only because Hanson's voice and her behavior break with the historical model, but also because, in that break, the text reconfigures the meaning of public testimony for Quaker women. For example, Elizabeth Hooten wrote about the persecutions she sustained because of her beliefs, and she communicated them to major political figures such as Cromwell and the mayor of London. Hooten did not confine herself to a testimony of personal sufferings but rather harangued authority figures for their dereliction in allowing other Quakers to be persecuted (Mack 27–30; Jones 105n5). Hooten's publications thereby present her as simultaneously a religious prophet and a social critic. Hanson's text, in contrast, offers a secularized and highly personal portrait of sufferings that she never relates to a specific religious or social context. Criticism of authorities, either military or religious, never emerges in the Hanson narrative, as it does to varying degrees in the earlier Puritan narratives and, certainly, in writings such as Fell's and Hooten's.[11] Rather, Hanson's voice remains intensely personal, disengaged from the larger forces that affect her life. Indeed, the only gesture at overt criticism appears parenthetically near the end of the narrative, where the text offers a brief snipe at established church practices: "But the next Day after I was redeemed, the *Romish* Priests took my Babe from me, and according to their Custom, they baptized it (urging if it died before That, it would be damned, like some of our modern pretended reformed Priests)" (34). Thus Hanson never assumes the authority to caution or criticize that is evident predominantly in the earlier Quaker women's writings and to a lesser extent in the publications of the Puritan women captives.

This reticence can be traced to a reevaluation of the value of women's public voices in the Society of Friends. By 1728, the utility of the literature of sufferings had changed from a means of protesting intolerant Calvinist and Anglican practices to a method of memorializing early martyrs. This new tradition established those martyrs as believers whose behaviors might be cherished but not reenacted. Thus the rhetoric of early eighteenth-century Quaker publications differed from that of the earlier period. Historian Arthur J. Worrall notes that "by the 1720's, one-time opponents were treating Friends with measured respect. Accompanying this change was development of a Quaker view of the Society's past. Hardened into virtual canon, this version of the sufferings of prophetic Friends provided a standard to which not even the faithful remnant among eighteenth-century Quakers could measure up" (42). Worrall's point is crucial to understanding the publication milieu that produced *God's Mercy,* particularly regarding the emergence of a Quaker history that in some measures counterposed Calvinist Providential histories.

One important consequence of this historiographic turn was that the public role of women changed. The history of women's activism in

Quaker society, as exemplified by Fell's writing and by the actions of the Dover missionaries, provided a pattern of aggressive female behavior that was no longer encouraged by the Society.[12] Whether an overt challenge, such as Alice Ambrose's retort to the magistrate, or a resolute engagement with the persecuting forces, such as Mary Dyer's return to Boston after banishment (knowing it would probably cost her her life), confrontation of any sort conflicted with a revised image of the Society's future. Accordingly, Hanson displays none of this aggressive female behavior in *God's Mercy*. Although Hanson clearly did not have a choice in the matter of her captivity, in the way that Dyer, for example, could choose whether or not to return to Boston, the narrative provides scant evidence of Hanson's self-assertion within the bounds of her captivity. Nor does a retrospective tone of defiance or indignation emerge from the text as the fictive Hanson tells the story of deprivation and degradation from her safe position as a redeemed captive, a tone that marks, for example, Rowlandson's complaints about "praying Indians." Rather than reproducing the heroism of assertive, resistant women and reinvigorating a model of Quaker female authority, *God's Mercy* presents Hanson as a woman utterly subject to her circumstances, acquiescing in her subjection: "There was no Resistance" (3).

Hanson's "I" maintains this strictly submissive aspect toward her master at all times, even excusing his cruel treatment of her six-year-old son or his threats to kill them all: "But I always observed whenever he was in such a Temper, he wanted Food, and was pinched with Hunger" (23). Ulrich reads this comment as Hanson's gesture at "humanizing" her master, portraying him as "a struggling human being" rather than as a "savage": "Dutiful service (and perhaps refusal to hate) were her witness against him" (*Good Wives* 232). Ulrich's reading is plausible, given Quakers' earlier sympathetic attitudes toward Natives. Yet the resignation and sympathy offered to her male master demonstrate as well that Hanson recognized and acceded to male power in a manner that earlier captives, and certainly the Quaker women missionaries, did not.[13] That is, Hanson's complete submission represents a variant captive figure—and a new version of a public Quaker woman—one who does not question the powerful agents or structures by which she is made to suffer.

One might argue that Hanson's agency appears—as Ulrich hints—in her capacity for acts of forgiveness and submission. In this case, her figure nevertheless differs from the vigorously resistant acts of earlier Quaker women. Her apparent *absence* of agency—the power and initiative to change or influence her state—from the narrative indicates that the author or authors of the text shaped Hanson's figure and voice to remedy what had come to be viewed as the excesses of the earlier female Quaker missionaries, in particular their aggressive public presence as instructors. Hanson thus became a model of women's comportment in contradistinction to that offered by the figures of Coleman, Hooten, or Dyer. The opening pages signal her vulnerability, indeed paralysis, by presenting Hanson as an almost detached spectator at the murders of her children: "two of these barbarous Salvages came in upon us, next Eleven more, all naked, with their Guns and Tomahauks came into the House in a great Fury upon us, and killed one Child immediately, as soon as they entred the Door, thinking thereby to strike in us the greater Terror, and to make us more fearful of them" (5). Notably, the text does not register Hanson's horror at the unnamed child's death; rather she explains the strategic value of this brutal act. The narrative repeatedly employs the strange tactic of interpreting Hanson's personal experiences from an Indian point of view, as when she excuses her master's behavior as a consequence of hunger. The result of this passage is to produce Hanson's voice as both informant and interpreter while her figure remains a suffering object. The tension between interpreting subject and interpreted object gives the text its eerily detached, analytical tone, so at odds with the convention of a captive's tortured self-portrait. This alienation effect appears most explicitly in the passage that describes her children's bodies being scalped:

> Now having kill'd two of my children, they scalp'd 'em (a Practice common with these People, which is, when-ever they kill any *English* People, they cut the skin off from the Crown of their Heads, and carry it with them for a Testimony and Evidence that they have kill'd so many, receiving sometimes a Reward of a Sum of Money for every Scalp) and then put forward to leave the House in great Haste, without doing any other Spoil than taking what they had pack'd together, with my self and little Babe Fourteen Days old, the Boy Six, and two Daughters . . . with my Servant Girl. (7)

The parenthetical explanation of scalping, coupled with the preceding rationale for the first child's death, not only downplays the narrative impact of the deaths but also interjects an anthropological commentary at a place where we expect personal response. These rhetorical disruptions might be interpreted as a form of psychological compensation, an attempt to distance the narrator from the painful memories of the murders. However, similar parentheticals are scattered throughout the narrative, as when, apparently at the end of her journey, Hanson describes the accommodations: "But here our Lodging was still on the cold Ground in a poor Wigwam, (which is a kind of little Shelter made with the Rinds of Trees and Mats for a Covering, something like a Tent.) These are so easily set up and taken down, that they oft remove them from one Place to another" (17). Moments such as these, when Hanson suspends the narrative flow of her captivity experiences in order to explain a particular Indian practice, signal the intervention of a shaping hand who shifts the tone from personal suffering to impersonal observation and interpretation. These passages impart to Hanson's "I" the authoritative tone of a rational, almost disinterested observer, one at odds with the voice of the beleaguered sufferer who seems reluctant to assert herself in any way.[14] That is, the tone of authority occurs precisely in those passages that are most clearly the work of the "transcriber"—the parentheticals—and the running narrative displays only submission, the voice of the captive as she relates the series of trials that befall her.

Moreover, the Hanson narrative selectively imports images of despair and persecution from the earlier Puritan women's captivity narratives without employing those stories' countering images of agency as well. For example, the Hanson narrative repeats the citation from Proverbs 27.7 that Rowlandson uses when she is first given unfamiliar and, to her, disgusting food. Eating bits of beaver-skin match-coats, Hanson states: "they gave us little Pieces, which by the *Indians* Example we laid on the Fire till the Hair was singed away, and then we eat them as a sweet Morsel, experimentally knowing, that *to the hungry Soul, every bitter thing is sweet*" (12). In an echo of the Rowlandson narrative, the biblical quote reappears on the next page in a discussion of eating a beaver without cleaning the "Guts and Garbage" (13). Additionally, like Rowlandson, Hanson quotes Psalm 137 ("By the Rivers

of Babylon there we sat down, yea we wept when we remembered
Zion"), but Hanson cites the entire passage, because in her case the
scriptural passage is literalized when her daughter's captors command
her to sing.[15] Clearly, some of the emblems found in Rowlandson's
and the other Puritan women's narratives recur here as a means toward authenticating Hanson's captivity experiences. The credibility
of *God's Mercy* thus depends, to some extent, on its alignment with
Puritan texts. However, Hanson's voice was not shaped by a Calvinist ministry for its ideological ends. We must turn to the first Quaker
Indian captivity narrative—the only one to precede Hanson's—in order to interpret her text within a genealogy of Quaker publications. A
comparison of Jonathan Dickinson's *God's Protecting Providence* and
Hanson's *God's Mercy Surmounting Man's Cruelty* extends the inquiry
into agency (or the apparent lack of it) in the Hanson text and suggests
that, while Hanson's passivity and submission seem to be peculiarly
Quaker characteristics in light of the Puritan texts, within Quaker contexts those qualities have become specifically gendered traits.

"Having Things Suitable"

Jonathan Dickinson's captivity followed a shipwreck off the Florida
coast in 1696. Dickinson kept a journal during his captivity that served
as the basis for *God's Protecting Providence* and, as I will discuss below, the publication of that journal became a priority in the Quaker
community of Philadelphia. The representation of Dickinson in the
text and the circumstances of the narrative's publication served as a
model to the composer(s) of *God's Mercy*. Although the Hanson text
drew language and imagery from the Puritan women's captivity narratives, its resonance with the publication of a coreligionist who endured captivity demonstrates a particularly Quaker use of the female
captive's voice. Not surprisingly, the following brief comparison of
the two captivity texts reveals that these narratives prescribed and re-
inforced the conventional gender roles prevailing at the time of publication. However, the comparison also underscores Hanson's nonresis-
tance in light of Quaker attempts to reconfigure and delimit women's
agency. Thus Hanson's female passivity, compared with Dickinson's
male assertiveness, subtends the Society's move away from the ear-

lier public and confrontational model of female action and toward a privatized, psychologized, much more quiescent role for its women members, especially those who came before the public in print.

Broadly viewed, the Hanson and Dickinson narratives seem to have little in common besides the fact of captivity. Dickinson's party, which included his wife and infant son, as well as the aged and sickly Quaker missionary Robert Barrow, was captured shortly after a shipwreck when they reached the shores of what is now Jupiter Inlet along the Florida Keys. Among the other captives were the captain and crew of their ship, the *Reformation*. This group was later joined by survivors of another ship in the convoy that had gone down in the same storm. Thus, all these captives were interjected into Indian territory and found there by their captors; unlike Hanson, they were not abducted. Another difference between the two captives is evident in their social positions: Dickinson was a wealthy Jamaican plantation owner, slave-holder, and businessman, while we know Hanson to have been an ordinary New Hampshire farm wife. However, these differences do not preclude a comparative reading, because the two texts share common themes and images. For example, both texts portray their narrators as prisoners under the control of unpredictable Indian masters and as victims suffering from hunger and exposure. Although Dickinson's wife is not the focus of the story, she, like Hanson, is described as an anxious woman trying to nurse her baby on a dwindling supply of milk. As well, in their respective narratives, Hanson and Dickinson are represented as heads of dispersed households, responsible for keeping their families alive and well. Moreover, for the purposes of this inquiry, the most significant element shared by the two texts is that they are the only first-person captivity narratives sanctioned by Quaker authorities over a nearly thirty-year period.[16]

Yet another similarity between the narratives may be found in the probability that Dickinson's *Journal,* although a first-person narrative, was not the product of his pen alone and was, like Hanson's, fashioned by a committee of concerned Quakers.[17] It is instructive to note that the text characterizes Dickinson as conventionally submissive to the will of divine providence while it simultaneously imparts to him an assertive personal agency, one that contrasts starkly with the self-abnegation evident in Hanson's character. The contrast suggests, then, that Quakers, or at least those responsible for the public representations of Friends through publication, did not emphasize passivity as a peculiarly Quaker trait. Rather, passivity was clearly a gendered trait by the second generation of the Quaker movement, that is, by the time the transformation from radical to mainstream religious organization was in full swing.[18]

The Dickinson narrative might be considered an interim text in this transformation. In its portrayal of the old missionary, Robert Barrow, and his consistent, profound faith in the face of impending death, the text tends toward hagiography. Barrow was a Public Friend, one of the first Quaker missionaries to come to America, whose sufferings for his religious convictions were well known. His exemplary death at the end of the narrative resonates with the documentation of the sufferings of the early Quaker martyrs. In fact, as the modern editors of *God's Protecting Providence* point out, title pages on later reprints of the narrative indicate that "if we study the size of the lettering used for the two names, Barrow becomes the real hero of the tale, and Dickinson remains merely the author" (Dickinson 18). Whatever the effects of these later title pages might have been, the first edition deftly provided two heroes, one the saintly, resigned Barrow, the other the more conspicuously resisting Dickinson. From the outset, Dickinson evidences a remarkable ability to seize the moment and remedy his situation (and that of his fellow captives). This image of capability is achieved early in the narrative, while Dickinson is still aboard ship. In an accident caused by high winds, the shipmaster's leg is broken, and the narrator describes the actions he takes: "which accident was grievous to him and us; but I having things suitable, with a little experience set it" (26).

Later, as a captive, Dickinson displays his reluctance to yield to the Indian master's wishes when they conflict with his own desires. The party and their captors, having rowed in the ocean all day en route to an Indian settlement, have not had a drop of water. Attempting to draw near the shore, they are prevented by swelling seas. Dickinson relates the following confrontation: "Our [Indian] master said it was impossible to get on shore alive: but I being under some exercise was desirous to be on shore, and thereupon did express myself to the rest of our people; they stated the danger; all which I was as sensible of as they, yet I could not rest but insisted on going ashore" (41). When they do not succeed in reaching shore, they stand off for the night, but Dickinson is relentless: "I began to persuade them to go on shore. All were desirous, but thought it impossible. At length we resolved to

venture" (42). By persuading the entire party to attempt the dangerous landing, he saves everyone from drowning in the storm that night,
including his captors. This rescue is attributed to divine intervention,
as the phrase "being under some exercise" indicates ("exercise" is a
familiar Quaker term for the workings of conscience, especially as a
mark of divine revelation). But the narrative also makes it clear that
God helped Dickinson because he helped himself, because he acted
on his "exercise." Similarly, in a later passage, the party puts ashore
among different groups of competing Indians, some who wish to kill
the captives and some to save them. A skirmish ensues, and the English are set walking through what might be considered a gauntlet: "We
dared not help one another; but help we had by some of them [friendly
Indians] being made instrumental to help us. My wife received several
blows, and an Indian came and took hold of her hair, and was going
either to cut her throat or something like it, having his knife nigh her
throat; but I looked at him, making a sign that he should not, so he
desisted" (45). Dickinson's personal authority, implicit in this encounter, appears in other passages as explicit command, as when he orders one of his surviving slaves to search for water. Therefore the first
Quaker Indian captivity narrative offers a male hero who, despite the
exigencies of hunger, exposure, and the illness of his wife, child, and
elderly friend, never seems to lose his composure or his sense of his
own authority. Both gender and class grant him the kind of distinction
that even the Spanish governor of St. Augustine recognizes when he
advances Dickinson credit for supplies. *God's Protecting Providence*
thus offers its readers two models of the Quaker public man: Barrow, whose time has literally and figuratively passed, and Dickinson,
who represents the future of the Society as a group of respectable,
respected, and highly competent men of business.

Dickinson's authority and personal command during captivity contrast sharply with the submission Hanson exhibits during her time
among the Indians. Where Dickinson reasons with and at times cajoles
his captors, Hanson shrinks from her master and removes herself and
her children from his sight if she perceives that he is in a threatening
mood. When Hanson's Indian master throws a sharp stick at her six-
year-old son, she relates that "he hit him on the Breast, with which my
Child was much bruised, and the Pain, with the Surprize, made him
turn as pale as Death." Yet in this direct attack on her child, Hanson

did not intercede. Rather, she says, "I intreated him not to cry; and though he was but six years old, and his breast very much bruised, he bore it with wonderful patience, not so much as once complaining. So that the patience of the child restrained his barbarity" (27). Unlike Dickinson, who could persuade an Indian to release his wife through sheer force of personality ("but I looked at him . . . and he desisted"), Hanson must be content to instruct her child in her own passive manner as a way of preserving his life.

This distinction between male authority and female subordination can be seen as well in the narrative's respective prefaces even before the first-person voices appear. Like the contextualizing materials of the earlier Puritan narratives, the opening commentaries in these texts both guide readers into a specific interpretation of the story and testify to the good reputation of the presumed author. However, the reputations are based on quite different criteria. The preface attests to Dickinson's authority, where an unknown writer preempts any questions concerning Dickinson's "credit": "I might very well here put a period to my preface; but that I foresee, some persons may be ready to say: here is an account of very strange passages, but of what credit is the relator? May we depend upon his authority, without danger of being imposed upon? To such I answer, He is a man well known in this town, of good credit and repute on whose fidelity and veracity, those who have any knowledge of him, will readily tell, without suspecting fallacy" (110). Clearly, the preface writer means to evoke Dickinson's "credit" as a moral characteristic, but the text also directs the reader's attention to Dickinson's standing as a successful businessman. As well, this passage comes at the end of an elaborate preface that explains, point by point, the meaning of some of the more notable events in the text. In contrast, the preface to the Hanson narrative consists of two paragraphs. The first paragraph, which echoes the Rowlandson preface in its invocation of "the Case of the *Israelites, Job, David, Daniel, Paul, Silas,* and many others," states the lesson to be learned from this text: that "we [?] may know he is *a God that changeth not, but is the same Yesterday, to Day and for ever*" (4). The brief second paragraph is one long sentence that neither emphasizes Hanson's social status nor draws attention to her "credit":

> Among the many modern Instances, I think, I have not met with
> a more singular One, of the Mercy and preserving Hand of God,

than in the Case of *Elizabeth Hanson,* Wife of *John Hanson* of *Knoxmarsh* in *Kecheachey,* in *Dover*-Township, in New-England, who was taken into Captivity the 27th Day of the 6th Month, call'd *August,* 1724, and carried away with four Children, and a Servant, by the *Indians;* which Relation, as it was taken from her own Mouth, by a Friend, differs very little from the Original Copy, but is even almost in her own Words (what small Alteration is made being partly owing to the Mistake of the Transcriber) which take as follows. (4)

The two prefaces illuminate the gender-differentiated versions of authority that condition the male and female captivity narratives. Dickinson's authority is explicitly invoked, and the preface writer assures the reader that his reputation for "fidelity and veracity" underwrites the narrative. Hanson is described simply as John Hanson's wife; the facts of her captivity, encapsulated in the prefatory sentence, register the authenticity of her experiences, but they do not confer a broad cultural authority on her. Dickinson's moral qualities and social standing testify to the value of his narrative, but the only credential Hanson's text offers is that it was "taken from her own Mouth." Quakers reading both of these captivity narratives therefore encountered two narrators whose differences in social status are apparent in the opening pages of the texts and who display highly gender-differentiated models of conduct during captivity. Given that, between 1699 and 1728, Dickinson's was the only Quaker captivity in print, we might ask what the Quaker publication establishment had in mind when they authorized the publication of another captivity narrative nearly thirty years later, one attributed not to a wealthy and eminent male Friend but to an obscure woman.[19]

"My Afflictions Are Not to Be Set Forth in Words to the Extent of Them"

That the Society of Friends was eager to publish Dickinson's *Journal* as *God's Protecting Providence* can be seen in the priority it received when Philadelphia Quakers finally set up their own press. Reiner Jansen, invited by the Quakers to operate the new press imported by the Society, was given the Dickinson manuscript to print before any other works. However, had Dickinson wished to publish his narrative immediately upon his return from captivity in 1697, he would have been prevented not only by the absence of a press but, more importantly, by the process through which all Quaker publications had to pass before they even reached the press. This censorship apparatus had been formalized over twenty years earlier. Louella M. Wright notes, "In 1672, when the Great Pardon of Charles II gave the Friends a temporary respite from persecutions, they grasped the opportunity for giving publicity to their books and tracts in a more systematic manner that had hitherto been possible" (80). The outpouring of Quaker publications was accompanied by a concern that the texts written by Quakers and/or produced by Quaker printing houses conform to the Society's aims.[20] In this spirit of regulation, the London Yearly Meeting directed the Second Day Morning Meeting to censor "all manuscripts published under the name of the Society" (Wright 97).[21] The effect of the directive was that all manuscripts written by Quakers, whether or not explicitly "published under the name of the Society," were screened.

The censors were particularly attentive to, and wary of, texts that contained incidents of enthusiasm and confrontation with other religions. For example, Wright discusses the difficulty the Morning Meeting had with Judith Bowlbie, who in 1686 wished to publish her contentious tract, *A Warning and Lamentation over England* (which was not published until 1751) (Wright 105). Not surprisingly, the censorship practices of the Morning Meeting reflected the Quakers' changing perceptions of the Society as a more conservative and mainstream religion. Publication was controlled, and even the tradition of traveling preachers was regulated by new directives requiring certification from the preachers' home meetings. As Mack notes, "Women felt the brunt of these restrictions on movement and behavior more than men" (366).[22] In the early years of the eighteenth century, the London Morning Meeting issued several warnings about "women's excessive speaking" and made it clear that public enthusiasm like that displayed in the early years would not be encouraged or abetted by the press. The institutionalized opposition to particular forms of Quaker expression can be seen in the records of those texts, like Bowlbie's, that were not sanctioned by the all-male censorship committee. Conversely, we may find in a narrative such as Hanson's precisely those themes and images the Society sought to foster.

Although the London Morning Meeting oversaw all texts published in England, it also noticed American publications and sent epistles to the colonies concerning publication there. Thus my reading of the Hanson narrative as a text that comes out of an English Quaker milieu concerned with self-regulation and sensitive to outside opinion attends to the narrative's transatlantic contexts.[23] Moreover, a group of men from the Philadelphia Yearly Meeting oversaw the press there until 1709 and after that year was replaced by a standing committee. Therefore the processes and structures for censorship had crossed the Atlantic well before Hanson's narrative was published (Frost 222). This committee would have seen and shaped the Hanson narrative to suit the ends of the Philadelphia Yearly Meeting in particular and the Society of Friends in general.

"Not to Be Set Forth in Words"

When Elizabeth Hanson arrives at the Indian fort, the story of her incessant discomforts and "sore trials" breaks to admit a moment of reflection. Here the voice is not enthusiastic, visionary, or prophetic, though her suffering is great. In contrast to the ecstatic experiences registered by Quaker women who underwent sufferings for their faith, Hanson's experiences under duress are self-negating and fearful. "Her" narration displays only concern for her children and the difficulty she has in maintaining a properly resigned state of mind:

> But while they were in their Jollity and Mirth, my Mind was greatly exercised towards the Lord, that I, with my dear Children separated from me, might be preserved from repining against God, under our Affliction on the one Hand, and on the other, we might have our Dependance on him who rules the Hearts of Men, and can do what pleases in the Kingdoms of the Earth, knowing that his Care is over them who put their Trust in him; but I found it very hard to keep my Mind as I ought, under the Resignation which is proper to be in, under such Afflictions and sore Trials, as at that Time I suffer'd, in being under various Fears and Doubts concerning my Children. . . . And herein I may truly say, my Afflictions are not to be set forth in Words to the Extent of them. (18–19)

As I noted above, Hanson's sufferings are caused by secular forces, although her responses throughout the narrative are spiritual. Thus, while the Hanson narrative portrays the suffering Quaker woman in a new setting, Indian captivity, it also presents her with a new rhetorical mode. This new mode invokes the memory of the early martyrs' persecutions without resorting to the incendiary rhetoric the early women used to publicize their sufferings and thereby publicly castigate their persecutors. The Society no longer wanted to project an image of divinely inspired female activists working toward thorough social reorganization, including radical gender egalitarianism. The more quiescent and anxiously maternal Hanson of *God's Mercy* offered a "properly resigned" woman whose attentions are focused on her private spiritual exercises and her children's welfare. This image, although less active than the earlier women's, carries with it a revised form of Quaker female agency. In this light, the images of Hanson's "insipid and confining femininity" — her utter submission to her Indian master, her resignation, her maternal and spiritual concernments — are neither insipid nor confining. Instead, they represent a use of rhetorical drag to accommodate the changes in the Society, which sought not to erase but to reconfigure, indeed, domesticate, the public authority of Quaker women.

Domestication was accomplished structurally through the separation of women's and men's meetings for business, where women's meetings focused primarily on family matters such as education of the young, marriage, and proper Quaker behavior.[24] We can find an echo of this model of women's cooperation in the Hanson narrative as well. Hanson's interactions with the Indian squaws offer the few glimpses of her where she is not either hiding from, being abused by, or otherwise submitting to her master's persecutions. The concern displayed by the Indian women pointedly contrasts with her master's brutality. For example, when her master tears Hanson's blanket from her and beats her son, the master's mother-in-law comes to Hanson and tells her through signs that he intends to kill her. Hanson states that the squaw advised her "by pointing up with her Fingers, in her Way, to pray to God, endeavoring by her Signs and Tears to instruct me in that which was most needful, *viz.* to prepare for Death which now threatened me; the poor old Squaw was so very kind and tender, that she would not leave me all that Night, but laid her self down at my Feet, designing what she could to asswage her Son-in-law's Wrath" (21).

This kind of female help is consistently available to Hanson: when she is too cold and feeble to obey the command to fetch water, another woman does it for her, and, notably, when Hanson's milk had dried up, the squaws teach her how to make a gruel from pounding walnuts. As well, Hanson is surprised by the squaws' attempts to intervene for her and her children when the master is abusing them. Although these instances of female cooperation are not strictly analogous to the Quaker women's meetings, they do represent a version of gender solidarity that does not disrupt an overarching patriarchal mode, just as the women's meetings never achieved an equivalent institutional authority to the men's, especially in terms of publication oversight or censorship. In these passages, then, the Hanson narrative presents a view of women who may not be autonomous but who exhibit, within certain strict boundaries, an agency and concern for the welfare of the women and children around them. In doing so, *God's Mercy* places Hanson within a wilderness domestic that emphasizes conventional female traits of sympathy and compassion, traits consonant with a model of eighteenth-century Quaker womanhood.

"A Short, but a True Account"

God's Mercy uses Hanson's voice, then, to mark the changes in women's public roles within the Quaker movement, to present a more reticent, more private, more conventionally feminized model of a female Friend. As I have noted, the Hanson narrative steers clear of any political or religious confrontation, instead employing Hanson's figure and voice to exemplify the early eighteenth-century accommodation with their former persecutors, the Congregationalists. This accommodation is most apparent in the narrative's generic affiliations with the earlier Puritan women's captivity texts. The Calvinist antipathy to the public authority displayed by Quaker women is amply documented. One need only open the pages of Mather's *Magnalia* to find a dialogue between a minister (a barely disguised Mather) and a Quaker in which the minister refers to two Quaker women who came naked into a public assembly as "These baggages" (*Magnalia* 2: 651). This dialogue appears in *Magnalia*'s reprint of the 1699 history of the Indian wars, *Decennium Luctuosum*. By the time of his death in 1728, however,

Mather had abandoned his enmity toward the Quakers and, like his fellow Congregationalists, came to see them as, at least, coreligionists (Silverman 405). Correspondingly, Quakers abandoned their pamphleteering and confrontational tactics such as disrupting (naked or otherwise) the Congregationalist services. One consequence of this shift in focus from persecution and dispute was that Quaker publication resources turned from merely documenting sufferings to interpreting and memorializing them. This expansion of the role of printed sufferings occurred within a broader Quaker historiographical project.

I have already discussed the utility of the Hannah Swarton and Hannah Duston captivities for various historiographical enterprises, initially Puritan, but later, secular and, in Thoreau's case, highly idiosyncratic and personal. Accordingly, this study of *God's Mercy* concludes with an examination of Elizabeth Hanson's usefulness to Quaker historians. Her voice, much mediated, anchors the text and, as the Puritan women captives did for Mather, certifies the authenticity of the account, even as the preface warns readers of the "small Alteration . . . partly owing to the Mistake of the Transcriber." Hanson's text is unique among the Quaker publications of the eighteenth century. It is not a journal; as the fictive Hanson states at the end of the narrative: "Thus, as well, and as near as I can from my memory (not being capable of keeping a Journal) I have given a short, but a true Account of some of the remarkable Trials and wonderful Deliverances, which I never purposed to expose" (40). Nor is it an autobiography in the sense of a long narrative that gives shape and purpose to a life. It is certainly not an epistle or a doctrinal tract. Rather, *God's Mercy* is that peculiarly American genre, a woman's account of captivity among North American Indians. As such, Hanson's narrative afforded the Philadelphia Yearly Meeting an opportunity to engage in making a distinctively American contribution to Quaker history while simultaneously constructing a new Quaker female voice, one that displays conventionally female traits. That is, like Swarton and Duston, Hanson represents an actual female figure whose captivity experiences were fashioned into a narrative that advanced the various ends of the men who sponsored (and to some extent, composed) her text. Significantly, the rhetorical drag employed to compose Hanson's text served a Quaker agenda that sought to curb, or at least to delimit, the public voice of women.

There is one curious personal gesture at the end of the narrative that both underscores Hanson's role as wife and mother and disputes the characterization of Quakers in a contemporaneously published Congregationalist history. The narrative does not close with the return of Hanson and her children from captivity; like Swarton, she laments the loss of her daughter to the French. The text goes on to explain that, although Hanson was grateful for the "many Deliverances and wonderful Providences of God" that she had received, her husband was not content: "But my dear Husband, poor Man! could not enjoy himself in Quiet with us, for want of his dear Daughter Sarah, that was left behind" (37). John Hanson is thus portrayed as a sensitive, feeling father whose concern for his family and his missing daughter ultimately costs him his life. In offering this portrait of John Hanson, *God's Mercy* directly counters the description of him in Samuel Penhallow's recently published *The History of the Wars of New-England*. There, Penhallow blames John Hanson for the deaths of the children murdered in the attack and the captivity of his other family members: "Some of [the Indians] fell on the House of *John Hanson* of *Dover*, who being a stiff Quaker, full of Enthusiasm, and ridiculing the Military Power, would on no account be influenced to come into the Garrison; by which means his whole Family (then at home) being eight in number, were all kill'd and taken. But some time after his Wife and two or three of his Children were redeemed with considerable Pains and Expense" (106). Of course, we cannot know whether Penhallow's accusations contributed to John Hanson's inability to accept his daughter's French captivity or to the Society's decision to publish *God's Mercy*. Nevertheless, the narrative clearly participates in the contest of representations by providing a view of Quaker familial concern and care that at least presumably matches Congregationalist expectations. By describing John Hanson's paternal anguish, *God's Mercy* challenges Penhallow's image of him as both a malfeasant father and a "stiff Quaker." Ironically, the tale of John Hanson's vigorous if doomed actions to rescue his daughter is told in Elizabeth Hanson's voice. "Her" words and actions mark a profound contrast to her husband's; the preternaturally passive and vulnerable Elizabeth Hanson of *God's Mercy* could never be charged with "enthusiasm," and, as such, her image offers a model for a new version of Quaker womanhood, fit for the Society's changing view of itself.

CHAPTER 4

"Affecting History"

Impersonating Women in
the Early Republic

> With all these misfortunes lying heavily upon me, the reader can
> imagine my situation.
> —*Narrative of the Captivity of Mrs. Johnson*

Concern with reputation and credibility, apparent in the prefaces to
colonial captivity narratives, recurs in two popular and distinctive
women's captivity narratives of the early Republic. Like the accounts
discussed in the previous chapters, the *Narrative of the Captivity of
Mrs. Johnson* and the two first-person versions of Jemima Howe's story
were written by men using the women's first-person voice to impart
such authentication. Unlike those earlier texts, which were published
soon after the women's return, both Johnson's and Howe's narratives
are distinguished by the lapse in time between captivity and publication. The relative immediacy of the earlier captivity stories imputed
a sense of currency and credibility to the texts and their "authors."
Thus, the nearly forty years between Susannah Johnson's and Jemima
Howe's returns from captivity and the appearance of "their" texts significantly differentiates these works from previous captivity narratives.
Moreover, whereas the political and social conditions that obtained
when the earlier captives were taken had not changed substantially by
the time of their stories' publication, the lag between captivity and the

publication of the Johnson and Howe texts spans a period that saw significant alterations in the women's status: as captives, Johnson and Howe had been British subjects; as authors, they were American citizens. The *Narrative of . . . Mrs. Johnson* and the Howe accounts thus offer versions of a woman's experiences that are specifically *historical* by the time of publication.[1] While invoking generic conventions of colonial women's captivity narratives, they also reveal the gendered discourses employed in representing the new nation's uneasy relationship to its own past.

The Revolutionary War and the subsequent establishment of the United States not only ruptured relations with Great Britain but also complicated attempts to construct a legitimating historical narrative of the new country. Accordingly, historians of the early Republic employed a range of theoretical frames in order to interpret the disruption. These frames, which included orthodox filiopietism, contemporary neoclassicism, and an emergent Romanticism, provided methods and images to explain the genesis of the new nation. Thus, when David Humphreys wrote his memoir of Revolutionary War hero Israel Putnam, he viewed Putnam through his own eyes, filiopietistically. A young military aide during the war, Humphreys saw in Putnam a respected elder, and he portrays Putnam as an American Cincinnatus, an image most often associated with Washington (Humphreys 10). But Putnam began life as a subject of the Crown, and, to be faithful to the biographical data, Humphreys includes a lengthy section detailing Putnam's service in the British Army during the French and Indian War. In so doing, he produces a Putnam whose life of consistent public service, first to the Crown, then to the Continental Congress, transcended the breach between colony and republic. The fissures in the political and social order wrought by the Revolution recede from view because Putnam himself is the focus, and his military career affords a continuity destroyed by political rupture. In this manner, history becomes biography; historical continuity and, with it, historical legitimation for the new nation, derive from the lives of its citizens.

It is instructive to note, however, that Humphreys' Putnam lived an intensely public life. In contrast with Susannah Johnson or Jemima Howe, Humphreys' Putnam moved across a landscape of great historical significance, making his reputation as a successful military leader. Indeed, as I argue below, in Humphreys' *Essay on the Life of . . . Putnam*, when Jemima Howe meets Israel Putnam during her own captivity, her private miseries counterpoint his heroic carriage in the text. How, then, do the Johnson and Howe narratives function in this public rhetoric of heroism, which is based on the image of the male patriot? And what do these narratives tell us about the cultural work of rhetorical drag, the fashioning of a woman's voice as historical informant, for the men who sought to shape the history of the new Republic?

If we approach these texts by attending to the elements and functions of rhetorical drag that they exhibit, we can trace some of the cultural imperatives of the early Republic. As in the previous narrative, the texts display a deep engagement with contemporary issues of gender and class structures. We must note, too, the category crisis addressed through these late eighteenth-century performances of gender impersonation: writers in the period's rapidly expanding print milieu continually wrestled with the problems of representation posed by the relationship between *private voice* and *public text* in the early national period.

As I will demonstrate, the practice of impersonated authorship articulates the disparate domains addressed in more recent debates on the textual and vocal dispositions of early Republic discourses.[2] When the impersonation crosses gender and class boundaries, this act of rhetorical drag produces a constellation of effects that display a deeply imbricated model of voice and text, of speech and writing, one premised on "appropriate" gender and class norms. Arguing for the cultural force of voice in the new Republic, Christopher Looby asserts "the difference between the abstract, alienated, rational polis of print culture and the more passionately attached, quasi-somatically experienced nation for which many Americans longed" (5). Authorial impersonation rendered in the first person bridges this difference by providing the textual marker for the speaking body, the "soma" that experiences and thereby creates a credible instrument when the author himself might lack the experience that underwrites that credibility.

Moreover, gender norms are crucial to this operation. As current feminist and queer theories indicate, when the voice is female, the text most commonly reproduces sex/gender regimes that recurrently, even obsessively, deploy an unstable mind-body split across a male-female axis. That is, the relentless *embodiment* of women (and other dominated or marginalized subjects) constitutes one of the most enduring practices in the social organization of gender.[3] The representation of a female speaking voice in print always constitutes an irruption of the ontological into our debates about the epistemological work of letters.

Male-to-female gender impersonated authorship, then, in manipulating gender figuration, represents a rhetorical gambit through which complexities and omissions in text/voice debates emerge. Employed in the production of a captivity narrative, gender impersonation reveals how the category of authorship compels recognition of gender regimes even as this recognition threatens to deconstruct those regimes. This threat becomes acute when we consider how gender-impersonated authorship may seek to consolidate conservative gender politics in the writing of public history. What might a man (or men) gain by inhabiting a woman's *speaking* body in his text? Might an erotics of rhetorical drag speak to the alienation that Looby notes?[4] How does personal expression, specifically the feminized expression of sentiment and affect, figure experiences that underwrite historiography?

A Narrative of . . . Mrs. Johnson provides a rich and complex text for these investigations. The Johnson narrative is discussed in several recent studies of women's captivity narratives,[5] and there are good reasons for scholarly focus on this text: it is, at 144 pages, one of the lengthiest captivity tales; it was popular, reprinted both as a single text and within collections, well into the nineteenth century; and, as I noted above, unlike most previous captivity narratives, it was published well after the events portrayed in it took place. Authorial attribution for the text has been truly confusing due largely to the dramatic force of the alleged Susannah Johnson's voice. Finally, if we believe that the alternative ascription of authorship to John C. Chamberlain by some scholars is accurate, we find Chamberlain working in a group of writers that included some of the most notable print characters of the period, Joseph Dennie and Royall Tyler, men deeply concerned with contemporary political events and their interpretation.

Since the *Narrative* is a product of gender impersonation, as I will demonstrate, the text reveals how male-to-female impersonated authorship seeks to capitalize on the social meaning of the female captive's voice. This rhetorical ploy seems initially to support the text's prefatory aims: the *Narrative* presents itself as history, a tale based on the actual experiences of the captive Johnson. Because the first-person voice is female, the narrator expresses her "self" in language derived from contemporary sentimental fiction, rhetorics identified with—and thus certifying—women's experiences. As an avowedly historical work, however, the text must negotiate the factive-fictive divide,[6] maintaining the precarious control that the *textuality* encoded in the historiographical narrative (with its official documentation and authoritative interpolations) exerts over the *vocality* represented by direct address and first-person narration. In certain passages, the rhetorical elements that signal the woman's voice/body threaten to undermine the elements that signal the historiographical project of the text. The composers of *A Narrative of . . . Mrs. Johnson* seemed to recognize this threat, and they employed several devices, such as footnotes and the interposition of third-person narration, in order to accommodate their desire to "speak" as Susannah Johnson while disciplining her voice within the rhetorical constraints of eighteenth-century historiography.

Historiography constituted a key element of the print world of the early Republic—the world that produced Susannah Johnson's voice because it attempted to shape an origin and justification for the establishment of the new nation.[7] Michael Warner has argued that this world, that is, the public sphere produced by print culture, emerged in contradistinction to the sphere of individuated experience founded on customary, personal, and familiar interactions.[8] Initially directing his study of the "letters" of the early Republic to political discourse, Warner theorizes a public domain in which printed political tracts appear differentiated from "the common exchange of society." That is, the public sphere "did not depend on an entire congruence between its norms and those observed in custom" (*Letters* 34), and he marks this shift in the location of textual authority as a move away from Calvinist theology toward emerging discourses of liberal political philosophy: "No longer a technology of privacy underwritten by divine authority, letters have become a technology of publicity whose meaning in the last analysis is civic and emancipatory" (3).

By the end of his study, however, Warner turns to a discussion of the novel to demonstrate how private, personalized modes seep back into the public sphere through the symbolic and sympathetic operations of fiction: "Simultaneously a *publication* subject to the diffusion of literature *and* a site of private imaginary identifications, the early American novel produces endless variations on the contradictory symbolic determinations of its own form" (170). This final discussion of his study includes Warner's most extensive statement about the discursive

formation of female gender in the republic of letters: "the early phase
of post-Revolutionary nationalism is marked by a gradual extension
of a national imaginary to exactly those social groups that were excluded from citizenship—notably women. Women were more and more
thought of as symbolic members of the nation, especially in their capacities as mothers" (173). Excluded from citizenship, a discursive formation founded on anonymity, disinterest, and dispersal, women and
other disenfranchised persons in the new nation appear as inhabitants,
members of the polity differentiated and instantiated through the medium of their bodies. Warner's argument about textuality and incorpo-
reality turns, finally, to the irrepressible, if symbolic, body to account for
a comprehensive version/vision of the "national imaginary."

Reinserting bodies into the body politic, Warner accurately argues
that women's bodies are the site of an emergent privatization, a re-
striction founded on their experiences as members of a polity who
do not have political agency.[9] Women's participation in the nation,
then, is most effectively, though not exclusively, enacted through the
performance of motherhood, an ontological role based on their status
as reproducing and caring beings. This kind of embodied status is
precisely the figuration that both Fliegelman and Looby emphasize in
their consideration of voice in the early Republic.

Fliegelman, in particular, repositions the body in text through his
discussion of orality and eloquence. He is especially concerned with
the ways in which eighteenth-century rhetoricians and philosophers,
including Jefferson, attempted to impart the sense of "spokenness"
to written text. Fliegelman argues that, for these men, the voice in
text presents a potent figure: "Because the human voice speaking ac-
cessibly and sincerely appears to be speaking truthfully, a prose that
registers that voice is potentially much more manipulatively powerful
than either traditional eloquence or elevated language. That is precisely why the plain style, which sought to redress rhetoric (in both
senses of the verb), ultimately came to dominate both fiction and jour-
nalism" (55). As well, Fliegelman cautions against reading orality and
print in stark contradistinction: "It is crucial to recognize that rather
than merely standing in opposition to print, orality can also be, and
in the eighteenth century often was, a defining characteristic of print,
a set of cues within a text that signal it is to be heard by the ear (as performance) as much as it is to be read by the eye" (218n50). This sense of

orality as a "defining characteristic of print," when examined in the context of gender dispositions and historiographical claims, complicates Fliegelman's reading of the body in text, especially if we pair it with Warner's disembodied model. The "human voice speaking" rendered into prose through direct address/first person appears gendered as soon as the speaker is identified, and identification of the historical informant is fundamental to establishing the credibility, accuracy, and value of her statements. The gendering of the voice as female, for example, the voice of the female captive, therefore makes possible a particular version of, in Fliegelman's terms, the voice's "manipulability" for its writers. Thus the female voice has a status and utility derived from female embodiment that distinguishes it from both male-identified models of depersonalized, textualized authority and male speaking "performances." Radically embodied, women's experiences come into the public through the emotive and affective modes of fiction, while speaking men may "sound" in a variety of modes: rational, sentimental, authoritative, and contestatory. Rhetorical drag mobilizes the different effects of gendered performance. The shifting and interpenetration of the documentary/factive modes and the sentimental/fictive modes provides the women's voices with male authority, while the male authors derive historical veracity from the women's authentic experiences related in their voices.

I am arguing, then, that, in reading the Johnson *Narrative* with attention to the operations of rhetorical drag, we find an exemplary text, one that recognizes and fuses the practices these theories of voice and textuality posit. Furthermore, in conducting a critical reading of the gender impersonation in *A Narrative of . . . Mrs. Johnson,* I contend that this text represents a historically valuable artifact in the study of gender roles and their meanings in the print culture of the early national period. Gender impersonation thus becomes not just an irksome or curious detail in a text's composition but another crucial element in its cultural capacity to shape historical knowledge and beliefs.

This capacity is enacted when gender-impersonated captivity narratives, relying on the symbolic force of the female body, produce representations of female experience that supersede the maternal. Captive women speak about political and military decisions that directly affected them (and their husbands and children), while they also offer observations about those who determine their fates. In constructing an

embodied female experience through the woman's voice, the impersonated texts display the persistent, resolute gender and class tensions in the
national imaginary that the textuality/vocality arguments of Warner,
Ziff, Fliegelman, and Looby seek to untangle. The men who write as
women, then, pursue a similar project: clarifying the historical processes
that formed the new nation by linking text to body, articulating the modalities of writing and speech for their political and cultural ends.

While Warner's final animadversion to the early American novel
posits the role of women as mothers, Cathy Davidson's groundbreaking study and the subsequent explosion of related scholarly work on
sentimental fiction make clear that some women assumed the role of
author as well. Yet even in these fictions by women, female characters were tethered to maternal or at least reproductive modes, never
detached from their ontological status as bodied beings. Emphasizing personal expression over impersonality and interested, experiential claims over disinterest, sentimental and seduction novels offered
female characters consistently speaking from their affected (seduced,
guarded, abandoned, appropriated, married, single, widowed, and, of
course, maternal) bodies.[10]

A Narrative of . . . Mrs. Johnson displays such a body. Yet in the
composition of visual and vocal display, in sounding like a woman,
this text both constructs the conditions for its credibility as a historically accurate text based on the experiences of Susannah Johnson
and threatens to dissolve into a novel, a genre it explicitly demurs
in its opening pages. Raymond Craig, in an unpublished paper, has
argued that prefatory materials most often reveal writers' attempts to
control "the interpretive practices of their readers" by "constructing
their readers, rejecting those who would not read them 'right' and
instructing others on how to read, how to interpret."[11] As I will argue
below, the introduction to the *Narrative* makes clear that the men who
produced the Johnson narrative hoped to instruct their readers, directing them explicitly to read the text as historiography, not fiction. For
these writers, gender impersonation offered the advantage of using
experience in its most rhetorically proximate form, the first person,
to authenticate their history. But in staging their account in the form
of first-person anecdote, they risked erasing the impersonal and disinterested narration that conveyed political gravitas and persuasion.
Thus, the unstable narrative formation weds vocality to textuality by

representing the speech of embodied beings (an ontological marker) to create historical meaning (an epistemological process). In so doing, the text recognizes and negotiates the fissures demarcated by gender in the print culture of the early Republic.

For these reasons, *A Narrative of . . . Mrs. Johnson* represents a key text in the studies of captivity narratives, of gendered discourses, and of the modalities and symbolic structures of voice/text that form the public-private continuum of the national imaginary. While earlier scholars usefully included the text in their investigations of "white womanhood" (Castiglia) or the increasing secularism of the genre (Ebersole), I focus on the *Narrative*'s self-proclaimed status as historiography to interrogate some of the cultural meanings of women's voices "spoken" in the text as official records. Reading *A Narrative of . . . Mrs. Johnson* with attention to its impersonated authorship and its imbrication within the print culture of the early Republic, we discover additional ways in which "the extension of the national imaginary" mandated the inclusion—and manipulation—of women's voices.[12] Additionally, the *Narrative* displays the struggles that this inclusion entailed: the destabilization of an authoritative, interpretive historiographical discourse dependent for its credibility, for its cultural force, on the personal, affective, putatively private voice of female experience.

Credibility

All the instances are authenticated in the most satisfactory manner;—some by deposition, and others by the information of persons of unexceptionable credibility.
— *The Affecting History of . . . Frederic Manheim's Family*

As this introductory claim indicates, readers of *The Affecting History of the Dreadful Distresses of Frederic Manheim's Family*, a collection of captivity narratives published in 1793, were to find the events portrayed in the text authenticated through two means: deposition and information. Moreover, the authenticating information would be produced by "persons of unexceptionable credibility." Authentication, then, derived both from the recognized authority of documents whose composition is the result of dialogue and legal form (as depositions imply that someone has been deposed by another) and from the reputation of informants (whose credibility underwrites the information). The persuasive value of the text, its historical authority as a representation of a set of events, thus depended on the reader's belief that both authenticating criteria were to be fulfilled at points throughout the collection.

Manheim's readers might recognize formal rhetorics associated with depositions and acknowledge their authenticating, juridical power, but how might they assess the credibility of the informants? Most readers, after all, would never meet the captives whose stories are told in the collection. Assessing credibility necessitates at the very least a consideration of the informant's reputation, because, if their stories were not elicited within the evidentiary rules of legal deposition, then they are not constrained by those authenticating rules and forms. Readers are left, finally, with their recognition and interpretation of the rhetorics of personal narrative. Thus, *Manheim*'s introductory statement seeks to position the collection as a historically accurate and authoritative text, in compliance with the rules of authentication, by infusing the cultural authority of deposition into the much more ambiguous—even untrustworthy—modality of the personal story.

Yet, as scholars have noted, many captivity narratives of this period, *Manheim* most definitely included, exhibit a marked fictionality. Abraham Panther's "A Very Surprising Narrative" (1787), certainly hyperbolic if not completely fictive, features a murdered giant and the demure "lady"—the informant—who killed him. Her voice, apparently unaffected by her lonely sojourn in the woods, exhibits all the delicacy of the parlor she forsook for an elopement. The Panther text, like contemporary seduction novels, produced women's voices that display specific textual characteristics (grammatical voice, patterns of imagery, and rhetorical forms) that function as gender indexes. As Davidson has noted of the period's novels, repeated narratorial intrusions insist on the text's instructive value; these intrusions construct an anxiety about misprision (then go on to allay that anxiety) while simultaneously indicating that the texts recognize and reproduce prevailing models of gendered behaviors. Deconstructing these characteristics, Davidson and others argue that women's texts simultaneously resist gender normativity by inverting these textual elements as strategies to challenge and refashion the very norms they are supposed to replicate and enforce. Gendered norms, figured in the contesting representations of the novels, infiltrate the factive accounts that also feature women's voices.

This infiltration of the fictive into the factive depends on gendered constructs as well as the ontological traces signaled by voice as the means by which experience is made manifest in text. As Joan Scott notes, "we need to attend to the historical processes that, through discourse, position subjects and produce their experiences" (25). The historical processes of the early Republic that most spectacularly positioned female subjects and produced their experiences, the processes and productions of print culture, gave rise to the novels of sentiment. Female experience, when rendered into text, entailed a fictive quality, the qualities of the emotive and sentimental. This fictive quality, then, is the slippery effect of written representations of female voice that gender norms produced. For women, the pressure to speak from experience as women resulted in a measure of self-alienation. Warner theorizes the textual basis for this apparently ontological effect: "Insofar as written contexts entailed dispositions of character that interpellated their subject as male, women could only write with a certain cognitive dissonance"; or, more succinctly, "To write was to inhabit gender" (*Letters* 15). For men, this print-based subject formation, too, presented problems because the move from individual to abstract, collective expression exacted a price—the loss of a "self"-generated text—and resulted in a "male collectivity formation of writing" (15) that relinquished specificity for a sense of complete, if completely dispersed, authority.

This bifurcation into gendered domains posed a significant problem for the writing of history that is reflected in contemporary debates about rational versus Romantic historiography. Mark Kamrath, for example, has shown that Brockden Brown worried about the paradox of historiography's reliance on "the evidence of others" while it sought to present an apparently disinterested and rationalist version of the past.[13] If, however, embodied experience authenticates, makes credible, the relation of historical events, gender impersonation allows for the articulation of that embodiment and the supervisory capacity to interpret the experience. Here, then, lies the utility of female expression and "female" authorship in an era of radically impersonal

writing. Publications attributed to women retain the power of the particular—the compelling, *ascribed* voice of experience that has been
lost in the rise of civic discourse.

A Narrative of . . . Mrs. Johnson cannily resorts to both modalities in its representation of experience and the interpretation of that
experience. Unlike Rowson's *Charlotte Temple*, Susannah Johnson
was an actual woman; her story was substantiated in the documents
(purportedly written by actual officials) pertaining to her captivity
and redemption, as well as in stories told by local residents.[14] The
Charlestown-Walpole vicinity was home to many Willards, Johnsons,
and Hastingses, and Susannah Willard Johnson, later Mrs. Hastings,
was herself living at the time of the *Narrative*'s publication. The facts
of her captivity experiences were therefore available not only in neighborly anecdotes but also most likely from her own personal testimony.
Her credibility, at least in her home district, could be ascertained. It
could also be appropriated; her story was "dictated by Mrs. Johnson"
then shaped and published by a local lawyer with strong connections
to the Charlestown-Walpole publishing scene.

The first edition of *A Narrative of the Captivity of Mrs. Johnson* is
listed in Evans' *American Bibliography* under the name of a Charlestown, New Hampshire, lawyer, John C. Chamberlain, and several
nineteenth-century sources corroborate that provenance.[15] Because
Susannah Johnson's first-person account purports to represent the authentic experiences of a woman whose captivity is recorded in local
history, it establishes the credibility of its informant and offers readers
a way to interpret historical events. Thus, the artifice of a woman's
narrative voice becomes an instrument in the hands of her male editors, in this case, her purported amanuensis, Chamberlain. Histori-
cizing this text and interpreting the meanings of its competing rhetorical strategies begins with a discussion of its actual author, John C.
Chamberlain, and with his likely collaborators, Joseph Dennie, Royall
Tyler, and those members of the New Hampshire bar who frequented
Craft's Tavern, located conveniently across the street from the print
shop of Thomas and Carlisle, in Walpole.

"Short Sermons for Idle Readers"

"My reputation as a man of letters is now producing me property.
This is everything, and soon it will render me independent."
—Letter to Mrs. Mary Dennie, 29 August 1796 (Pedder, 154)

While living in Walpole, New Hampshire, in 1796, Joseph Dennie
shifted his interest—and means of gainful employment—from the law
to newspaper writing. He reassured his patient and infinitely supportive mother that the change from lawyer to "man of letters" would
provide him not only with an improved income but also with a literary reputation. Significantly, this reputation and Dennie's claim were
based on the response to his pseudonymous Lay Preacher essays, a
series of articles in the *Farmer's Weekly Museum,* the most popular
magazine "from Maine to Georgia" and a venue that published the
work of many of his Craft's Tavern cronies as well.[16]

The Walpole men's conception of authorship can be viewed in
both their disposition of the figure of the author and in their writing
practices, each of which demonstrates an interconnection among authorship, reputation, and credibility in the early Republic. Publishing
pseudonymously, anonymously, collaboratively, and sometimes even
under their own names, the Walpole group reconfigured traditional
connections between author and voice, between author and self-representation, in artifices mirroring those of the *Spectator* essays. As
Dennie's note to his mother illustrates, the New Hampshire men were
concerned with reputation; their writings, and the pseudonyms under which they published them, demonstrate a canny awareness of
the effects of a first-person voice detached from an actual person but
simultaneously invoking an individual experience or opinion. In this
respect, it is not surprising to find that Chamberlain, possibly with the
collaboration of some of the Walpole writers, composed Susannah
Johnson's captivity narrative, drawing on *her* reputation as a former
captive and appropriating her name to publish a historical account of
colonial history with Carlisle's press.

Carlisle's most successful publishing venture began in April 1793
when he initiated publication of the *New-Hampshire Journal.* As Dennie's letter home attests, by 1796, Carlisle had engaged him as editor

and chief writer. While editing, Dennie published many of, but not all, his essays under the byline of "the Lay Preacher." He had begun his magazine writing a few years earlier with contributions to the Vermont publication the *Farrago*. Soon thereafter, Dennie entered into an alliance with another Harvard-educated scholar, the lawyer Royall Tyler, and together they published pseudonymously both prose and poetry selections from the "Shop of Messrs. Colon and Spondee."[17] Joseph Buckingham, Carlisle's printer's devil and, later, an editor and printer in his own right, described their compositional practices, practices that aptly illustrate Warner's model of a "male collectivity formation." As Buckingham noted, the men seemed to view their publications as literary property in common:

> Dennie wrote with great rapidity, and generally postponed his task till he was called upon for *copy*. It was frequently necessary to go to his office, and it was not uncommon to find him in bed at a late hour in the morning. His *copy* was often given out in small portions, a paragraph or two at a time; sometimes it was written in the printing-office, while the compositor was waiting to put it in type. One of the best of his Lay sermons was written at the village tavern, directly opposite to the office, in a chamber where he and his friends were amusing themselves with cards. It was delivered to me by piece-meal, at four or five different times. If he happened to be engaged in a game, when I applied for copy, he would ask some one to *play his hand for him, while he could give the devil his due.* When I called for the closing paragraph of the sermon, he said, *call again in five minutes.* "No," — said Tyler — "I'll write the improvement for you." He accordingly wrote a concluding paragraph, and Dennie never saw it till it was in print. (Buckingham 197)[18]

The Craft's Tavern group described by Buckingham included Harvard graduates Roger Vose and John C. Chamberlain as well as Thomas Green Fessenden of Dartmouth. These men published their *Farmer's Museum* pieces, following "Messrs. Colon and Spondee," under names such as "Christopher Caustic" and "Simon Spunky" (Fessenden), and "the Hermit" and "Tim Pandect" (Chamberlain).[19] The pseudonymity chosen by these authors illuminates their linkage of first-person voice to the authorial practices. A "caustic" writer evokes strikingly different readerly expectations from those of a "lay preacher," yet neither of these authorial postures indicates that the text expresses the opinions or full experiences of an actual person in the community. That is, the fiction of the author is bound expressly to that piece (or series of pieces) alone, a patent artifice in which the authorial persona is positional and circumstantial, conditioned by the essay's argument or topic. Drawing upon pseudonymous pieces from the *Farmer's Weekly Museum,* I wish to articulate the use of disguised authorship in the newspaper with the Walpole writers' impersonation of Susannah Johnson to demonstrate the ways in which gendered discourses might be used to produce politically and culturally authoritative texts.[20]

For John C. Chamberlain, accustomed to employing pseudonymity to construct both his persona and his topic, assuming Susannah Johnson's voice presented certain opportunities inhering both in contemporary views of women's authorship and in local legend. Although Susannah Johnson's "I" imparts the credibility based on her experience, the themes, images, and shape of the text—its rhetoric—emerge from Chamberlain's hands. The *Narrative . . . of Mrs. Johnson* displays the tensions arising from this artifice, and in those tensions we may discover why Chamberlain chose to "cross-write" as Susannah Johnson. Before he fashioned Johnson's story, however, Chamberlain needed the facts of the forty-year-old captivity, and it is likely that Johnson herself related her memories to him, because the introduction mentions that Johnson "dictated" it. As well, the Johnson family was large and had lived in the area for some time; indeed, Caleb Johnson owned a general store in Walpole, for which the *Farmer's Weekly Museum* carried a regular advertisement. Therefore the facts concerning her captivity were probably not hard to come by in the small towns of Walpole and Charlestown. The facts are as follows:

Johnson, her husband James, and sister Miriam Willard; their neighbors, Peter Labarree and Ebenezer Farnsworth; as well as the Johnson children, Sylvanus (six), Susanna (four), and Polly (two), were captured in a raid on Charlestown on 30 August 1754. On the day after the attack, during the trek through the forest, Johnson gave birth to a daughter, later named Captive. After nine days, the party arrived on the shores of Lake Champlain and took passage to Crown Point, where the French commander received them with "hospitality" (*Narrative* 54), but four days later they pushed on, finally arriving in the Indian settlement of St. Francis. There the captives were distributed among different Indian families: James Johnson was sent to Montreal for sale to the French, followed by Labarree, Farnsworth, Miriam Willard, and the two older girls. By 15 October 1754, Johnson was left with Captive; Sylvanus had been sent off with a hunting party. In early November, she and the infant went to Montreal, where her captors agreed to try to sell her to the French as well. She joined her husband and found that her sister and daughters had been sold.

Here, halfway through the text, the story transforms from an Indian to a French captivity tale.[21] In January 1755, James Johnson obtained a two-month leave on parole and returned to New England to gather sums for ransom. Provided with letters of credit from New Hampshire authorities, to be drawn on men in Albany who traded with the French and Indians, he set out for Montreal but was called back by Massachusetts governor Shirley. This order postponed his return to Montreal until June and thus violated his parole. Although James Johnson had been attempting to settle accounts through the men in Albany, the new governor in Montreal imprisoned him in July, and a Frenchman posing as a friend absconded with the silver that friendly St. Francis Indians had retrieved from Albany for the Johnson family. By late July 1755, Susannah and James Johnson, with Polly and Captive, were imprisoned in the criminal jail in Quebec City.

From July 1755 to July 1757 the family endured imprisonment, during which all contracted smallpox and Susannah Johnson gave birth to a son who died within hours. However, through a French agent, they successfully petitioned the governor for relief, and Susannah, Miriam Willard (who had rejoined them), Polly, and Captive were permitted to sail to England in a prisoner exchange, although James Johnson remained a prisoner. Susannah Johnson sailed to England, then back to New York, and made her way to Lancaster, Massachusetts (erstwhile home of Mary Rowlandson), where, on 1 January 1758, she was reunited with her husband. James Johnson, whose commission as a lieutenant had further complicated the parole violation, set out for New York to attempt again to resolve his accounts but was "persuaded by Gov. Pownal to take a Captain's commission, and join the forces,

bound for Ticonderoga, where he was killed on the 8th of July following" (*Narrative* 136). Of the others captured with Susannah Johnson,
Sylvanus returned in October 1758; Johnson's brother (called in the
Narrative "my brother in law") was captured with his family in the
summer of 1760 but returned after the French surrender of Montreal
with Johnson's daughter Susanna. Peter Labarree had escaped; Ebenezer Farnsworth "came home a little before" Susannah. Johnson
returned to Charlestown in October 1759, where she was living with
Captive when "she" inscribed the last page of her narrative "Charlestown, June 20, 1796."

Johnson's voice imparts credibility to the *Narrative* because she
actually experienced Indian captivity and French imprisonment from
1754 to 1758. The introduction, however, cautions the reader that even
a credible witness is prey to some unreliability. The following proviso
appears on the verso of the introductory page and alerts readers to
the text's conditions of production: "PART of the following pages
were dictated by MRS. JOHNSON, now MRS. HASTINGS, herself,
and part were taken from minutes, made by MR. JOHNSON and
herself, during their imprisonment. She is much indebted to her fellow prisoner, MR. LABARREE, by whose assistance many incidents
are mentioned, which had escaped her recollection." The *Narrative*
thus constitutes itself from fragments, both oral and textual: part
dictation, part previously inscribed notes of Mr. Johnson, part the
unspecified "assistance" of Mr. Labarree, and part the memories of
Susannah Johnson, now Hastings—a *re*-collection indeed. The introduction acknowledges that the sources of the *Narrative* are cobbled
and multifarious. How much is dictation? Which passages are based
on the notes? How many episodes are recovered by the helpful Labarree, shoring up the fragments of Mrs. Hastings's failing memory?
The notes themselves would have been forty years old, papers carried
through several changes in residence and preserved since 1758, when
James Johnson died.[22] The reliability of both Hastings's and Labarree's testimony must be considered in light of their ages in 1796—she
was sixty-seven, he seventy-two—and, most significantly, in light of
the forty-two-year lapse since their capture.

Moreover, the evasions in the *Narrative*'s attribution appear before
the introduction. On the title page, the text announces itself as "A

Narrative of the Captivity of Mrs. Johnson," "published according to an Act of Congress," with no separately designated author's name. Johnson's *Narrative* appears under the new secular—and impersonal—authority of the U.S. Congress. The title's preposition simultaneously invokes Johnson as author and defers her, making her both subject and object of the text. Ultimately, then, it is the first-person "I" that simultaneously substantiates (the fiction of) Johnson's authorial voice and establishes her credibility.

This hedging on the title page is directly linked to the dispersal of authenticating elements found in the prefatory note. As in the introduction to the *Manheim* collection, this introduction asks its readers to consider multiple authenticating phenomena, both historical "minutes" and the "recollection" (here, somewhat unreliable) of Susannah Johnson, assisted by Peter Labarree. Thus the introductory materials hint that Susannah Johnson's voice is at least provisional, if not wholly purloined, and that her credibility depends upon the corroboration of her memories by Labarree.

The subsequent interplay of this compromised voice with specific imagery and various interpolated texts produces a literary farrago that reflects contemporary discourses on women, politics, and literary conventions, an amalgamation that assumes both the embodied voice of experience and the disembodied commentary that interprets that experience. Thus, the model of "dueling textual voices" found in earlier captivity narratives sublimes into a model of overdetermination, wherein several of the text's rhetorical effects—most significantly, Susannah Johnson's voice—are mobilized to work for the historiographical and political ends of the male authors.

These goals are mutually dependent: the Johnson *Narrative* enacts the historiographical goal of interpreting the past so that its readers will be directed to a politicized reading of their present. This mutuality would be familiar to contemporary readers of the *Farmer's Weekly Museum,* who were barraged with descriptions of current events through continuous reportage on the French Revolution alongside the Lay Preacher's (Dennie's) demonizing characterization of Jacobins and their dangerous influence on American Republicans. Like most newspapers of the period, the *Museum* was a fiercely partisan—in this case, Federalist—organ. Consequently, the *Narrative*'s representations

of the midcentury French and British forces that brought so much suffering to Johnson and her family transform into frightening images of
French and American Republicans.[23]

"The Miseries of a 'Frontier Man'"

The *Narrative*'s utility to Federalist partisans inheres in its depiction
of French and British perfidy, although the French who imprison the
Johnsons are by far the greater villains. Similarly, its dialogue with
contemporary literature celebrating the new nation while excoriating
the French Revolution affiliates the Johnson text with Federalist positions. The Federalist project of extending a centralized, protective
shield over all the states is served by the discussion of frontier vulnerability. Indeed, the introduction echoes Crèvecoeur's "Distresses of a
Frontier Man" in his *Letters from an American Farmer* (1782) as the
text declares that "A DETAIL of the miseries of a 'frontier man,' must
excite the pity of every one who claims humanity" (3).

The tensions and ambiguities of rhetorical drag manifest at the
outset here, because the Johnson introduction clearly portrays these
frontier miseries as a man would experience them; the language closely
parallels the opening of Crèvecoeur's passage where a discussion of the
word "misery" occasions sentimentalized effusions about lost community and endangered families from James the Farmer. Johnson's
Narrative, although the story of a woman's experiences, thus opens
with a general appraisal of *male* frontier life, albeit in a form that truly
muddles gendered figuration through its recourse to the language of
sentiment: "If the peaceful employment of husbandry is pursued, the
loaded musket must stand by his side; if he visits a neighbor, or resorts
on sundays to the sacred house of prayer, the weapons of war must
bear him company; at home, the distresses of a wife, and the fears
of lisping children often unman the souls that real danger assailed in
vain" (4).[24] Although "unmanned," this representation of male experience belies the putative authorial voice, and the introduction continues to portray the "distresses" of a frontier man's life as husband and
protector. In these initial passages, then, the text evades the reality of
the purported author's gender and in its stead presents frontier life as a

man might experience it (albeit a man inhabiting a domesticated space perched precariously on that frontier). Describing wilderness miseries through the eyes of an unidentified male, the introduction evades personal specificity in order to invoke the rhetorical authority of, in Warner's terms, the depersonalized mode of male public discourse. What the text relinquishes in consistency—the fiction of the female narrator—is compensated by its invocation of this powerfully authoritative register of the nonspecific, unidentified frontier man whose image corresponds with the popular figure of the citizen/frontiersman.[25]

Describing the epoch in which Johnson and her family were captured, the *Narrative* maintains this tone of authoritative, depersonalized, third-person historical narration. For example, the text attacks two notable public men, Massachusetts governor Shirley and New Hampshire governor Wentworth, and decries the absence of "an organized government, to stretch forth its protecting arm" (4–5). Politico-historical commentary saturates the introduction for several pages more, ridiculing "the supine" Wentworth and Shirley's "visionary schemes" and "quixotic expedition to Louisburg," his "impolitick" and "wild" projects (5–6). Forestalling entry of Johnson's voice, the introduction continues in this impersonal yet polemical tone for eight of its nine pages.

Finally, however, Susannah Johnson's voice must be introduced if the narrative is to elicit the value of credibility deriving from her actual experiences, and accordingly, the *Narrative* shifts from historiographical commentary to personal revelation. Paradoxically, but to great effect, the text diminishes the individualized—that is, personal—import of Susannah Johnson's distresses, while it simultaneously uses those very personal sufferings to construct a tale of broad historical significance. Johnson here most clearly emerges as an object of history, not a subject of her story:

The air of novelty will not be attempted in the following pages; simple facts, unadorned, is what the reader must expect; pity for my sufferings, and admiration at my safe return, is all that my history can excite. The aged man, while perusing, will probably turn his attention to the period when the facts took place, his memory will be refreshed with the sad tidings of his country's sufferings, which gave a daily wound to his feelings, between the years forty

and sixty; by contrasting those days with the present, he may rejoice, that he witnesses those times, which many have "waited for,
but died without a sight." Those "in early life," while they com-
miserate the sufferings which their parents, and ancestors endured,
may felicitate themselves that their lines fell in a land of peace,
where neither savages, nor neighboring wars embitter life. (8)

The end of the introduction not only brings Susannah Johnson into
the book under the pronominal adjective "my," but it also inserts her
into a recognizable scheme of representation whereby the particulars of her life are transformed from personal story to a history from
which all, young and old, can benefit. Her voice ("my sufferings")
is buried within the third-person interpretive apparatus. Notably, the
text eschews the "air of novelty," that is, of novels, while claiming the
same instructional aims that a novel such as *Charlotte Temple* avers.
Johnson's "simple facts, unadorned" intend to be a historical lesson,
not an imaginative flight. The emphasis on fact verifies her story and
confers its status as historiographical matter. The *Narrative* thereby
portrays a secularized, progressivist dream of the Republic, in which
individual experience is subsumed into the impersonalized discourses
of public history, while that experience simultaneously resists absorp-
tion through the very personalized—voiced—rhetorics that structure
it. The voice threatens to infuse the *Narrative* with the very elements
the introduction seeks to suppress, the "air of novelty."

Contemporary images of sensibility and theatricality—particularly
melodrama—inform the opening passage, and they recur throughout
the *Narrative* in striking descriptions of Susannah Johnson's female
body and feminized imagination.[26] "During the year 1753, all was har-
mony and safety," the *Narrative* asserts, as James Johnson established
"his occupation of trade" with the local tribes (11). By 1754, "another
rupture between the French and English" exploded over disputed Canadian boundaries; however, James Johnson deemed the threat remote enough to travel to Connecticut on business, leaving his family
alone in the new border settlement. When a family is captured down
the Merrimack River from Charlestown, Susannah Johnson's fears are
"beyond description," "baffle description" (13). Thus the narrative
initially elicits the heightened sensibility of the seduction novels of

the period, evoking a topos of inexpressibility to underscore both the physical threat of Indian attack and Susannah Johnson's emotional and psychological vulnerability.

This vulnerability emerges in response to the awful power of her imagination, which itself constitutes another level of danger, that of misreading one's own experiences: "Imagination now saw and heard a thousand Indians; and I never went round my own house, without first looking with trembling caution by each corner, to see if a tomahawk was not raised for my destruction" (13). As the danger of misprision haunts the female novel readers of the period, Susannah Johnson is haunted by her fears that she might misread the signs of attack. The fears transform her from a rational subject to a creature at the mercy of "imagination," which itself literally assumes the subject position in the sentence. Before the actual attack, the narrative voice has already assumed a recognizably feminized position of victim, harassed by both external and internal forces—Indians and imagination.

The text stresses that lack of information enhances this imaginative capacity for terror. The problem of reading the situation accurately, then, is compounded by a breakdown in lines of communication, as when Johnson notes that "the Indians were reported to be on their march for our destruction, and our distance from sources of information gave full latitude for exaggeration of news, before it reached our ears" (12). This absence of real reportage and the consequent outbursts of imagination ("exaggeration") reinforce the importance of nonfiction in policing the destructive drift of fancy, especially in light of the *Narrative*'s connection to a group of newspaper writers. Nevertheless, the introduction's promise of "simple facts, unadorned," falters because the fiction of the female author's voice requires a subject who is prey to imaginative flight.

This representation of Johnson as a victim of her imagination thus offers a first-person voice of striking instability. The language here directly contrasts with the authoritative tone of the introduction, in which historical exposition and political commentary predominate. Thirteen pages into the text, the fragmented, discontinuous, and unstable quality of the *Narrative*'s authorial/narratorial presentation— alternately authoritative/declamatory and familiar/expressive—reveals the gendered construction of the impersonated authorship in its most confusing aspects. The same "I" ranges across both geopolitical and

intensely emotional terrain; that is, it exhibits both the depersonalized, civic rationality of Republican discourse and the personal, private irrationality of a woman at wit's end from the immanence (and
imminence) of lethal attack. This internally inconsistent subject, at
once dispassionate and hysterical, depends for its narrative coherence
on the actual body housing the speaking "I." Unsurprisingly, the figuration of Johnson's body cannot hold the fiction of her authorship
together with any greater effect than that of her speaking voice.

The disjuncture between the authority who writes in the introduction and the actual victim of the first chapter, whose sufferings ("my
sufferings") infiltrate the introduction's historical discourse, recurs in
a literally melodramatic moment of physicality. During the attack,
James Johnson opens the door to admit Peter Labarree, and "by opening the door he opened a scene—terrible to describe!! Indians!" (16).
Readers are explicitly directed to the stage set of Charlestown circa
1754 to view the scene through Susannah Johnson's eyes. While James
Johnson, Peter Labarree, and Ebenezer Farnsworth are bound, the fictive Susannah surveys the situation: "I was led to the door, fainting
and trembling . . . and to complete the shocking scene, my three little
children were driven naked to the place where I stood. On viewing
myself I found that I too was naked. An Indian had plundered three
gowns, who, on seeing my situation, gave me the whole. I asked another for a petticoat, but he refused it" (16–17). The narrative artifice
of a woman not noticing her nakedness strains credulity; at the least
it underscores a heightened emotionalism generated by "the shocking
scene." It is important to note that Susannah Johnson was in the "last
days of pregnancy" (14), a time when few women can easily forget the
state of their bodies. Moreover, the phrase "on viewing myself" medi-
ates a male gaze, here, reappropriated to the speaking female subject
whose voice is supplied by the male author or authors. The deliberative tone of the phrase contrasts with the immediacy of the adjacent
descriptions and reveals the bifurcation in the narrative voice: Susannah Johnson, subject, views Susannah Johnson, abject object.

This figure of the naked, heavily pregnant woman and her children
in the midst of plundering Indians offers a sensationalized image of
utter vulnerability; the addition of a group of bound, impotent white
men completes the abjection.[27] The scene's theatricality and spectacularly naked woman resembles the famous passage in Edmund Burke,

in which Marie Antoinette is roisted, "almost naked," from her chamber, victim of wild Jacobins as "savage" as Canadian Indians. Burke's
description of the attack on the royal family and their subsequent treatment uses language familiar to readers of North American captivities:
"the royal captives who followed in the train were slowly moved along
amidst the horrid yells, and shrilling screams, and frantic dances, and
infamous contumelies, and all the unutterable abominations of the
furies of hell, in the abused shape of the vilest of women."[28] Women's
bodies anchor both these texts as the figure through which Jacobins
metaphorize into Indians, Indians into Jacobins.[29]

   While Burke's text echoes captivity narratives, the writers in the
Farmer's Weekly Museum explicitly cite Burke. The convergence of
commentary on the French Revolution in the newspaper with the
Walpole writers' historiographical concerns erupts in the *Museum* of
16 August 1796. On the first page of that edition, "Messr. Colon &
Spondee" write to defend Marie Antoinette, noting that she had "been
stigmatized as an abandoned courtezan." In column two, we find a
piece entitled "Reason" wherein "*French* reason" is characterized as
"a prostitute. A courtezan, assuming the garb of virtue." That piece
ends with the argument that "Burke's phillippick was not so severe a
satire against the revolution in France as that which the Goddess of
Reason uttered to surrounding pikemen."

   Finally, that same *Museum* edition of 16 August 1796 contains, in column three, a long disquisition by the Hermit (Chamberlain) in which he
visits a local farmhouse in order "to amuse [him]self with the artless tales
of its tenants." Juxtaposed to the Marie Antoinette and Burke/"*French*
reason" texts, this Hermit piece demonstrates the deeply imbricated relationship of *A Narrative of . . . Mrs. Johnson* with the newspaper and
its writers. The Hermit listens as the "good landlady" of the farmhouse
discusses the bad old days of "the persecution of witches and quakers,"
and she "blesses her stars, for permitting her to see these better days."
She might "see these better days," but her "white headed husband," we
are told, had a hand in shaping them. Initially he relates "some Pequod
anecdotes, [and] this leads him to give the history of a battle in the Indian War, when he bore a dangerous share, and saved his Colonel from
a scalping knife." The old man is both historical agent and informant,
qualified to relate the history of the vicinity. He tells the Hermit that
"in that upper pasture, stood a house from which the Indians stole two

children. But . . . I have lived to see the Indians extirpated, I have fought for my country's freedom, and live in its perfection, by my own labor." Here in the pages of the *Farmer's Weekly Museum*, then, the old couple perform for the Hermit precisely those functions of the "aged man" in the Johnson introduction, whose memory is "refreshed" by reading the *Narrative*, and who might "rejoice, that he witnesses those times, which many have 'waited for, but died without a sight'" (8).

Given that the *Farmer's Weekly Museum* of this period continually ran reports on military engagements with various Native peoples on the western frontier, this language resonates as well with contemporary concerns for frontier settlers.[30] The Federalist writers of the *Museum*, in equating Jacobin policy with Indian barbarity, deliberately link the dangers of French Revolutionary excess to the unstable, war-ravaged western frontiers, and the *Narrative of . . . Mrs. Johnson* strengthens this linkage.[31] Thus a naked Susannah Johnson, viewing herself, figures simultaneously the immediate horrors of Indian attack and the threat of Democrat Jacobins disrupting a "land of peace, where neither savages, nor neighboring wars embitter life" (9).

The timing of this 16 August edition is noteworthy: the original proposal for subscriptions for the Johnson narrative appeared in the 10 May 1796 edition of the *Museum*, and the 20 September 1796 edition notes that the "amusing and instructing Book" is "just published."[32] Within this time span between composition and publication, *A Narrative of . . . Mrs. Johnson* was shaped by the predominant ideologies and discursive practices of the Walpole newspapermen; as the Hermit's column indicates, these men consistently constructed versions of the voices of local people in order to represent current memories and past experiences, which they would then go on to interpret. In so doing, they sought to fashion both public opinion about contemporary issues and a Federalist interpretation of the new Republic's history.

"The Reader Can Imagine My Situation"

In earlier captivity narratives, the initial attack serves up horrific images of Indians performing gruesome and apparently gratuitous acts of violence against settlers. The Johnson *Narrative* follows this convention, but the sensationalism, the emphasis on the woman's exposed body, echoes more contemporary captivities. The transition to late eighteenth-century sensibility—and especially, sensationalism—can be tracked in the extent to which the captive's body in these narratives is stripped and penetrated.

Infliction of specific physical torments depended on the practices of the capturing tribes, and these changed as the locations of the narratives shifted. In the post-Revolutionary period of the publication of the Johnson narrative, other captivity narratives, such as the Panther Captivity and those collected in the *Manheim* anthology, were set in the western territories. These highly sensationalized, fictive accounts contrast sharply with the New England captivities of Johnson and Jemima Howe ([1788, 1792] discussed below), which present narrators who are actual persons, whose sufferings are within the pale of common understanding (no giants, no gruesome, graphic tortures). Yet the factive narratives must be read in light of the contemporary fictive texts because they aspire to the popularity of those exorbitant tales and echo anxieties concerning narrative credibility characteristic of women's writing in the period.

While the Panther Captivity's layered narration includes a familiar epistolary opening—"I now sit down, agreeable to your request, to give you a account of my journey" (9)—as well as "an agreeable, sensible Lady" (11), who relates the story of her captivity within that letter, its pretense to authenticity is suborned by the fantastical elements of the tale itself: gothic horror reenacted in the wilderness, with caves substituted for dungeons and a sexually threatening giant rather than a randy Monk.[33] It is difficult to believe that even the most credulous reader would consider this a factual account of captivity. Conversely, as the epigraph to the *Manheim* collection attests, that anthology insists that "all the instances are authenticated in the most satisfactory manner" (1). These "instances" are short, and of the nine entries, four purport to be first-person accounts, all by men, all taking place in the western wilderness. Of these, only Jackson Johonnot's harkens to the (by 1793) old conventions of providential dispensation, probably because he was born and raised in the Congregationalist stronghold of Falmouth (now Portland), Maine.[34] Massey Herbeson's story as well as Experience Bozarth's ("Extraordinary Bravery of a Woman") are brief third-person texts of western events as well. None of the *Manheim* tales ranges into the geographic or historical territory of the Johnson *Narrative*. The anthology, as its introductory note indicates, stakes its authentication on the "unexceptionable credibility" of each entry's eyewitness testimony, an attestation similar to the prefatory notice in Johnson. What *Manheim* lacks in duration (the events of any one entry rarely span more than a few weeks), it compensates with gory detail, particularly in the torture and murder of the Manheim daughters.[35]

The Johnson *Narrative*'s eschewal of this type of lurid detail differentiates it from the western captivity narratives. The differences derive from both the sources and the ends of these texts: *Manheim* and Panther are quick and dirty, tidbits of excess for popular consumption; the Johnson text, from the hands of Harvard-educated elites, exhibits a belles-lettristic concern for its own historiographical methods.[36] These differences, as we have seen, are not absolute, because the Johnson text is suffused with sensationalized language and images. Yet its length and temporal duration, together with alternating tones of impersonal historiographical authority and personal testimony, mark its more ambitious scope.

Although the Johnson *Narrative,* in its complexity and comparatively low-key images of blood and gore, contrasts with contemporary narratives, it shares with them the problem of substantiating the first-person narrator's credibility. The epistolary format, found in the Panther Captivity and many of the *Manheim* selections, pretends to a first-person authenticity while it complicates the narration with the additional layer of a correspondent/informant model, and this format recurs in the popular captivity narrative *The History of Maria Kittle.*[37] Because novels of the period frequently employed the ruse of letter writing,[38] the first-person narrator/letter-writer imparts a fictive status that undermines its function as credible witness. *Maria Kittle* is graphically constructed as correspondence, a tale related "In a Letter to Miss Ten Eyck," with place and date in the upper left corner of the first page and the salutation "Dear Susan" preceding the body of the text.[39] However, the author/correspondent's name never appears at the end of the "letter": the missing signature, presumably made superfluous because Ann Eliza Bleecker's name is on the title page, complicates the text's claim to credibility.[40] This text, too, opens with a dismissal of novels:

> HOWEVER fond of novels and romances you may be, the unfortunate adventures of one of my neighbours, who died yesterday,

will make you despise that fiction, in which, knowing the subject
to be fabulous, we can never be so truly interested. While this lady
was expiring,

Mrs. C— V—, her near kinswoman, related to me her unhappy history, in which I shall now take the liberty of interesting
your benevolent and feeling heart. (3)

The opening simultaneously derides novelistic topics and establishes
a hierarchy based on interest in which this purportedly true "history"
supersedes the merely "fabulous." Yet Miss Ten Eyck would find this
story "interesting" because she possesses a "benevolent and feeling
heart." Therefore the passage, in attempting to establish the text as
more than mere fiction, turns to that very seat of emotionalism that
sustains (and craves) novel reading, the "feeling heart." These discursive contortions, appearing in an allegedly personal writing between
two women, demonstrate the tangled state of female authorship, whose
didactic intentions—stated in prefatory material—and final productions often do not jibe. Critics such as Davidson notice the eighteenth-
century women's novels' internal discrepancies and attribute to them
a subversive effect, specifically a barely disguised critique of the early
Republic's patriarchal social structures. But she argues as well that the
novels "are ultimately about silence, subservience, and stasis . . . the
form itself—or the writer—cannot imagine a life beyond her society's
limitations without violating the essential social realism on which sentimental fiction . . . is ultimately based" (*Coquette*, xix).

While Davidson's term "social realism" might seem premature
from a literary historical perspective, her point—that readers found
the novels' events and characters plausible, within the range of their
own experiences—is crucial to an interpretation of the gender structures in the Johnson text. That is, the realism of the novels is intensi-
fied in women's captivity narratives such as Johnson's because, unlike
the novels, they make unambiguous claims to actual experience. But
the claims recuperate novelistic rhetorics while maintaining the reality
of the narrator's sufferings. For example, Mary Kinnan's 1795 narrative, purportedly based on her actual captivity experiences, elicits both
the language and tone of a sentimental novel: "Whilst the tear of sensibility so often flows at the unreal tale of woe, which glows under the

pen of the poet and the novelist, shall our hearts refuse to be melted with sorrow at the unaffected and unvarnished tale of a female, who has surmounted difficulties and dangers, which on a review appear romantic, even to herself?"[41] The internalized "romantic" discourse therefore explains the narratives' novelistic style: Kinnan (or her male author) claims for her work a "tear of sensibility," invoking the powerful affect of an "unreal" tale for an "unvarnished" one.

The Johnson *Narrative*'s reliance on emotional affect indicates that women's renderings of their experiences cannot be written outside the fictive register. Intensifying the effect of the speaking voice, the text employs apostrophe to enhance/expand its representation of expressive female discourse. Ironically, these apostrophes constitute a conspicuous rhetorical device popular for its instructional value in contemporary women's novels. Johnson's *Narrative* deploys apostrophe not so much to instruct as to create empathy for the fictive Susannah's experiences: "I will only detain the reader a few moments longer in this place, while I eat the leg of a woodchuck, and then request him to take a night's sailing in the canoe with me across the Lake. Though I sincerely wish him a better passage than I had" (52). Here, the woodchuck's leg denotes the true wilderness experience, but it is embedded in a rhetorical construct that undermines the image's authenticity. The use of the present tense intrudes on the narrative's consistent use of the past—the historiographical preterite—while the direct address to the reader echoes the pathos of epistolary novels. Several apostrophes appear in the Johnson *Narrative*, most often pleading for the reader's commiseration in Johnson's specifically female woes. When Johnson recounts her labor and delivery in the forest, she interrupts the events with just such a request: "Here the compassionate reader will drop a fresh tear, for my inexpressible distress . . . none but mothers can figure to themselves my unhappy fortune" (27). Sentimental, sensational, pathetic, these moments authenticate the *Narrative* as a true relation of the captive's experiences while deploying the images of a suffering, maternal body associated with women's fiction. Although Johnson's historicity is not in question, her status as a credible informant necessitates these moments of recognizably female sensibility. Without them, the *Narrative* could not maintain its posture as the authentic recollections of an actual woman, because "real" women wrote in the language of sensibility. To authenticate Johnson's voice, the text must encode her as a fictional character; that is, Susannah Johnson must sound like Charlotte Temple or Eliza Wharton.

Yet a consistent reliance on this feminized voice of sensibility, grounded in images of the body, is not sustained throughout the *Narrative* because of the danger that the text would be misread as fiction and not as an accurate record of the Republic's colonial past. In a publishing milieu where first-person narrators were employed with little or no pretense toward authenticity, and the term "history" was synonymous with "story," and where, conversely, readers insisted on finding real people behind the fictional characters (the cult of Charlotte Temple comes to mind), the credibility of the Johnson *Narrative* could not depend solely on the voice of Susannah Johnson. Thus, the text employs supplementary devices, historiographical credentials, inserted to assure its readers that the Johnson *Narrative* represented not merely the dramatized voice of experience but also the text of history.

"The Space of Forty-five Years"

The Johnson *Narrative* persistently demonstrates extraordinary self-consciousness about its historical meaning. In addition to the political contextualization offered in the introduction, the text interpolates footnotes, letters from colonial authorities, and ethnographic details.[42] All these components support the narrative "I," supplementing personal claims of veracity with text, an apparatus of scholarly documentation that maintains the text's dialogue between the female voice of experience and the dispassionate (disembodied) textual markers of interpretive authority. The *Narrative*'s structure thereby produces two distinct modes to tell its tale. The first half of the text (to page 76) describes the Indian captivity; the last, the family's tribulations while imprisoned by the French. This dual focus echoes the bifurcated narrative apparatus of subjective speech and objective historiography. While the Indian episodes are told from the narrator's "eyewitness" position, the later passages set in Canada interpolate official documentation. The contrast between the two sections, the two modes, is striking and illuminates the *Narrative*'s inner dialogue in which the woman's voice is made subject to historiographical and political imperatives.

These imperatives include a clear dehumanizing and distancing of Johnson's Native captors. While staying with the Indians, she is expected to function as one of the group because she is, according to custom, adopted by her master. Although she refers to some of the Indians as "my new sisters and brothers" (66), it is clear that Johnson cannot adapt to Indian life. The descriptions of ritual, such as the captives' forced dancing and singing (53–54) and the arrival at St. Francis, delineate the distinctions between Johnson and her captors: "My new home was not the most agreeable; a large wigwam without a floor . . . [with] tools for cookery, made clumsily of wood . . . will not be thought a pleasing residence to one accustomed to civilized life" (61). On a fishing expedition, Johnson cannot keep up with her companions, and her "sister" calls her "no good squaw" (70). Thus the *Narrative* effectively avoids the assimilationist images found in male captivity narratives of the Revolutionary period such as Filson's Boone and the spectacular Ethan Allen.[43] Johnson remains a pathetic, tormented victim, who, in surveying the Indian life around her, may soften her attitude toward her captors but never loses her own "civilized" self. Furthermore, the French who appear in the first section of the narrative are uniformly hospitable and helpful. However, the transition between chapter 5, the last section dedicated to Indian captivity, and chapter 6, the beginning of the French sojourn, offers a rehabilitative version of the Indians, contrasting their general courtesy—they share their scant food with captives and adopt them into their families—with the fate Johnson considers if she "had fallen into the hands of French soldiery" (76). This marks the shift in Susannah Johnson's circumstances, while it simultaneously signals a change in the *Narrative*'s mode.

Chapter 6 begins with the erasure, or at least, displacement, of Susannah Johnson's voice: "The reader will leave me, and *my family*, under the care of our [new French] factor, a short time, and proceed with Mr. Johnson" (77; emphasis mine). James Johnson sets out for Boston, via Albany, "to apply to Governor Wentworth, at Portsmouth, for money to redeem *his family*, and the English prisoners" (78; emphasis mine). Wentworth and the General Assembly approve the funds, and their letter of credit specifying James Johnson's obligations, signed by the committee, is reprinted in the text and appended with a list of captives taken from New Hampshire. As well, the text reproduces

Governor Wentworth's "passport" requesting all British subjects to aid James Johnson in his mission. "With these credentials, Mr. Johnson proceeded with alacrity to Boston" (84). Once in Boston, he receives similar credentials from Governor Shirley, the same man called "impolitick" and "quixotic" in the introduction. The *Narrative* then proves its introductory allegations by reprinting a letter, dated 15 February 1755, from Shirley to James Johnson, forbidding him to press on to Albany and Quebec because intelligence indicates that imminent invasions by the French would make his passage unsafe. This is the order that causes James Johnson to violate his parole and leave "his family exposed to the malice of exasperated Frenchmen" (86); here, the first person resurfaces, and Susannah notes "the gradual change in my friends, from coldness to neglect, and from neglect to contempt" (89).

The official status of these documents brings the private history of Susannah Johnson and her family out from the cabin and wigwam and into the theater of international politics through the medium of James Johnson. Between British and French colonial administrations, the Johnsons are caught in impossible strictures. According to the *Narrative,* Shirley does not consider, or does not care about, the effects of his order on the captives in Canada. The French governor, Vaudreuil, consigns the family to prison upon James Johnson's return because his concern is with the broken parole and unreimbursed redemption funds paid by French persons to the Indians on the Johnsons' behalf.[44] No one in either colonial administration demonstrates an awareness of the consequences of their orders for the people on the frontiers. Their bumbling is documented, as are the layers of bureaucracy that keep the family incarcerated.[45]

Other letters, sent to Susannah Johnson while she was in England, establish her reputation as a "defenceless woman" (124) who has been sorely tried. Unlike the official documents, directed to James Johnson and recounting the colonial administrators' unfeeling errors, these letters record personal interest in Susannah Johnson herself evinced by private agents from New Hampshire in England. The text apologizes for their inclusion, whereas the reproduction of the earlier official letters went unremarked: "While on board the Royal Ann, I received the following letters; the reader will excuse the recitation; it would be ingratitude not to record such conspicuous acts of benevolence" (124–25). These include the "benefaction, of the charitable Ladies" of Plymouth, England, who collect money for Susannah Johnson. The letter of one Hannah Grove manifests a pathetic, feminized tone, citing Johnson's "distress": "Only believe me, madam, you have my earnest prayers to God, to help and assist you. My mama's compliments with mine" (127–28). With these interpolations, the text provides proof of its historical import as well as a critique of colonialist malfeasance, while it maintains separately gendered spheres of public and private life. As credentials, the letters produce a publicly active, officially noted James Johnson over against Susannah's passive victim, dependent on the kindness of strangers.[46]

The Johnson *Narrative* also employs yet another authenticating historiographical technique, footnotes. Most of these appear in the early pages, filling in details that Johnson could not have known at the time of the attack, that is, in narrative time. In the first note there is a factual error, when the narrator states, "My father, Mr. James Willard, was then second in command" (18n). Susannah Willard Johnson's father's name was Moses Willard, and he is mentioned later in the text when she is told in Canada that he had been killed in an Indian raid. The next note recurs to the "assistance" Johnson received, mentioned in the prefatory remarks, while composing the *Narrative*. Here, Johnson's tentative tone is meant to reinforce the artifice that she is writing this account: "Mr. Labarree is very positive, and I think Mr. Johnson was of the same opinion, that seventeen Indians attacked the house" (21–22n). Both these notes supplement the narrator's version with correctives from men that simultaneously summon historical "facts" into the personal narrative and prove the author/narrator's credibility.

The last footnote underscores Susannah Johnson's function as both experienced captive and actual author of her text. In a passage describing Johnson's attempts to keep her family together and fed when her husband is first imprisoned, the *Narrative* aligns Susannah Johnson with the famously pathetic captive, Jemima Howe. Plunging into high sensibility, the narrator states: "Our own misfortunes had taught us how to feel for the sufferings of others, and large demands were now made, on our sympathetick powers" (93). More English captives appear in Montreal, among them the daughters of Mrs. Howe, Polly and Submit Phips, "two children belonging to Mrs. How [*sic*], the fair captive, celebrated in Col. Humphrey's [*sic*] life of Putnam. Mrs. How was then a prisoner at St. Johns" (94n). Howe's captivity narrative had been published first in 1788 in David Humphreys' biography of Israel Putnam, and several versions had appeared by 1796. Her account, also composed in the first person and written by a man (as were subsequent editions), renders Howe as the first "self"-consciously aestheticized, melodramatic female captive. It is likely that the Walpole writers read or, at the least, were familiar with the Howe narrative and viewed it as a precursor or even a template for their work on Johnson. Significantly, in February of 1796, just a few months before the "proposal" for the Johnson narrative appeared in the 10 May *Farmer's Weekly Museum*, Royall Tyler had met Jemima Howe while stopping for supper at her son's house.[47] The Johnson *Narrative*'s reference to Howe, and Tyler's recent interaction with her, links Susannah Johnson to the "fair captive" and establishes both the Howe and Johnson accounts as key texts that demonstrate the use of gendered markers to define, combine, and give meaning to distinctive linguistic modalities in the print culture of the early Republic. The cultural authority of both texts depends on a deft integration of women's speech and men's interpretive narration.[48]

Moreover, in the Howe footnote, the *Narrative* achieves a seamless blend of feminized personal expression and impersonal interpretation that foregrounds the text's means and ends. The rhetoric of literary sensibility saturates the footnote, but the format of the note itself marks the use of scholarly documentation—in Derounian-Stodola's terms, the union of the fictive and the factive. Therefore the troublesome lapse of forty years is elided by a contemporary appeal to readers' familiarity both with a literature of female sensibility (how a woman should sound) and with historiographical practices.[49] The combination provides a potent rhetorical formula for the actual writer or writers by allowing them to exploit both Susannah Johnson's experiences and her gender to produce a belles-lettristic account of local history.

In the publishing milieu of Walpole, the importation by the "men of letters" of Susannah Johnson as speaking subject of "her" narrative extends their practice of pseudonymity to gender impersonation. This use of rhetorical drag literally refigures the ways in which personal expression might be converted into literary property through the textual appropriation of a credible voice. In the use of gender impersonation, the Walpole writers superseded the playful connection between a lay preacher and his "sermon" or a Christopher Caustic and his acerbic text; rather, first-person voice, as an index of an actual person's experi-

ence, becomes a crucial corner in the triangulated relationship of text
to presumed narrator to actual author. What the Walpole men achieved
in writing Susannah Johnson's *Narrative* was entry into the world of
belles lettres through the backdoor of impersonation; the popularity
of the text, due to its credible source in Johnson's experience, ensured
that the Walpole writers' Federalist positions in contemporary political
debates might be read back into the prehistory of the Republic.

Their version of Susannah Johnson's experiences did indeed become history. By 1870, a descendant of Peter Labarree's had assigned
the same mistaken authorship that some of our contemporary critics
presume in their studies of Susannah Johnson's voice. In a dedica-
tory address for a monument to early Charlestown settlers, Dr. Benjamin Labarree, Peter's grandson, referred to Susannah Johnson as
the text's author and declaimed that "her character and deeds create
history—*her graphic pen records it.* That little book, though small,
has produced a sensation in the world. It is a book of authority and is
quoted by all who have attempted to write the history of Charlestown"
(quoted in Saunderson 305). Labarree's characterization indicates that
the Walpole men's ruse succeeded; their gender-impersonated text had
become "a book of authority."

Thus the Johnson and Howe narratives, composed in the familiar
sentimental language of the period's novels, nevertheless continue to
be viewed as authentic representations of the captive women's experiences, expressed in their own voices. At the time of publication, *A Narrative of the Captivity of Mrs. Johnson* convincingly represented the
subject's personal testimony as an alternative to depersonalized public
discourse, even as that subject became an object within the historical-
political composition of the Federalist men. The daily presence of Susannah Johnson and her family in the towns of Walpole and Charlestown
permitted the male impersonators to fashion the woman's experiences
into Federalist revisions of the French and Indian War. For these men,
Johnson provided a ground on which to write a history contrasting the
current peace against the depredations of colonialism, both French and
British. Accordingly, the *Narrative* concludes with Susannah Johnson
looking back over her whole life. Like the "good landlady" who told
her tale to the Hermit, Susannah Johnson is grateful to be living in a
different time: "That I have been an unfortunate woman, all will grant;
yet, my misfortunes, while they enriched my experience, and taught me

the value of patience, have increased my gratitude to the author of all those blessings, whose goodness and mercy have preserved my life to the present time" (141).

In the concluding pages of the narrative, the text maintains the tension between historiographical discourse that interprets the facts of Johnson's captivity and the sentimental voice that speaks her experiences. While a Romantic but impersonalized voice argues that "the gloomy wilderness . . . has vanished away; and the thrifty farm smiles in its stead," Susannah finishes with an intensely personal, familial note: "My numerous progeny, often gather around me, to hear the sufferings once felt by their aunt or grandmother, and wonder at their magnitude. My daughter, Captive still keeps the dress she appeared in, when brought to my bed side, by the French nurse at Ticonderoga hospital; and often refreshes my memory with past scenes, when showing it to her children. These things yield a melancholy pleasure" (144).

Gathered to hear her story, the family, like the reader, wonders at the sufferings Susannah Johnson experienced. The Walpole men who were responsible for writing her narrative recognized the power of the story-telling voice and the wonder it produced, and they harnessed it for their ends. Certainly, *A Narrative of the Captivity of Mrs. Johnson* demonstrates the ways in which captivity narratives "provided an instant tradition for a society that, in a European sense, lacked a past" (Washburn xxii), but it also provides an intriguing and complex example of processes and products of rhetorical drag as a complex negotiation of the modes of vocality and textuality in the early Republic. This practice extends the meaning and value of pseudonymity and offers a broader scope for the men who "spoke" by writing occasionally as "saunterers," "hermits," or even, phantasmagorically, as "colons" and "spondees" (textual markers that categorically refuse the possibility of embodiment and speech). Trading the ambiguity/anonymity afforded by these pseudonyms for Susannah Johnson's "I," the composers of the *Narrative* appropriated her captivity experiences through her voice. By means of rhetorical drag, the Walpole writers fashioned Susannah Johnson's credibility from this voice and thereby made possible—made *authentic*—their written history of the new nation.

A Fair Captive

After having long been the sport of fiction, [the reader] will perhaps probably run into the opposite extreme, and give up all confidence in the annals of ancient as well as modern times: and thus
the easy-believer of fine fables and marvellous stories will find, at
last, his historical faith change to scepticism and end in infidelity.
    —David Humphreys, *Essay on the Life of . . . Putnam*[50]

Susannah Johnson's encounter with Jemima Howe's daughters and
the footnote discussion of Mrs. Howe herself presume readers' familiarity with the Howe captivity. Jemima Sartwell Phips Howe Tute
(1713?–1805), as her full name indicates, outlived three husbands; bore
at least seven children; and, like Johnson, lived to a good age. Her
fame, however, derived from the circumstances of her captivity.

The details of her captivity, according to these sources, are as follows. On 27 July 1755, Mrs. Howe was taken captive during an Indian
raid on Hinsdale, New Hampshire, in which her husband, Caleb Howe,
was killed. Howe, two female neighbors, and their eleven children were
forced to march north through the wilderness. Approximately ten days
later they arrived with their captors at Crown Point and spent nearly
a week there; some of the captives were taken to Montreal to be sold
to the French, including Submit Phips, Howe's daughter whom Susannah Johnson met. The remainder moved on to St. Francis where Howe
was assigned to a Native woman whom she convinced to sell her to
the French. The attempt was unsuccessful because, the narrative states,
when the French housewife saw Howe's six-month-old baby, she would
not buy a woman who had a child to care for. Howe returned to St.
Francis, where her baby was taken from her, and she spent the winter
with Indians who told her that two of her children, including the youngest, were dead, but she later found one alive. After a dispute with her
Indian master, she was sold to one Saccappee, a Frenchman living in
the nearby fort. The change in circumstances allowed her to aid other
captives brought from St. Johns, because Saccappee and his wife were
good masters, although both the older Saccappee and his son became
enamored of her. She was rescued from this situation by Peter Schuyler
on the orders of Governor Vaudreuil. Her two daughters were placed in

a convent; one returned with Vaudreuil to France at the end of the war
and married a Frenchman named Cron Lewis. The other stayed in the
convent well after Howe's redemption and resisted Howe's attempts to
repatriate her until Howe asked for, and received, the intervention of
the new governor. Howe herself was redeemed through the offices of
several men, one of whom was the ubiquitous Schuyler.

By 1796, Howe's story had appeared in separate works by two eminent men of letters, David Humphreys, one of the Connecticut Wits,
and Jeremy Belknap, founder of the Massachusetts Historical Society.
Additionally, her captivity was retold in a pamphlet issued by the Rev.
Bunker Gay of Hinsdale, New Hampshire. Like the Johnson *Narrative,*
Howe's experiences were published many years after her capture (July
1755) in a first-person account. Unlike Johnson's, however, Jemima
Howe's first-person text did not inaugurate her appearance before the
public. Howe's personal testimony was preceded by Humphreys' version
of her experiences and Belknap's references to her first-person account
in the second volume of his *History of New-Hampshire.* So Chamberlain and the Walpole circle, in fashioning a public Susannah Johnson
and evoking Jemima Howe, can be situated within an expanded genealogy of male gender impersonators writing as female captives in the print
world of Revolutionary and early Republic letters.

This line, of course, begins with the Mathers, particularly Cotton
Mather's writing of Hannah Duston. As we have seen, as Duston's
historicity became more remote, her figure and actions became more
encrusted with imagery drawn from her revisionists' cultural concerns
about behavior appropriate to gender regimes of their own historical
moments; the Puritan goodwife transformed, over time and through
ideological grids, into the "bloody old hag." These ideological and aesthetic mutations produced a significantly more romanticized Hannah
Duston from the figure in Mather's sermon and his history, *Decennium
Luctuosum.* But even in the Duston third-person accounts, we trace a
shift from (much-mediated) historical subject to imaginative object.
Howe's editors/ghostwriters/revisers—it is difficult to assign one term
for the impersonation—reverse this order of representation. The result
is that, when it finally appears, Howe's "I" steps into a shape already
fashioned for it, a rhetorical construct undermined by previous renditions of her figure. In large part this is due to Humphreys, because
his astoundingly sentimentalized and eroticized third-person version

adumbrated the subsequent renditions of Howe even as Belknap and Gay attempted to reclaim her voice for their "correct" historiographical ends.

Christopher Castiglia notes that "the paradoxical situation of the captive in the hands of her editor is best encapsulated by Jemima Howe" (79). Echoing the actual movement "between men" that Howe experiences in captivity, her first-person narrative passes from Gay to Belknap.[51] Thus, "the captive's narrative no longer serves, as those of earlier captives purportedly did, for moral edification; rather, the body of her text—like her body within the text—exists solely for the pleasure and 'amusement' of the men who traffic in it" (79–80). Castiglia, citing Eve Sedgwick's theorization of male homosocial desire, anticipates what I characterized previously as "an erotics of rhetorical drag." He argues that "through their traffic in the shared female object, the men ensure their own position as subjects in control of a symbolic economy in which the women figures only as a prized commodity" (206n20). Both the Johnson and Howe narratives should be read within the "symbolic economy" that encompasses gender (as well as race and class) regimes pertaining at the time of publication. Understood within these systems of representation, the captivity narratives' enactments of rhetorical drag demonstrate how impersonation provides the male authors with the instruments whereby they might experience the "pleasure and 'amusements'" of a culturally powerful subjectivity. As writing subjects, they produce the objects, such as Susannah Johnson and Jemima Howe, whose textual figures confirm the men's historical claims. The claims emerge, however, from the specific rhetorical choices they make in order to substantiate the claims. For example, recall the scene of abjection wherein Johnson "finds" herself naked and vulnerable, while her husband and male neighbors stand by, immobilized by their captors. The text makes clear that the historical actors could not take action; there is no agency here at all, only paralytic suffering.[52]

Howe's body does serve as a source of textual pleasure, but that objectified and titillating Howe is much more evident in Humphreys' text than in the Belknap and Gay versions Castiglia reviews. The trajectory of her figuration demonstrates that a first-person female captivity account offers a site for the kinds of pleasures male impersonators might derive from portraying her as *sexually*, as well as physically and psychologically, vulnerable. First embedded in Humphreys' history, and then "taken from her own mouth," Howe's story exemplifies as well how a woman's voice might suit the ends of ambitious literary men who seek to compose local histories. As Johnson did for Chamberlain and the Walpole circle, Howe retrieves the memories of long-ago suffering for Belknap's and Gay's versions of the events that lead, ineluctably, to the new Republic.

"The Career of Her Miseries"

Humphreys' prefatory remarks in the *Essay on the Life of the Honorable Major-General Israel Putnam* recall the earlier captivity narratives' "dispensations" while emphasizing his subject's reputation: "An essay on the life of a person so elevated in military rank, and so conversant in extraordinary scenes, could not be destitute of amusement and instruction, and would possess the advantages of presenting for imitation a respectable model of public and private virtues" (iii–iv). Putnam made his reputation as a commander in the Revolutionary War and confidant of Washington. As the text reveals, Humphreys fought alongside Putnam, and he conspicuously signs his remarks from "Mount Vernon, in Virginia," simultaneously evoking the authenticity of the eyewitness (privy to Putnam's *personal* virtue) and the name invested with paramount national authority. The *Essay* obviously has a more ambitious end than mere "amusement and instruction": Humphreys rashly asserts that "the inclosed manuscript justly claims indulgence for its venial errors, as it is the first effort in biography, that has been made on this continent" (iv). Previous historical efforts to portray famous men as "respectable models," such as the Mathers' hagiographic sketches, are ignored in Humphreys' determination to be the first.[53]

Despite the prefatory pretensions toward a factual representation of Putnam's life, Humphreys' own melodramatic impulses overwhelm his subject. William Bottorff observes that "the biography is also an early American historical romance, and its author a herald of many mythmakers to follow. He anticipates such romantic novelists as Charles Brockden Brown and James Fenimore Cooper" (xi). If, as Humphreys insists, the *Essay* illuminates Putnam's "domestic, manly, and heroic virtues" (14), then the inclusion of Jemima Howe's story provides the female counterpart to the virile Putnam. The captivity episode, in which

Putnam is taken prisoner during the French and Indian War, introduces Jemima Howe as if she is the heroine of a novel. Humphreys describes Putnam's "squalid" conditions and his rescue by Colonel Schuyler, the indefatigable comforter of Canadian captives (whose letter testifying to James Johnson's good faith appears in that narrative). At Schuyler's home, Putnam meets Mrs. Howe, "a fair captive, whose history would not be read without emotion if it could be written in the same affecting manner, in which I have often heard it told" (74). Here, Humphreys reinserts himself as Putnam's own confidant while establishing Jemima Howe's reputation as the "fair captive," whose story is, presumably, already known. Putnam drops out of the *Essay* for the next six pages while Humphreys traces "the career of her miseries" (75) in what appears to be his attempt to recapture that "same affecting manner."

The description of Howe owes much more to the literature of sentiment and seduction than it does to any previous captivity narrative. Although a forty-two-year-old woman, who had borne seven children and lived on the New Hampshire frontier most of her life, Jemima Howe appears to have weathered her sufferings extremely well:

> She was still young and handsome herself, though she had two daughters of marriageable age. Distress, which had taken somewhat from the original redundancy of her bloom and added a softening paleness to her cheeks, rendered her appearance the more engaging. Her face, that seemed to have been formed for the assemblage of dimples and smiles, was clouded with care. The natural sweetness was not, however, soured by despondency and petulance; but chastened by humility and resignation. (Humphreys 74)

Echoes of Puritan "humility and resignation" vie with sentimental discourse—"the assemblage of dimples and smiles"—in the appealing Howe. Physical attractiveness soon proves a disadvantage, however, and when new miseries threaten Howe, Humphreys takes off on a melodramatic tour de force. Saccappee, the elder Frenchman who bought Howe from her Indian master, admires/desires her but "gaze[s] respectfully on her beauty." His son, a backwoods Lovelace, besieges Howe because "the impetuosity of youth was fired to madness by the sight of her charms" (77).

One day the son, whose attentions had been long lavished upon her in vain, finding her alone in a chamber, forcibly seized her hand and solemnly declared that he would now satiate the passion which she had so long refused to indulge. She recurred to intreaties, struggles and tears, those prevalent female weapons, which the distraction of danger not less than the promptness of genius is wont to supply: while he, in the delirium of vexation and desire, snatched a dagger and swore he would put an end to her life if she persisted to struggle. Mrs. Howe, assuming the dignity of conscious virtue, told him it was what she most ardently wished, and begged him to plunge the poignard through her heart, since the mutual importunities and jealousies of such rivals had rendered her life, though innocent, more irksome and insupportable than death itself. (77–78)

Although young Saccappee is ordered to Detroit, Howe fears his return and worries about her children. Schuyler, "the friend of suffering humanity," was in the vicinity, and "she came with feeble and trembling steps to him. The same maternal passion, which, sometimes, overcomes the timidity of nature in the birds when plundered of their callow nestlings, emboldened her, notwithstanding her native diffidence, to disclose those griefs which were ready to devour her in silence" (78–79). Howe's deeply feminized figure conflates both maidenly and matronly attractions, a powerful combination that doubles the gendered, embodied effect of her experiences. The passage emphasizes her physicality, her delicacy, and—significantly—her ability to tell her tale: "While her delicate aspect was heightened to a glowing blush, for fear of offending by an inexcusable importunity, or of transgressing the rules of propriety by representing herself as being an object of admiration; she told, with artless simplicity, all the story of her woes" (79). Although Howe wishes to save herself and her children, she risks sacrificing propriety in the attempt by representing herself as "an object of admiration." She cannot remain silent, yet she should not tell her (salacious) tale. Therefore, her own recitation must be "artless," devoid of the very sensationalism Humphreys so effusively supplies. This helpless Howe counterpoints the heroic (and despicable) acts of the men around her.

Soon after Schuyler rescued her, he "recommended the fair captive to the protection of his friend Putnam" (79), a shift that allows Humphreys to parade the major's manly virtue. Young Saccappee returns "with his passion rather encreased than abated by absence" (80), and his relentless pursuit terrifies Howe, who "was obliged to keep constantly near Major Putnam, who informed the young officer [Saccappee] that he should protect that lady at the risque of his life" (80). The situation elicits a most spectacular figure of frustrated sexual impulse, which, understandably, requires an explanatory footnote. Saccappee's passion for Howe is so overwhelmingly physical "that while he was speaking of her the * blood would frequently gush from his nostrils" (80). The footnote reassures readers: "*This physical effect, wonderful as it may appear, is so far from being a fictitious embellishment, that it can be proved by the most solemn testimony of more than one person still living" (80n). Thus, the perhaps incredulous but titillated reader finds the psychosexual image of the amazing, gushing nosebleeds corroborated in the authoritative format of the footnote. Alluding to eyewitness testimony, Humphreys establishes the authenticity of Howe's sheer physical attraction; that is, Howe's body provokes a sensational textual moment that elicits, indeed, necessitates, a historiographical marker in the form of a footnote.

It seems no wonder that a woman who displayed such erotic power should become a legend before she ever told her story. In his rush to produce a spectacular version of Jemima Howe, Humphreys stumbles across the very gender categories he seeks to incarnate in the figures of Howe and Putnam. On their march back from captivity in Canada, Howe, "though endowed with masculine fortitude . . . was truly feminine in strength and must have fainted by the way had it not been for the assistance of Major Putnam" (81). Howe simultaneously displays both masculine and feminine traits, but finally—essentially—the female weaknesses must be supported by the manly Putnam.

The *Essay* leaves Jemima Howe immediately before the Revolutionary War, demonstrating her "acknowledged superiority" in her designation by the people of Hinsdale as agent in a New Hampshire land dispute. "But the dispute was fortunately accommodated . . . without their being obliged to make use of her talents" (82). Howe's superior (in every respect) figure channels Humphreys' historiographical and stylistic impulses and provides the canvas on which he can paint Putnam's virility and honorable behavior over against her eroticized vulnerability, the stock of sentimental fiction. Humphreys' emotionally and sexually charged tale, rhetorically overwrought and filled with historical characters, contrasts with the representation of "artless simplicity" in the story Howe tells Schuyler to enlist his aid. Thus novelized, Howe passes into history, and not long after, into Belknap's *History.*

"The Subscriber, Being Engaged in Continuing the History . . ."

So begins Jeremy Belknap's 1790 broadside soliciting historical information. From "the Ministers and other Gentlemen of note, in the State," Belknap "begs the favour of them to collect and transmit to him such information as can be obtained on the following heads." Item 2 reads: "The sufferings of the people by French and Indian wars; the number and names of the killed, wounded and captived; their treatment by the enemy; their death or redemption, with particular dates." One minister, Bunker Gay of Hinsdale, responded to this request with the story of Jemima Howe. Belknap refers to Howe twice in the *History* but only once interpolates Howe as narrator of her own experiences. Like Swarton and Duston, then, Howe becomes material for ministerial ends. However, as Castiglia notes, late eighteenth-century historiography, especially in the hands of Belknap, traded the sense of divine instrumentality in the earlier narratives for a more secularized figure of historical informant.

Belknap's literary mentor was Thomas Prince, another minister whose "passion for factual accuracy" passed to his better-known disciple.[54] Prince initiated the practice of circulating questionnaires to gather information on local towns. Conscious of his descent from the Mathers on his mother's side and guided by Prince, Belknap became the foremost practicing historian in the early Republic. Post–Revolutionary War interest in local histories supported works such as Belknap's, although the publication delays between each volume of the *History* seem to have reduced sales. The delays were caused by Belknap's famous penchant for accuracy: his exactitude is apparent in the 1790 broadside's specificity and itemization, and that exactitude was the product of a man deeply concerned with his own reputation. "I consider my reputation as at stake the moment I consent to undertake the work," Belknap writes to Matthew Cary, explaining his compositional methods as well as personal anxieties.[55] To ensure that his *History* held to his own scrupulously high standards, Belknap included citations of the texts on which he based his own discourse in the margins of the published volumes. The preface to the first volume describes the method and its provisos: "The authorities from which information is derived are carefully noted in the margin. Where no written testimonies could be obtained, recourse has been had to the most authentic traditions, selected and compared with a scrupulous attention, and with proper allowance for the imperfection of human memory. After all, the critical reader will doubtless find some chasms which in such a work it would be improper to fill by the help of imagination and conjecture."[56] Thus, Belknap's history conducts a textual dialogue with the marginal authorities.

When Belknap recurs to the events surrounding Howe's captivity, the marginal notation cites "Gay's MS letter," but he does not quote directly from the letter. Rather, in a footnote, Belknap invokes the reputation conferred on Howe by Humphreys' *Essay* and issues a slight corrective, not to the outrageous sentimentality of Humphreys' description, but to the final mention of Howe's public service as a New Hampshire agent. Describing the captives, Belknap writes,

> One of these, the wife of Caleb Howe, was the FAIR CAPTIVE, of whom such a brilliant account is given in the life of General Putnam, published by Col. Humphrey [*sic*]. She is still living at Hinsdale, and has obliged the author with a particular narrative of her sufferings and deliverance. This account, drawn up by the Rev. Mr. Gay, is too long to be here inserted, and too entertaining to be abridged, but will probably be published at some future time. As to that part of the story, that the people of Hinsdale chose her to go to Europe, as their agent in a case of disputed lands; it was never known or thought of by them till the life of Putnam appeared in print.—Gay's MS letter. (2: 295n)

The *History* takes issue with a minor question, the mooted commission, but lets stand, unexceptionably, Howe's portrait as "the FAIR CAPTIVE," and, in so doing, indicates the value of Howe's tale for early Republic historiography. Having mined the Gay account for "real" history to counter Humphreys' imperfect version, Belknap consigns

Jemima Howe's voice, "too entertaining" a text to be excluded from his full history, to an appendix in the third volume. The entertainment value of Howe's narrative, like her sobriquet, had already been established by Humphreys. The historiographical utility of her experiences is urged in Gay's documentation of the Hinsdale events in the manuscript letter responding to Belknap's broadside. Like the Swarton narrative, Howe's first-person text, "drawn up by the Rev. Mr. Gay," serves as a testimonial voice of suffering, contextualized by the appropriate ministerial hand and submitted for the use of his history.

"Taken from Her Own Mouth, and Written"

The Gay letter appended to Belknap's third volume was issued separately in 1792. Here we apparently find Howe's own voice, at least what appears to be her own "I," not hidden in an appendix but curiously embedded in Gay's personal text, the letter addressed to Belknap. The sliding subjectivity of *A Genuine and Correct Account* offers a clumsy but telling variant on rhetorical drag and its performance of a woman's voice. Specifically, the rhetorical subject Howe, marked by her first-person pronoun, is policed and subsumed by Gay's "I," which not only brackets Howe's relation but ensures that the relation includes all the particulars Belknap requires.

The title page's claim that this work is both "genuine" and "correct" positions Gay's text as the truthful alternative to "the mistakes of Col. Humphreys, relating to Mrs. Howe, in his 'life of General Putnam.'"[57] Humphreys' account might be "brilliant," as Belknap notes, quoting Gay, but it lacks the historical accuracy that is supplied by Howe's apparently authentic first-person voice. As well, the Howe narrative answers Belknap's call in his broadside for documentation about phenomena beyond the sphere of human action. Thus, Howe's recollection of her movements with her Indian captors includes a night "remarkable on account of the *great earthquake*," the date of which is supplied in the footnote (10). The alternation of recognizably historiographic forms and sentimental language foreshadows the contending voices in the Johnson *Narrative*. Here, however, the feminized, emotionally charged passages are not nearly as emphatic as in that text, and they certainly never approach Humphreys' over-the-top eroticism and sentimentality. This diminution in tone can be attributed both to Gay's recognition of Belknap's discursive preferences and, perhaps, to Gay's ministerial reserve. An early passage describing Howe's first winter with the tribe displays this conjunction of the historical and the personal: "And now came on the season when the Indians begun to prepare for a winter's hunt. I was ordered to return my poor child to those of them, who still claimed it as their property. This was a severe trial. The babe clung to my bosom with all its might; but I was obliged to pluck it thence, and deliver it, shrieking and screaming, enough to penetrate a heart of stone, into the hands of those unfeeling wretches whose tender mercies may be termed cruel" (9). The stiff formality of "And now came on" contrasts with the pathos in the "heart of stone," and the piece ends with a biblical echo from Cotton Mather's description of Indians as "Tawnies," whose "tender mercies are cruelties." Furthermore, the fiction that Howe related her story to Gay in this language fails here, and in similarly dissonant passages, because it is so obviously, at the least, a Matherian "improvement."

The first four and a half pages of *A Genuine and Correct Account* maintain no such fiction. They are, rather, the words of Bunker Gay to Jeremy Belknap, providing specifics of the initial moments in the Hinsdale attack. Gay describes in detail Caleb Howe's mortal injuries and lingering death, but his authorial "I" does not appear explicitly until the story concerns the three women: "Their husbands, I need not mention again, and their feelings at this juncture I will not attempt to describe" (4). However, that is exactly what Gay goes on to do, noting how "extremely anxious" they were and citing their "inexpressible disappointment and surprise" (4). Listing the number of captives, including the children and their ages, and clarifying the parentage of Howe's two elder daughters, Gay performs admirably as a Belknap informant.

Gay's assertion that "it was from the mouth of this woman that I lately received the foregoing account" (5) signals the textual transition from Gay's text to Howe's. A disturbing qualification of Howe's account coupled with a syntactical breakdown then leads into the graphic demarcation between the man's and the woman's words. Along with the description of the "foregoing account," that is, of the initial attack, Gay writes, "She also gave me, I doubt not, a true, though to be sure, a very brief and imperfect history of her captivity, which I here insert for your perusal. It may perhaps afford you some amusement, and can do no harm; if after it has undergone your critical inspection, you should not think it (or an abbreviation of it) worthy to be preserved among the records you are about to publish" (5). The last phrase goes begging and reveals Gay's attempt to ingratiate himself with the historian. He inserts Howe's "brief" and "imperfect" testimony because it is also "true" and therefore a plausible record possibly "worthy to be preserved." Paradoxically, Howe's truthfulness relies on Gay's shaping hand. Employing a milder version of feminized sentimentalism than Humphreys' alongside Belknapian detail, Gay guarantees historiographical value from even this unreliable informant. To drive the point home, Howe's discourse is set off from his own first-person epistolary text with a single quotation mark (never closed at the end of the narrative), followed by the parenthetical "she says," after which "I" presumably indicates Jemima Howe's voice. Both the complex syntax and the contesting tones of the text belie the "I."

Like Swarton in Mather's harangue against the French Catholics who try to convert her, Gay's Howe holds her own in Canada, although her daughter succumbs to "this school of superstition and bigotry" (17). The prejudice the narrative displays against those who actually saved Submit Phips from Indian captivity retrieves the Calvinist tone of those earlier anti-Catholic polemics. Intent on vilifying the nuns, the narrative loses its sense of temporal progression, and the fictive Howe apologizes for the disruption: "But I have run on a little before my story, for I have not yet informed you of the means and manner of my own redemption" (18). That is, the story has Howe returning to Canada to rescue her "extremely bigoted" daughter from the "customs and religion of the place" before it narrates the circumstances of her own deliverance. This discontinuity in an otherwise chronological narrative suggests psychological verisimilitude in the voice; it also performs a critique of Catholicism likely to be endorsed by a Protestant minister.

The transition back to Gay's "I" lacks a graphic marker and therefore produces some confusion in the crossover. Howe expresses her gratitude to Schuyler: "He accompanied and conducted us from Montreal to Albany, and entertained us in the most friendly and hospitable manner a considerable time, at his own house, and I believe entirely at his own expense" (18–19). The next sentence begins a new paragraph: "I have spun out the above narrative to a much greater length than I at first intended"—here, we still read Howe for "I," but the conclusion of the sentence explodes that identification—"and shall conclude it with referring you, for a more ample and *brilliant* account of the captive heroine, who is the subject of it, to Col. Humphrey's [*sic*] history of the life of Gen. Israel Putnam, together with a few remarks upon a few clauses in it" (18). So closely does Gay impersonate Howe's voice that he misses the disjunction in his own rhetorical construct, reappropriating the "I" he never really relinquished: "I have spun out the above narrative."

The struggle for rhetorical primacy emerges clearly here, a struggle that is the direct result of the conditions that make possible rhetorical drag. The impersonation of Howe's voice depends on language that convincingly represents Howe's memories, and this language must sound like Howe. For Gay, the value of the text inhered in its historiographical propriety, its observance of accuracy and veracity. Significantly, Howe's voice and Gay's writing conflict in these last passages. In referring to Humphreys' "*brilliant* account," Gay warns his readers that Humphreys' description of Howe might be too "romantick and extravagant" and asserts that, in some details of her experiences, "the Colonel must needs have been misinformed." However, Gay states that Howe herself initially maintained the truthfulness of the Humphreys' version. When Gay read her an extract of it, she was "well-pleased and said, at first, it was all true." The passage continues:

> but soon after [she] contradicted the circumstances of her lover's being so bereft of his senses when he saw her moving off in a boat at some distance from the shore, as to plunge into the water after her, in consequence of which he was seen no more. It is true, she said, that as she was returning from Montreal to Albany, she met with young Saccapee on the way, that she was in a boat with Col. Schuyler, that the French officer came on board the boat, made her some handsome presents, took his final leave of her, and departed to outward appearance, in tolerable good humour.

The last paragraph of the text follows this third-person confession, but in it Howe, according to Gay, insists that when she returned to Canada for her daughter, "she met with him again, that he showed her a lock of her hair, and her name likewise, printed with vermilion on his arm." Thus, Gay reports, Howe retrieves her own "romantick and extravagant" role in Saccappee's life (her "lover"), even after she revises Humphreys' account of it. Howe's body is reduced to a memento (a lock of hair), her name transferred to the body of Saccappee in a tattoo (a body memento) and her voice now transmuted into more formal and familiar historiographical indirect discourse. Gay's imposture thus gives way to the exactitudes of supervision, and he concludes his account of Howe's experiences in the mode that Belknap practiced, authoritative and distanced. In shifting to this mode, Gay continues to correct Humphreys, charging that the people of Hinsdale never considered Jemima Howe as an agent until after reading that portion of his *Essay*. Although it was untrue, Humphreys "inserted it as a matter of undoubted fact" (20). These accusatory words close *A Genuine and Correct Account,* which itself purports to be the real thing in historiography by employing the impersonated voice of the "fair captive."

These two women's captivity narratives of the early Republic, marked by the sensibility of the period's novels, nevertheless continue to rely on the voice of a suffering woman to impart credibility to the histories they tell. Both *The Narrative of the Captivity of Mrs. Johnson* and the Howe accounts represent the rhetorical subject's personal testimony—her voice speaking her captive experiences—as a counter to post-Declaration depersonalized political discourse. The experiences of Susannah Johnson and Jemima Howe provided male editors/impersonators with material for their historical accounts of the French and Indian War. For Chamberlain and the Walpole writers, Johnson's captivity grounded a Federalist reverie that contrasted the current peace against the depredations of colonialism, French and British. Howe's three revisers recognized different degrees of utility in her story and accordingly represented first her figure then her voice. Particularity, regional identification, physicality, and the sheer historicity of their captivities combined to make Johnson and Howe fit objects for their impersonators' practice of rhetorical drag. Their voices, performed by imitating and invoking the styles of women's writing in the early Republic, entered into history as affecting and credible impersonations.

EPILOGUE

"I'm Just an Advertisement for a Version of Myself"

Versions

When I first heard these lyrics from David Byrne's song "Angels," I was struck by their encapsulation of the practices and consequences of rhetorical drag. Byrne's figure of postmodern self-imaging proves an aptly ironical emblem for my research and writing on early American rhetorical drag because of its recognition that a subject's position is never solely its own to inhabit. The subject, "I," concatenates into an "advertisement," a "version," and a "(my)self." This self occupies multiple positions in a reiterated linguistic costuming, a set of possibilities that never stabilizes into a real, or unified, subject. However, the "I" does speak, asserting its identity with all the potential subject positions named by the sentence; we understand that this subject, this "I," comes into being because it performs itself.

Initially, I placed these lyrics as an epigraph in the chapter on Hannah Duston, but as the project progressed, it became clear to me that I could use Byrne's words to connect contemporary feminist theories to all the early captivity narratives I examined. As I researched the origins of each impersonated text and sought to read them within their historical contexts, Byrne's lyrics suggested both the means and the ends of early American rhetorical drag: the performance of female-gendered subjectivities by men to "sell" a particular historical view. Advertising a version of the captive, each text *turns* (as the Latin root of both "advertise" and "version" connotes), transforming the woman into an

instrument—exemplar, informant, site of identification—of men who
wrote the histories, colonial and national, of early America.

In the historical narratives the impersonators composed, the practices of rhetorical drag emphasize the centrality of gender formations.
It is crucial to view these practices in light of the performances they
set out to achieve. The successful impersonation of the women's voices
depended on the men's fundamental recognition that gender is the key
to signify a speaking subject, because gender so profoundly signals
the subject's disposition in the world. As Judith Butler writes, "it is
unclear that there can be an 'I' or a 'we' who has not been submitted,
subjected to gender, where gendering is, among other things the differ-
entiating relations by which speaking subjects come into being" (*Bodies* 7). Finally, it is this "being," this characterization of the woman
as an experienced person in the world, that the impersonators wanted
to recapture for their historiographic projects, because the woman's
voice verifies the authenticity of the text's evidence. As we have seen in
those women's captivity narratives produced by men, the ontological
status of captivity *and* of being female grounded the men's versions of
history and the ways each history should be understood.

American literary studies abound with texts whose primary goal is
to make moral, ethical, political, and historical claims on the basis of
subjective experience. Notably, an examination of the problems and
potentialities white abolitionists encountered in speaking *for* and *as*
enslaved persons, as Karen Sanchez-Eppler demonstrates, leads to an
understanding of how those abolitionists came to imagine and represent personhood. Yet, while slave narratives composed or sponsored by
white abolitionists did often feature gender as well as race crossing, their
primary aim was not historiographical. The men who impersonated female captives, however, sought to fashion historical informants, witnesses to events that they deemed suitably historical and therefore fit for
the official chronicles of the colony and early Republic. White women,
although not enfranchised, might still speak to the public (provided the
appropriate dispensations were in place), while most people of color
held a different social or even ontological status; indeed, in many cases,
they were not granted the basic acknowledgement of personhood. One
use of rhetorical drag as a hermeneutic, then, would be in a comparative investigation into the practices of authorial impersonation in slave

narratives and in narratives of white captives. This study could lead to a better understanding of how historiographical discourse privileges and marginalizes certain voices on the basis of gender, race, and class. That is, how do impersonators represent and distinguish the voices of those they deem suitable "speaking subjects" of history?

Similarly, reading for the traces of rhetorical drag directs us to texts of uncertain provenance or vexed attribution, and it can also reveal the cultural work of texts whose authorship appears suspect, if undisputed. I have in mind here the convent captivities rediscovered by Nancy Lusignan Schultz. As Schultz notes, these melodramatic stories of the early nineteenth century "are connected to the older, more established genres of the gothic, Indian captivities and a long European tradition of anti-Catholic literature" (*Veil* xix). Convent "captives" Maria Monk and Rebecca Reed each present figures of abject female vulnerability and suffering, and both Monk and Reed had powerful male sponsors who saw their stories into print. Using the theory of rhetorical drag, we might examine these texts, particularly their images of abjection and victimization, and consider whether these are male fantasies of female experience and what that would tell us about gender formations in 1830s Boston. Are these images, spoken through the erstwhile nuns' voices, generated in order to delineate proper gender behavior? Do representations of female suffering elide or enhance the legibility of other kinds of subject positions, notably those of class or ethnicity or religion?

These published stories of capture, confinement, coercion, and return are carefully constructed to be so remarkable that they must be represented and interpreted within a broader terrain than the merely personal. A slave's story exemplified precisely those evils the abolitionist writer/sponsor confronted, while Reed's escaped nun's tale, sponsored by some of Boston's Protestant elite, ultimately led a mob to destroy a Catholic convent.[1] But the products of rhetorical drag have a more capacious role to play: they are *historical* actors, agents in the march of history as envisioned by their producers. The captive's meaning derives from her body and voice as they are placed in a historical frame, in the expanded political and social field that historiography constructs. As the instances of rhetorical drag illustrate, specifically, the captive woman's gender, her *embodied* otherness, characterized her as an apt instrument for the male historiographers.

"Gender is a field of structured and structuring difference," writes Donna Haraway, "where the tones of extreme localization, of the intimately personal and the individualized body, vibrate in the same field with global high tension emissions" (195). The practices of rhetorical drag trace the connections between the "extreme localization"—for example, Increase Mather's notion of Mary Rowlandson's "particular knowledge"—and the "field" generated by the male impersonators' visions/versions of history. Moreover, Haraway's conceptualization of gender as a field with "nodes," and "inflections in orientations," resonates with the rhetorical choices made by the impersonators as they offer readings of warfare and suffering. That is, they speak through an array of discursive regimes, figurative language, and textual forms to write effectively and convincingly as embodied captives. After all, as Haraway argues, "embodiment is a significant prosthesis; objectivity cannot be about fixed visions when what counts as an object is precisely what world history turns out to be about" (195).

It is, finally, the prosthetic function of rhetorical drag that allows each of the impersonators not only to describe a historical moment but also to inhabit that moment and *speak from it*. A reconsideration of what I called earlier "the erotics of rhetorical drag" is useful here. Readers of captivity narratives, as Michelle Burnham argues, might experience a sympathetic identification with captives, but what of the writers? For those men who so ably manipulated the representations of gendered embodiment by speaking as the suffering and abject captives, and even for the revisionists who wrote to speak for Hannah Duston, the pleasures of the text were manifold. Through rhetorical drag they could write history as male authorities and live that history as the women who experienced it. Although we cannot properly characterize the erotic imaginary of Cotton Mather, neither can we ignore that he, like the other gender impersonators, chose to write *as* rather than write *about* a captive woman. What did that textual embodiment offer Mather and the others? Rhetorical drag provided for these men a powerful doubled position of subject and object, the vantage from which to inhabit gender as writing male and speaking female, the means to decide "what counts as an object" and to form that object as well.

In addition to the specific historical contexts that conditioned each narrative, I think this pleasurable position, with its discursive power, accounts for the choices these men made to write in the first person.

When their costume slips, when their control of the female voice falters, we find those moments that some contemporary scholars find "resistant" or counterhegemonic in the narratives.[2] However, by considering the cultural work of rhetorical drag, we identify alternative feminist readings of the women's captivity narratives. These readings do not search for images of resistance to oppression, to exploitation, and to appropriation inscribed by the captive woman in the interstices of the text, although those critical interpretations offer powerful feminist analyses. Rather, recognizing rhetorical drag reveals the conditions that structure gendered subjects in their historical and historiographical manifestations: it tells us how impersonated captivity narratives both created the "objects of history" and sought to fit them into prevailing gender regimes. We know those regimes were, indeed, oppressive, exploitative, and appropriative, but we don't know how they worked discursively until we examine the language of gender structuration, the "nodes" and "inflections of orientation" observed and adapted by the male impersonators.

Advertisements

As the analysis of captivity narratives in the previous chapters demonstrates, the writing practices that constitute each instance of rhetorical drag emerge from various and distinctive contexts. While each narrative displays the "inflections of orientation" that its writer or writers used to mark a female-gendered subject, all the narratives exhibit tensions regarding the first-person voice of a woman speaking about her experiences in print and thereby entering into historical discourse. The textual traces of these anxieties appear, for example, in the fictive Hannah Swarton's apology for her faulty memory; in Susannah Johnson's reliance on external documentation; or in Bunker Gay's "(she says)" parenthetical conflation of Jemima Howe's voice with his own writing. These moments within the impersonated texts indicate that the male writers sought to establish constraints or limitations on female authorship and, more particularly, on women's agency in *interpreting* for readers the meanings of their own experiences. One goal of rhetorical drag, then, is to convincingly hide the impersonator while letting the captive woman articulate her own authorial limitations.

Later captivity texts, such as *A Narrative of the Life of Mrs. Mary Jemison* (1824) and *Captivity of the Oatman Girls* (1857), which both employ the first person, do not exhibit the same species of dissembling rhetoric. These texts purport to be "as-told-to" tales,[3] accounts whose actual male authors were named on the title pages. In his preface to *A Narrative of . . . Mary Jemison,* James E. Seaver assures his readers that the work is "a piece of biography, that shows what changes may be effected in the animal and mental constitutions of man [*sic*]; what trials may be surmounted; what cruelties perpetrated, and what pain endured, when stern necessity holds the reins, and drives the car of fate" (xix). Seaver asserts that "strict fidelity has been observed in the composition; consequently, no circumstance has been intentionally exaggerated by the paintings of fancy, nor by fine flashes of rhetoric," and that, because of Jemison's age (she was around eighty years old), "any error [should] be overlooked . . . or charitably placed to the narrator's account, and not imputed to neglect, or want of attention in the compiler" (xx). As "the compiler" of "the narrator's account," Seaver defines himself unambiguously as the man in control of the language and rhetoric of the narrative.

Although he employs Jemison's "I" to ground the narration, Seaver's preface emphasizes Jemison's incapacity to interpret her own significance: that task falls to him as compiler. In his hands, Jemison's "I" cannot be read in the conventional grammatical space of subjectivity because Jemison is, from the text's opening pages, a narrator whose figure and experiences emerge in the ill-fitting garb of Seaver's sentimentalized nineteenth-century prose style. Unlike the men who impersonated the earlier captives, Seaver overtly positions himself as the interpreter of Jemison's meaning, and his preface directs his audience to the right reading of her: "it is fondly hoped that the lessons of distress that are pourtrayed, may have a direct tendency to increase our love of liberty; to enlarge our view of the blessings that are derived from our liberal institutions; and to excite in our breasts sentiments of devotion and gratitude to the great Author and finisher of our happiness" (xxi). Living outside those "liberal institutions," Jemison, who remained with her captors and assimilated into Seneca society, relates her experiences to Seaver as a distanced and diminishing revenant against whom readers can measure their own fortunes.

Similarly, in *Captivity of the Oatman Girls,* R. B. Stratton recreates Olive Oatman's direct discourse (and, intermittently, the speech of her brother Lorenzo, who was not captured). Like Seaver's Jemison, Stratton's Olive Oatman offers readers the exotic and mysterious figure of a captive who may have transculturated during the long years of captivity.[4] But Stratton chose not to limit himself to a first-person point of view. His prose muddies the sources for his text's descriptions and commentary: in some passages, Olive Oatman's "I" is bound within quotation marks, in others it floats freely, "speaking" about her five-year-long captivity. Again, like Seaver's compilation of Jemison's words, Stratton's composition of Oatman attempts to invigorate the text with the voice of the speaking captive while it simultaneously, and quite obviously, controls that voice for certain ends. In the last pages of the narrative, Oatman's voice is subsumed into Stratton's overwrought figure for a chorus of dead captives, who speak to us from their graves: "But there is a voice coming up from these scattered, unmonumented resting-places of their dead; and it pleads, pleads with the potency and unerringness of those pleadings from '*under the ground*' of ancient date, and of the fact and effect of which we have a guiding record" (287). This voice trails off without specifying the object of its pleading, and the book ends with a florid plea for the westward expansion of American "civilization."

While the Jemison and the Oatman accounts certainly propose specific models of female behavior, the texts were not written through the ruse of authorial impersonation. These narratives provide different lenses for the understanding of gender formation and regulation from those of the earlier women's captivity narratives written by men. Yet these texts are good candidates for elaborating and extending critical methods for the interpretation of instances of rhetorical drag because they provide "speaking" women whose voices readily reveal the artifice of their rhetorical forms. The obvious artifice of Jemison's relation and Oatman's dialogue imitates the conventions of fictional characterization, although both Seaver and Stratton assert the historicity of the captives.[5] Clearly, Susannah Johnson and Jemima Howe serve as drag foremothers to the captive figures of Jemison and Oatman in their sentimentality and resonance with fictional discourse. Readers should approach Seaver and Stratton with an eye toward their representation of the captives *as women* through the voices they assigned to them.

The kind of feminist reading I argue for here and throughout this book certainly privileges gender as the category of analysis. As well, reading for and through rhetorical drag compels us to consider how gender formation helps to structure other subject assignments, such as race, ethnicity, and class—other kinds of ontological and epistemological inflections.[6] In this way, gender becomes the entry point for a critical analysis that attempts to complicate and redefine what we mean by agency. Particularly, when we investigate historical texts, it is crucial to uncover problematic claims about agency in light of the text's contexts and conditions of production. Reading for rhetorical drag, at the very least, puts into question the relationship between agency and instrumentality.

Women's captivity experiences remain powerful cultural emblems in current nationalist and imperialist discourses, and, unsurprisingly, gender ideologies continue to shape the contours and meanings of current captivity narratives. Over the time that I researched and wrote this book, the United States has engaged in several wars, most recently the wars in Iraq and Afghanistan, and it persists in prosecuting an ambitious, if highly ambiguous, "war" on "terror." The position of women as combatants in these contemporary wars has changed some of the ways in which women's captivity may be read by today's audiences. While early American women captives were assuredly noncombatants, contemporary captives such as Jessica Lynch and Shannon Johnson proceed into war zones as part of the forces deployed by the U.S. Army, and these women become symbols in domestic conflicts as well as imperial warfare.

Earlier in this study, I cited Anne Myles's compelling discussion of the links between the Lynch captivity versions and early American literary texts, such as Rowson's *Slaves in Algiers,* and several Barbary captivities. Her study cogently sets out the disturbing affiliations between anxieties and ambitions apparent in literary texts of the early Republic and those in our own media. Myles offers an illuminating model of reading early captivity narratives in dialogue with contemporary texts for both students and teachers. That dialogue, after all, is what allows us to consider early American texts useful, instructive, and even pleasurable in our own day. With this dialogic model in mind, I have often asked students in early American and women's studies courses to consider the figuration of gender in captivity tales as both a historical and a contemporary phenomenon. More at home on the Internet than in rare book rooms, students researched historical Web sites as well as blogs and found that Jessica Lynch's captivity elicited a range of responses eerily similar to those found in the earlier texts. Approbation or disapprobation of her behavior, manipulation of her image, and interpretation of her experiences emerged as readily from those recent events as did similar approbations, manipulations, and interpretations in the seventeenth and eighteenth centuries. Significantly, many bloggers—twenty-first-century variants on the early journal writers whose works scholars continue to scour—became obsessed with interpreting Jessica Lynch.[7] These cybertexts sought to fit Lynch's experiences into broader social (and presumably personal) agendas; she became a ground on which to assert "proper" female roles and behaviors.

The aspect of Lynch's story that so compelled the bloggers and talk radio hosts—whose Lynch chatter overwhelmed the airwaves in the early days of the Iraq war—is the very feature that makes her tale resonate with early narratives: the disturbing image of a suffering and vulnerable woman.[8] As well, Lynch did not at first comment publicly on her experiences, and so, although no one spoke *as* Lynch, several spoke *for* her, notably the producers of the apparently heroic rescue-operation video and the American doctors who cared for her during her recovery. Lynch's captivity tale thus shares with all the captivity texts I have discussed the elements of preemption and substitution. Using these techniques, people who hold positions of cultural authority—here, Pentagon spokespersons—compose specific versions of the woman's captivity experience and seek to control the interpretation of those experiences. However, unlike Mather or even the nineteenth-century antiquarians such as Dwight or Whittier, who sought both to depict and to explain Hannah Duston's acts for their readers, the Pentagon could not contain the explosion of readings that Lynch's captivity generated in contemporary mass media culture.

For example, while Lynch remained silent and the Pentagon attempted to fashion her as *the* heroic figure in the Iraq war, conservative commentators and bloggers attacked these representations. Their versions of Lynch's captivity and redemption excoriated new army regulations that place women in combat situations. Lynch became, in this formulation, not an unfortunate victim of warfare but a woman out of bounds, put there by spineless Pentagon leaders who capitulated to the ineluctable demands of feminists for equal access to military positions. When Lynch's version of events finally appeared in *I Am a Soldier, Too: The Jessica Lynch Story,* the book's author was not Lynch, as one would suppose from the title, but rather Rick Bragg, "a renowned chronicler of American lives" (according to the dust jacket). Like the complex conditions that produced the early captivities written by male impersonators, the contexts of Lynch's story must be read as a field full of category crises that have beset contemporary U.S. culture: conflict over the roles of women in the military; concerns over the ways that the Pentagon produces information for public consumption; military service as a substitution for other kinds of meaningful employment; and, most significantly, the determination of "appropriate" female behavior.[9]

Of course, the nature of the crises or debates addressed by rhetorical drag changes over time, as do the models of appropriate or exorbitant behavior designated by gender. Nevertheless, the early versions of Jessica Lynch, like the versions of Hannah Duston (and those of the other women captives), represent performances, "tricky texts" that, under examination, reveal the artifice that produced them. When readers deconstruct the artifice, we gain critical insights into the ways people use gender formations to control and contain the meanings of a "speaking" subject. An impersonated female captive represents not only an object of history but also an advertisement for a particular version of what her impersonator imagines history to be.

Notes

Introduction

1. Castiglia also asserts that "no captivity is, finally, an individual experience" and that "no captive survives by her wits alone, but must comprehend and assimilate the cultural codes of her captors . . . as well as those technologies of reincorporation . . . that will allow her to 'return' home" (127). Rhetorical drag functions as one of those powerful "technologies."

2. Anne G. Myles's essay, "Slaves in Algiers, Captives in Iraq: The Strange Career of the Barbary Captivity Narrative," is a provocative and convincing example of how to read and understand current events by examining critically their antecedents in early American popular culture.

3. Esther Newton argues that "'drag' can be used as an adjective or a noun. As a noun it means the clothing of one sex when worn by the other sex" (3) and "'drag' has come to have a broader referent: any clothing that signifies a social role, for instance a fireman's suit or farmer's overalls. The concept of drag is embodied in a complex homosexual attitude toward social roles" (3n). My study views drag as a set of performances, attitudes, and *writing practices* concerned with social roles, particularly gendered roles, that are not necessarily correlated to sexual practices.

4. Jameson argues that "parody capitalizes on the uniqueness of these [modernist authors'] styles and seizes on their idiosyncrasies and eccentricities to produce an imitation which mocks the original" (113).

5. Of course, some drag performances inhabit characters as acts of homage, as in John Kelly's performances of Joni Mitchell. As objects of historiography (not cabaret), however, the female captives were neither mocked nor admired so much as appropriated for the male writers' historical ends.

6. See Derounian and Fitzpatrick for arguments concerning the shaping hand of the sponsor in Rowlandson's text.

7. Strong, in reading the 1697 Hannah Swarton narrative, asserts that because "the Swarton narrative lacks the typifying epithets characteristic of [Cotton] Mather's descriptions of Indians," the narrative must be attributed to Swarton herself, although this "does not, of course, imply that Cotton Mather refrained from 'improving' it to his satisfaction" (124). As I argue below, Mather, practicing rhetorical drag, extends and enriches the kinds of "improvement" he might make in the Swarton text; that is, precisely because Mather fashions the text as a woman's text, he must forego his normal style.

8. I am not arguing here that men always maintained the same status in captivity that their gender afforded them in their home cultures. Foster examines the plight of Puritan male captives in *The Captor's Tale,* and he argues that these men were subjected to "rituals of unmanning" by their Iroquoian and Algonquian female captors (10). When they were sold to French Catholic nuns, they resisted the gender role reversal that transformed them into domestic laborers at the command of powerful women. However, the female captivity narratives in this study must be seen as cultural productions, written texts that, for the most part, reproduced conventional gender behaviors in order to underscore the female experience at the heart of the texts. The captive women "wrote" about life inside the teepees and French households from a vantage most men did not have.

9. Significantly, Foucault maintains that one component of a "socio-historical analysis" would be "studies of authenticity and attribution." Some questions he asks, and that I seek to answer in terms of these captivity narratives, are: "What are the modes of existence of this discourse? Where has it been used, how can it circulate, and who can appropriate it for himself? What are the places in it where there is room for possible subjects? Who can assume these various subject functions? And behind all these questions, we would hear hardly anything but the stirring of an indifference: What difference does it make who is speaking?" (120). The "difference," or the stake in this line of questioning, is a more nuanced and complex understanding of how we might historicize gender and historiographic practice in early American contexts.

10. In the preface to Rowlandson's narrative, Ter Amicam asserts that Mary Rowlandson experienced a "strange and amazing dispensation" (65) and that the "works of the Lord (not only of Creation, but of Providence)" (65) can be read within her text.

11. According to Toulouse, "The Mather attribution is made by David Richards in a 1967 unpublished Yale College honors thesis, '"The Memorable Preservations": Narratives of Indian Captivity in the Literature and

Politics of Colonial New England, 1675–1725,' 20–30" (674n3). As Toulouse notes, most scholars concur that Increase Mather was Ter Amicam, the author of the preface.

1. *"Being Read with a Greedy Attention"*

1. Mather, *Ornaments for the Daughters of Zion* 9. Holmes notes that the original publication date is questionable, but he sets the probable date circa April 1692; see entries 266-A through C, 2: 771–76.

2. Lyle Koehler notes that "only four women are among the authors of the 911 works published in seventeenth-century New England" (54). As I will argue, assuming that women wrote texts to which their names are ascribed as author is problematic, given internal textual evidence and the text's conditions of publication.

3. In "'Vertuous Women Found': New England Ministerial Literature, 1668–1735," Ulrich argues that "a collection of ministerial literature cannot tell us what New England women, even of the more pious variety, were really like. Nor can it describe what 'most Puritans' thought of women. It can tell us only what qualities were publicly praised in a specific time by a specific group of men. In spite of personal idiosyncrasies and the acknowledged predominance of Mather, this literature is remarkably consistent" (59). Ulrich examines the advice directed toward women, particularly the representations of piety and proper social behavior in Puritan sermons but argues that "in a very real sense there is no such thing as *female* piety in early New England" (64). Yet Mather's figuration of the church specifically as a virtuous woman emphasizes reliance on gender roles in the representation of piety, a figuration he bases in large part on the Song of Songs.

4. William Andrews's study of Mather's funeral sermons yields these revealing statistics: "Of the fifty-five sermons, twenty-four (44 percent) are on women, twenty-three (42 percent) on men, and eight (14 percent) on children. That Mather delivers funeral sermons for so many women is interesting in light of the fact that in the other funeral sermons of the period the subjects are men in three out of four cases." Andrews accurately notes Mather's "inordinate stress on the example of female piety" and argues that "his motives are at the same time general—aimed at the women of New England—and specific in two ways—paying tribute to a particular woman and providing 'Instruments of Piety' for relatives" (31). The function of this last trope of instrumentation provides a basis for my thesis that the social roles of women fit them most aptly for their construction as instruments. Ulrich notes in *Good Wives* "a conscious effort to elevate the public image, if not the status,

of women. Because Cotton Mather, the chief exponent of the new emphasis, was also the most prominent historian of the Indian wars, living heroines of the northern frontier took their place in these years beside pious Boston matrons eulogized in countless funeral sermons" (178). Ulrich presents "a study in role definition," which, while providing historical context for the images of women presented in her study, elides the problems of control, dissemination, and use of those images.

5. Pattie Cowell notes that *Ornaments'* three editions (1692, 1694, 1741) "testify to its popularity, and contemporary references indicate the seriousness with which it was read" (xii). See her introduction to the 1741 reprint for an overview of Mather's concern with female piety and its uses.

6. The style of Emerson's statement suggests Mather edited her testament heavily or at least directed Emerson to confess that her most grievous sin had been disobedience to her parents: *Warnings from the Dead* is addressed especially to "young persons."

7. Much scholarly interest in this tension focuses, naturally, on Bradstreet's poems, but Teresa Toulouse's convincing work on Rowlandson's "credit" addresses the problem from the specific instance of captivity.

8. Jeannine Hensley writes, "As for American poetry, except for the *Bay Psalm Book,* no volume of poetry had been printed in New England before *The Tenth Muse* was published in London in 1650" (xxviii). John Harvard Ellis notes in his preface to *The Works of Anne Bradstreet* that "the first edition appeared in London in 1650, under the title of 'The Tenth Muse, lately sprung up in America' a neatly-printed volume in small 16mo, xiv, and 207 pages. The second edition was printed in Boston by John Foster, in 1678. It contained additions and corrections of the author and several poems found amongst her papers after her death" (v).

9. Mather continues in his "application": "The petulant Pens of some forward and morose Men, have sometimes treated the Female Sex with very great Indignities; Blades, I guess, whose Mothers had Undutiful Children, or whose Wives have but Cruel Masters" (46). Apparent in this passage is Mather's continuing concern with the roles women play—mother and wife— and their relationship to the "petulant Pens."

10. See "The Copy of a Valedictory and Monitory Writing, Left by Sarah Goodhue" in Waters (519). As well as Sarah Goodhue's letter, see also the 1712 *A Dying Mother's Legacy,* by Grace Smith, "Late Widow to Mr. Ralph Smith of Eastham in New-England." The title page of Smith's text states that the work was "Left as a Perpetual Monitor to her Surviving Children; as it was taken from her own Mouth a little before her Death, by the Minister of that Town where She Died." Interestingly, the Smith text opens with a twenty-line poem, a remarkable feat for a woman on her deathbed.

11. See Koehler's chapter on "Sex-Role Stereotyping" (28–70) for a full discussion of social hierarchies and gender roles. Mather designates the role

of teacher as a necessary function of motherhood in *Ornaments* (106–7) and, with great circumspection, indicates that in some cases a woman may "remind her Husband of what was delivered in the Church. Truly, tho' a Woman may not speak in the Church, yet she may humbly repeat unto her Husband at home what the Minister spoke in the Church, that may be pertinent to his Condition. Thus every Paul may have Women that labour with him in the Gospel" (96).

12. Here, I consider the complete printed text, with prefaces and epilogues. So, although Joseph Rowlandson appears in Mary Rowlandson's account of her captivity only in the passage describing the initial attack on Lancaster, he does get the last word in the Boston edition (1682) by virtue of his appended sermon. See Derounian's discussion in "Publication, Promotion, and Distribution" (242–43).

13. "If thou couldest ask me a reason why I thus declare myself?—I cannot answer no other but this; that I have had of late a strong persuasion upon my mind, that by sudden death I shoud be surprized, either at my travail, or soon after it " (523).

14. Mather advised women that the most powerful way to counter the "petulant Pens" was to display pious behavior: "If any Men are so wicked (and some Sects of Men have been so) as to deny your being *rational* Creatures, the best means to confute them, will be by proving yourselves religious ones" (46).

15. John Winthrop remarked in his journal that Mrs. Hopkins's "sad infirmity" arose from "her giving herself wholly to reading and writing, and [she] had written many books" (Hosmer 1: 225).

16. Sontag begins her inquiry by quoting Virginia Woolf's claims about photographs from the Spanish civil war, wherein Woolf states that photographs "are not an argument; they are simply a crude statement of fact addressed to the eye." Woolf continues, "The eye is connected with the brain; the brain with the nervous system. That sends its messages in a flash through every past memory and present feeling" (26).

17. Burnham cogently traces the complex network of cultural practices that are brought to bear on the text because of this demand for sympathetic identification in the reader. See pp. 10–42 and especially 41–42.

18. In *The Doctrine of Divine Providence*, Increase Mather offers theodicy couched in terms of the exceptional. He cautions readers not to rely too much on their own understanding or reason: "To make things depend chiefly upon the decrees and wills of man, is to place Man in the Throne and to dethrone him that sitteth in Heaven. We must therefor know, that all Events of Providence are the issues and executions of an Ancient, Eternal, Unchangeable decree of Heaven" (8). Explicitly, the verb "to dispense" speaks both to this "decree" and to the interpretation of the exceptional: "There are also extraordinary mercies and extraordinary judgments, which the Providence of God does sometimes dispense towards the children of men" (47). The use of

"dispensation" in the preface, which so closely aligns with Increase Mather's language in the *Doctrine,* supports the scholarly consensus that he was indeed Ter Amicam.

19. Toulouse argues that it is precisely the anxiety of a captive woman to redeem her social value within the "hierarchical social discourse" of Puritan New England that informs the Rowlandson narrative. She notes that Rowlandson's social standing derives not only from her minister husband but also from her father, John White, "Lancaster's wealthiest citizen" (670). Also, Salisbury's edition of the narrative offers important contextualizing materials that discuss the White family's emigration and settlement in New England; see Rowlandson 16–17.

20. Again in *Doctrine of Divine Providence,* Increase Mather writes, "Things act sometimes otherwise than according to their natures and proper inclinations, which is a clear demonstration that they are over ruled by a divine hand" (23).

21. Recently, scholars have been turning to cultural studies to examine the phenomenon of the captive as celebrity; in particular, since Disney's release of *Pocahontas,* there have been several studies of her, including Faery's. Castiglia's chapter on Patty Hearst brilliantly inaugurated this kind of investigation.

22. Ter Amicam notes the "atheisticall, proud, wild cruel, barbarous, bruitish (in one word) diabolicall creatures" (67) who captured Rowlandson, and the folly of a premature determination "that the Army should desist the pursuit, and retire" (63) in their battle against the Narragansetts. Thus, Ter Amicam's preface places Rowlandson's tale within a broader range of Puritan concerns, from the diabolical provenance of the Narragansetts to the ill-executed military strategies of "the Forces of *Plimouth* and the *Bay*" (63).

23. Castiglia, Burnham, and Strong each provide readings of the captive as a culture-crossing subject operating in a liminal space between English and Native cultures.

24. Fitzpatrick characterizes the "dueling textual voices of the captives and their ministerial sponsors" as "palimpsests, engraved by authors whose exegeses are in dialogical relation to one another." Acknowledging "the clergy's attempts to impose a socially and doctrinally unified and orthodox interpretation of the captives' experiences," Fitzpatrick reads in the tensions between these voices a "gendered site of . . . narrative formation" (2). The subversive effect of the woman's voice, noticed by many scholars, including Fitzpatrick, in studies of Mary Rowlandson's narrative, meets an unusual obstacle in Cotton Mather's treatment of Hannah Swarton's story.

25. Fitzpatrick argues that "primary tellers of their tales, the women captives became the active authors of their own histories, defying if never escaping the traditionally masculine authority and authorship central to the Puritan sexual order" (5). The defiance, I think, is greatly mitigated by the

text's recurrent concern with the process and achievement of spiritual salvation and by its structural adherence to orthodox rhetorical practices. Most significant, however, is that any sense of defiance must be read within the historical context that includes the internal politics of the narrative: its ideological and material aims (religious conversion and territorial expansion). Strong's more recent study considers ministerial "hegemony" in light of her broader project. Working from Raymond Williams's concept of "selective tradition," Strong seeks to redress the "decontextualization" she finds in recent scholarship on captivity narratives. To accomplish this recontextualization, especially to reintroduce the dimension of American Indian experiences, Strong considers the processes of "typification" ("a representation of collective identity—one that was constructed, challenged, and transformed through identifiable social processes") that shape the "Captive Self" (8–9). Ministerial hegemony, particularly ministerial access to and manipulation of print culture, constitutes a key component of these social processes.

26. "Our Family being now gathered together (those of us that were living) the South Church in Boston hired an House for us: Then we removed from Mr. Shepards, those cordial Friends, and went to Boston, where we continued about three quarters of a year: Still the Lord went along with us, and provided graciously for us. I thought it somewhat strange to set up House-keeping with bare walls; but as Solomon sayes, Mony answers all things; and that we had through the benevolence of Christian-friends, some in this Town, and some in that, and others: And some from England, that in a little time we might look, and see the House furnished with love" (111). It is clear from the list of "friends" that the Rowlandsons enjoyed a great deal of support after their trials. The breadth of support, from various towns and from England, speaks to the relative importance of the Rowlandson and White families and to the text's implication in an emerging Puritan secular historiography, as somewhat distinct from the metanarrative of providential history. That is, the Rowlandsons' and Whites' experiences become part of a more immediately recognizable version of the Puritan "errand's" temporal realities.

27. The Rowlandson family then moved from Boston to Wethersfield, Connecticut.

28. Kenneth Silverman in *The Life and Times of Cotton Mather* argues that Mather's impulse to write and publish is inextricably bound with his overarching ambition: "The intensity of Mather's conflict over his writing may be judged from the evident abundance in his works of unconscious strategies for resolving it, stammerlike devices that at once express and cancel. In trying to make peace between his ambition and his guilt, he often simultaneously concealed and revealed his authorship" (200). Silverman continues his discussion of Mather's strategies by noting the curious introduction to *Decennium Luctuosum,* the language of which I examine below.

29. In an earlier published version of this chapter, I erroneously stated that the "church-history" to which Mather refers here was his projected *Biblia Americana*. I thank Terry Catapano for clarifying inaccurate details that appeared in the earlier study.

30. The diary contains many references to Mather's visitations among his congregation during which he disseminates his own work.

31. "When I have readd thro' a Book, at any time, I would make a Pause; and first, give Thanks to the Father of Lights, for whatever Illumination He has by this Book bestow'd upon me. Secondly, If the Author be in his Book an useful Servant of the Church, I would give Thanks to God, for His Raising up such an Instrument, and Inclining and Assisting of him to this Performance" (*Diary* 2: 226).

32. Ebersole notes that Mather's New England readers could not fail "to recognize the author—not only is Mather's style distinctive, the volume included a flyleaf at the end advertising the publication shortly thereafter of two sermons by Mather. Moreover, a lecture delivered by him in Boston on July 27, 1698 . . . was appended" (67).

33. See the "Instructions to Matthew Cary."

34. Edward Tyng was commander of Casco fort until 1688, when he was appointed governor of Annapolis by Phips. He was returning to Maine when he was captured onboard John Alden's sloop. Alden was in the service of the colony "to provide provisions and clothes for the force at Falmouth" (Coleman 1: 70n5). Both Tyng and Alden were carried to France, and Tyng died in prison there. Alden returned, only to be charged in the 1692 witchcraft trials (when he was 70 years old). He escaped from a Boston jail and hid until the furor passed. See Coleman 1: 70n5.

35. Coleman traced a history of John Swarton ("spelled on Canadian records: Soarre, Shiard, Shaken, Soüarten, Sowarten, Schouarden, Souard"): "John Swarton of Beverly received a fifty acre grant in North Yarmouth. In his petition he said he had fought with Charles II in Flanders," and she notes that "Church mentions 'One Swarton, a Jersey man' whose language he could hardly understand" (1: 204).

36. Because my concern with the Swarton narrative includes its publication history, I use two versions of the text. The first, hereafter referred to as *Humiliations,* is a facsimile of the Boston edition, published by B. Green and J. Allen for Samuel Phillips (1697). The second version, "A Narrative of Hannah Swarton," appeared in *Magnalia Christi Americana* (1702), here called *Magnalia Swarton.* The variants are discussed below.

37. See Ulrich, *Good Wives* 175–80.

38. The petition accuses the Massachusetts Bay leaders of dragging their heels in dispatching aid to Maine during the Indian attacks waged in the summer of 1688. It not only praises the work of Governor Andros in providing

relief to the province upon his return from New York and getting a full report of the depredations, but it also charges the "Change of Government" (after the insurrection of April 1688) with supplying the Indians "with stores of Warr and Amunition by vessels sent by some in Boston to trade with them, and thereupon [the Indians] took new Courage and resolution to Continue the Warr; and having got to their assistance other Indians, who before were unconcerned they presently burnt and destroyed the several Fortifications which the Forces had deserted." See "Petition of the Inhabitants of Maine" in *The Andros Tracts*. The petition was signed 25 January 1689, almost a year after the anti-Andros uprising in Boston, and shortly before the attack on Casco.

39. Mather later wrote about the dangers of living without benefit of a minister in his 1702 *A Letter to Ungospelized Plantations*.

40. See Holmes 2: 492. Holmes asserts that "Cotton Mather wrote this Narrative some time between November, 1695, the month of Hannah Swarton's return, and November, 1696—probably nearer the latter date—when he wrote his advertisement for *Great Examples*, the work in which he first intended to print the Swarton Narrative" (493). See Holmes 1: 452–53 for an extended discussion of the trajectory of the Swarton text. It was advertised as part of the forthcoming "Great Examples of Judgment and Mercy," which probably was never printed.

41. As Colley asserts, Mather did not confine himself geographically; rather she states that he "built much of his ruthlessly successful clerical and publishing career on the backs of multifarious captives [and] devoted at least two sermons to the threat that Barbary and Islam represented to seamen in England and New England both" (154).

42. Strong also argues that the narrative's disposition of pronouns presents Swarton as, at times, included in the group of captors, a point I make both below and in the earlier version of this study, to which Strong refers. However, my extended consideration of the text's positioning of Swarton in, among, and apart from her captors reads these pronominal locations in light of the narrative's focus on Swarton's captivity among the French, an element ignored in Strong's study.

43. As I noted above, the impersonation is still successful and, as in 1697 and 1702, its success derives from the reader's response not only to the text's immediacy and identification, an effect of first-person narration, but also from the interpretive frame that seeks to control the text's meaning.

44. Kolodny, *Land* 20; see pp. 19–26 for Kolodny's extended reading of the *Judea capta* emblem.

45. Holmes initially states that the Duston narrative "as it now stands is almost certainly of Cotton Mather's authorship or editing" (2: 491). However, in a longer consideration of the timing of the sermon and Mather's other attempts at fact gathering, he concludes, "We are inclined to believe,

therefore, that the original of the Hannah Dustan Narrative was written by the Rev. Benjamin Rolfe of Haverhill, but that its statements were confirmed by Cotton Mather's interview with the principals, and that the printed text received his editorship" (2: 492). This view is supported by the title page's presentation of the story as an "improvement."

46. The variant of the Duston episode in *Decennium Luctuosum* provides information about the specific rewards received by Duston, Neff, and Lennardson.

47. See Holmes 3: 1198–1200 for notes on the sermon, *Warnings from the Dead*. Emerson's "Instrument" was reprinted in Mather's *Pillars of Salt* (1699) and in the *Magnalia*. Ulrich reports that Emerson was severely beaten by her father and suggests that this abuse could account for her "rebellion" (*Good Wives* 197–98).

48. If Ebersole's argument that lay Puritans were steeped in scripture is accurate, and I believe it is, provided we attend to variables such as location, social status, gender, and access to education, this does not account for Swarton's proficiency in theological *debate*, a discursive form not commonly practiced among women. We need only to turn to Anne Hutchinson to find that women were particularly discouraged from engaging in this practice.

49. Fitzpatrick argues that Swarton was "converted at the hands of apostates, whose challenges to the 'true religion' prompted Swarton's profession of Puritan faith." She sees this as a subversion of the notion that conversion should occur within "the communal covenant," which would offer nurturance within Puritan social order and the congregation.

50. See the controversy surrounding the publication of *Publick Occurrences,* an anonymously published criticism of the government's campaign on the eastern frontier, and Mather's "slippery" disavowal of his authorship in Silverman (*Letters* 75–76). Mather's dodging is evident in his letter to John Cotton, dated 17 October 1690, in which he protests that "the publisher had not one line of it from me, only as accidentally meeting him in the high-way, on his request, I showed him how to contract and express the report of the expedition at Casco and the east" (27). These are the expeditions that should have prevented the Indian attack on Casco that resulted in Swarton's capture.

51. Mather reminds his audience in the sermon that "words that are spoken in an *Ordinance* of the Lord Jesus Christ, carry with them a peculiar Efficacy and Authority" (*Humiliations* 48).

52. "I desired to see all my Sins, and to Repent of them all, with all my Heart, and of that Sin which had been especially a Burden to me, namely, That I Left the Public Worship and Ordinances of God, to go to Live in a Remote Place, without the Publick Ministry" (*Humiliations* 67–68).

53. According to church records, Swarton's daughter, whose whereabouts were unknown at the end of the narrative, remained in Canada and converted. See Levernier and Cohen 31–32.

54. Colley argues that the captivity experience caused much anxiety for early Euro-Americans because "it could lead to assimilation into Native American societies, or into rival Catholic empires." Discussing the Swarton narrative, she writes, "It was in this context that insisting on her Englishness in her printed narrative appeared crucial. It testified to any doubters, and also to herself, that she had successfully preserved her national and religious identity" (151). Although Colley reads the narrative as Swarton's production, her point concerning the critical issue of identity pertains; indeed, it supports the prevailing tone of Mather's anti-French tirade. "Swarton's" protestations express an *intracolonial* anxiety about "Englishness," which, according to Colley, did not necessarily extend back to the metropolis: "Manifestly, then, before 1750, printers and publishers in Britain reached the commercial decision that there was only limited domestic demand for tales of settler captivity at the hands of Native Americans" (152). Colley provides a useful and much broader context in which to read the captivity narratives in "America: Captives and Embarrassments," part 2 of her exhaustive study of captivity in various zones of the British Empire.

55. The story of seven-year-old Sarah Gerish, "a very Beautiful and Ingenious Damsel," foreshadows the sensationalism of later captivity narratives in its sentimental rendering of the little child imprisoned in a wilderness with a "dragon" for a master. The Gerish account is notable, too, for its representation of sexual threat when Sarah's master commands her to "loosen som of her upper-Garments." "God knows what he was going to do," the account continues, but no harm comes to the child, and she is eventually restored to her family (*Decennium Luctuosum* 36–39).

56. See Lincoln's note in *Narratives of the Indian Wars* 190.

57. From the title page of *Magnalia*, book 6: 339.

2. "Peculiar Efficacy and Authority"

1. Sewall's diary entry reads, "*April 29. 5th day* is signalised by the Atchievment of Hannah Dustun, Mary Neff, and Samuel Lenerson; who kill'd Two men [Indians], their Masters, and two women and 6. others, and have brought in Ten Scalps." His 12 May entry records indirect discourse attributed to Hannah Duston and is the closest that contemporary accounts come to rendering her thoughts at the time: "Hannah Dustun came to see us; I gave her part of Conecticut Flax. She saith her Master, whom she kill'd, did formerly live with Mr. Rowlandson at Lancaster: He told her, that when he pray'd the English way, he thought that was good: but now he found the French way was better. The single man shewed the night before, to Sam Lenarson, how he used to knock Englishmen on the head and take off their

Scalps; little thinking that the Captives would make some of their first experiment upon himself. Sam. Lenarson kill'd him" (1: 372–73). This testimony about Indian praying practices resonates with the Swarton narrative's quotation of Hannah Swarton's Indian mistress, who had been raised with the English at Black Point but chose the more "careful" French instruction.

2. I do not argue that Rowlandson, or indeed any captive, was complicit or complaisant during captivity. Many studies of Rowlandson's text correctly demonstrate that Rowlandson manipulated her environment with a great deal of savvy. However, she remained in captivity until ransomed, as did most captives, and this fact marks the difference between Duston and other female captives who returned.

3. Here Mather's account may differ from Sewall's, because Sewall writes that the "single man" showed Lennardson how to kill.

4. See note 45 in preceding chapter on Holmes's attribution of the passage in quotation marks to the Rev. Benjamin Rolfe of Haverhill. Whitford cites R. W. G. Vail, rather than Holmes, as the source for the Rolfe attribution (although she names him "John Rolfe").

5. See Gilmore 55–64 for an explanation of this form of "interruption" in the "truth" of autobiographical discourse.

6. See Whitford as well as Arner for surveys of the many authors who take up the Duston story. Just as her story is transformed by each author, Hannah Duston's name undergoes transformation at the hands of her various revisionists; different authors spell it "Duston," "Dustin," or "Dustan."

7. I am indebted to Whitford's study for its analysis of the moral lineaments each writer assigns to (or withholds from) Duston and for its consideration of nearly all versions (although she does not discuss Leverett Saltonstall's account). Whitford follows the story through the late nineteenth century and into the twentieth, and she correctly notes that "as Hannah's historians became further removed from frontier life, they increasingly admired women rather for their frailty than for their hardihood. The new crop of authors, fascinated by Hannah's story, yet deploring her conduct, insisted upon the harsher details of her exploit, while religious ardor and ethical judgment faded before social convention" (324). While Whitford reprints the *Magnalia* version in its entirety as the source text, she does discuss the story's original appearance in the *Humiliations* sermon. She goes on to claim that "a careful reading of the work makes clear that Mather learned the story from Hannah herself" (310). As well, she argues that Mather, in providing the "legalistic" justification for the killings, was "apparently quoting Mrs. Dustin" (311). Whitford gives no textual reasons for this personal provenance deriving from her "careful reading," however, and never refers to the problem of the quotation marks, probably because she uses the Duston text from the *Magnalia*, already once removed from *Humiliations*. My study delineates and interprets

the implications of the omission of Duston's voice. It necessarily begins with Duston's silence and extends Whitford's inquiry into a more detailed analysis of the specific rhetorical strategies each male reviser used to figure Duston as a historical agent, but one who doesn't compose/publish her own tale.

8. These interjections serve to support Holmes's claim that the text is the work of Benjamin Rolfe or another minister who relayed it to Mather shortly before the sermon was preached. As well, they also further my contention that Mather had very little time in which to edit and emend it. See also Vail 189.

9. Mather's second aside addresses the audience as a gathering of neighbors as well: "Syrs, can we hear of these things befalling our Neighbours, & not *Humble* our selves before our God!" (*Humiliations* 46).

10. "You will seriously consider"; "And you will sincerely Render your very selves unto the Lord"; "Let me tell you"; "Become the sincere servants"; "Deny not the Lord"; "I tell you truly."

11. The Duston episode from *Decennium Luctuosum* is reprinted without variation in book 7 of the *Magnalia*.

12. Arner's study, like Whitford's, follows the various versions of the Duston story and notes the variants characterizing each version. Arner's final comment reveals that, for him, Hannah Duston is a failed national hero and as such serves as a mere literary curiosity: "Hannah is emphatically not a feminine charmer like Pocahontas, nor does she reflect the American character. With the decline of Puritanism, she lost her relevance as a culture hero and became only a slayer of Indians. Furthermore, she belonged only to a particular place—the shores of the Merrimac, which cannot support a national legend" (22). While Arner's study is useful for its bibliographical information and its emphasis on the pictorial value of the story, his theoretical bias toward a universal "American character" and Hannah Duston's insufficiency as either a "feminine charmer" or a "national legend" illustrates precisely the vague, uncritical, and dehistoricized practices my argument seeks to remedy. In particular, feminist criticism's emphasis on particularity, locality, subjectivity, and agency renders Duston a major figure in the studies of female representation.

13. Derounian-Stodola and Levernier explain the historical meaning of the word "comfortable" as a spiritual quality; it was not normally a term used to connote a physical condition in Puritan contexts (135–37).

14. Lang argues that Cotton Mather elaborates Anne Hutchinson's story from religious debate to gendered political-historical emblem: "Antinomianism . . . emerges from the *Magnalia* as a heretical form of individualism discernible in the bearing of the heretic and peculiarly typified by the Woman." She notes "the shift away from narrow doctrinal concerns and toward the formulation of the antinomian controversy as a battle between masculine reason and female enthusiasm" (70).

15. See, for example, Dwight's portrait of the Indians of Stonington, Connecticut, in his "Journey to Provincetown." His description of the descendants of the original Pequot inhabitants reveals his disgust: "The whole body of these Indians are a poor, degraded, miserable race of beings. The former, proud, heroic spirit of the Pequot, terrible even to other proud heroic spirits around him, is shrunk into the tameness and torpor of reasoning brutism. All the vice of the original is left. All its energy has vanished. They are lazy in the extreme, and never labor unless compelled by necessity. Nor are they less prodigal than lazy" (3:14). We can trace a parallel track here, one, European/American, ascending from a rough beginning to a civilized contemporaneity; the other, Indian, descending into degradation and oblivion.

16. See Arner for subsequent illustrations of the Duston story in which the emphasis remains on Thomas Duston. As Arner correctly notes, "A portrait of Hannah, hatchet in hand, standing over the sleeping Indians or lifting a scalp in triumph might have served allegorically as Revenge but would otherwise have invoked the moral issue" (20). Interestingly, the 1973 Jim Beam liquor bottle (see image page 56), with its illustration of luridly red scalps dangling from Hannah Duston's hands and unproblematic characterization of Duston as the "heroine of the massacre," marks a strange moment in American marketing history.

17. Both Arner and B. Bernard Cohen assert that Hawthorne's sources, in addition to Mather's *Magnalia,* include *Peter Parley's Method of Telling about the History of the World to Children* and B. L. Mirick's *History of Haverhill, Massachusetts.* These last two "supplied him details which were not in Mather's book" (Cohen 236–41). I will discuss these sources below in reference to Hawthorne's version of the Duston story.

18. The exception is Thoreau's Duston, but his enterprise so diverges from earlier historiographic practice that it might be considered a new genre (as he intended it).

19. Although not direct quotation, the account of captivity and escape that Duston gave to Samuel Sewall might stand, in some part, as a fairly close version of her words, especially given the brevity of the entry in the *Diary* and Sewall's lack of an expanded commentary on her relation.

20. Similarly, Hawthorne refers to Anne Hutchinson as "the Woman," thereby embodying in Mrs. Hutchinson all the follies, pride, and failures he sees in women, on which he elaborates in the opening to his short piece, "Mrs. Hutchinson." See discussion below on Hawthorne's Duston.

21. Whittier specifically refers to the "earliest settlers," which would exclude eighteenth-century captivity narrators such as Elizabeth Hanson, Jemima Howe, and Susannah Johnson.

22. In 1832, Whittier wrote to Sarah Josepha Hale, the editor of *Ladies Magazine,* "If you have not seen a copy of 'N. E. Legends'—it is not my fault

as I expressly directed my publishers to send you a copy" and, in the same letter, "I meant to have given you a bit of rhyme for your magazine, but my harp is hung on the willows for the present.—I dare say however you have enough of it. Miss Gould [Hannah F. Gould] of N. P. [Newburyport] is a good writer. Do you get much from Mrs. Sigourney: I admire that woman" (24 January 1832, in Pickard, *Letters* 1: 72–73).

23. See *Letters of Lydia Maria Child,* for which Whittier wrote a biographical introduction. In it, he praises Child's "power of description and characterization" and attributes her writing success to its "tone of healthy morality and good sense" (vii).

24. Joseph M. Ernest, Jr., notes that Whittier's "appreciation of the intellectual and artistic talents of women came from the Quakers, who were leaders in the belief that both men and women had access to spiritual inspiration, or the Inner Light. One remembers that in Quaker meetings the women are as free as the men to stand and testify when moved by the spirit." Ernest's perusal of thousands of letters in Whittier's correspondence led him to conclude that "an authoress had only to request his help to obtain it, provided that he considered the general influence of the applicant and her work morally wholesome. From the 1830's to the 1890's he gave liberal encouragement and practical help to a great many female writers, including over a third of the forty-four women who . . . gave a feminine cast to mid-nineteenth century America" (184–96). As the discussion below indicates, this "feminine cast" was problematic for some male writers, notably Hawthorne.

25. See his review "Susannah Rowson, *Charlotte's Daughter*" in Cady and Clark (15–18). Whittier ends the review with an observation on Rowson's "many imperfections" as a writer but attributes them to her busy schedule of teaching and editing the *Boston Weekly Magazine.*

26. These observations are found in "The Prose Works of Milton" (1828), "Robert Burns" (1828), "Sir Walter Scott" (1829), and "American Literature" (1829).

27. This problem of "credit" echoes Teresa Toulouse's contention that Mary Rowlandson's text is her attempt to retrieve social status lost during her captivity. Duston's "trophies" thus substitute for a literal text and become the sign of her authenticity as captive and heroine. That they also brought fifty pounds into the family coffers through bounty rewards is a fact that Whittier elides but Hawthorne condemns.

28. In "The Boy Captives," a story also set in Haverhill, but appearing later than *Legends,* Whittier conflates Hannah Duston with her companion, Mary Neff, and condenses her tale to a ridiculously long and digressive parenthetical: "At the garrison-house of Thomas Dustin, the husband of the far-famed Mary Dustin, (who, while a captive of the Indians, and maddened by the murder of her infant child, killed and scalped, with the assistance of a young boy, the

entire band of her captors, ten in number,) the business of brick-making was carried on" (*Complete Writings* 6: 397–98). Whittier finally produced his own fictive text with the publication of *Leaves from Margaret Smith's Journal in the Province of Massachusetts Bay, 1678–79*. There, in a prefatory note, he acknowledges, "That there are passages indicative of a comparatively recent origin, and calculated to cast a shade of doubt over the entire narrative, the Editor would be the last to deny, notwithstanding its general accordance with historical verities and probabilities." "Margaret Smith" abjures "any Vanitie of Authorship," echoing Whittier's own attestation in the letter quoted above to Sarah Josepha Hale (January 1832) that "I have not enough of the vanity of authorship to induce me to shake my fist in the face and eyes of the world."

29. Among the many readers who note Hawthorne's egregious treatment of the Duston legend are Ulrich (*Good Wives*) and Derounian-Stodola and Levernier. Ulrich remarks on Hawthorne's "blunt" account and his "aversion to Hannah" because of her "unfeminine manner" (172). Derounian-Stodola and Levernier, in a brief examination of several of the Duston accounts, aptly contrast Hawthorne's "totally unsympathetic" version with Thoreau's "mythic overtones" (176). Earlier in the study, Derounian-Stodola and Levernier argue that women's captivity narratives "stress that captivity's main metonymy was the dramatic and decisive fracturing of the original family unit" (112), and this observation is useful in addressing Hawthorne's treatment of the genre. The fracture of "The Duston Family" results in a reconstituted domestic scene, Thomas Duston and his children safe in the garrison; as Hawthorne makes quite clear, the family is infinitely improved by the absence of the demonic Hannah.

30. See Poovey 79–105.

31. T. Walter Herbert observes that models of early nineteenth-century American democratic individualism, following Emerson, depend on a shift in the conception of sovereignty from the monarch to the ordinary man. "Yet to enact this royal autonomy, men must become womanly. As the competitive struggle remodeled male-male relations to resemble international relations, it was discovered that each individual sovereignty needed a privy council. Survival in the public arena required the maintenance of an inward forum where policies could be evolved in the freedom of creative disarray and uncertainties could be entertained that must be hidden from view in public exchanges with other sovereignties. . . . A subtle, intuitive, and inscrutable interiority—the sacred essence of nineteenth-century 'femininity'—lies at the heart of self-made manliness" (72–73). Herbert traces Hawthorne's own "womanliness" to his childhood among strong women but goes on to argue that androgyny—not a specifically female identity—governed both Nathaniel's and Sophia Hawthorne's understanding of his creative character. In this image of the andro-

gynous writer, Herbert follows Nina Baym and Leland Person, and all three discuss the Hawthornes' marriage to substantiate their claims about his work. Herbert clarifies the often confusing terminology: "Women are in fact distinct from the 'inner women' of men, however. . . . I have sought to keep these issues clear by maintaining a degree of distance from the terms *woman* and *man* as applied to aspects of the Hawthornes' inner lives. It is possible to say that Nathaniel and Sophia's narcissistic marital collusion involved his projecting an 'inner' woman on her and her projecting an 'inner' man on him; but this mutual projection should not imply an 'equality' that cancels awareness of the fundamental difference in social power between them and Hawthorne's interest in preserving that difference" (299–300n). The persuasive crux of this critical argument is that Hawthorne's creative work depended on his imaginative reconfiguration of gender roles. "The Duston Family" bears close scrutiny within this approach to Hawthorne criticism because, unlike the later stories and novels on which these critics base their studies, this story presents a fully realized feminized yet heroic man. The historical woman is utterly superfluous, even demonized. Because Hawthorne wrote this sketch before he married Sophia Peabody, we must view it as an important attempt to compose a domestic reconfiguration before he actually assumed his own patriarchal role.

32. As mentioned in note 17, Cohen asserts that, although Mather furnished the main reference, Hawthorne "seems to have consulted two other books during the composition of his sketch . . . *Peter Parley's Method of Telling about the History of the World to Children,* written or edited by Samuel B. Goodrich . . . and B. L. Mirick's *The History of Haverhill, Massachusetts"* (236–37). Cohen notes the similarities between the illustration accompanying Hawthorne's story and the *Parley's* text and, more importantly, the close professional relationship between Goodrich and Hawthorne. He suggests that Goodrich might have shown Hawthorne the Duston story and its engraving and requested that he write an accompanying sketch. Thus, in an unusual reversal of publication practices, Hawthorne's text would have been commissioned to "illustrate" the engraving.

33. Mirick does not name the "inconsistent" sources.

34. Strong notes that Mather's text at one point describes Duston's captors "as an 'Indian family' that put many a 'prayerless' English family to 'shame.'" She goes on to suggest that Mather may have "fabricated" this interaction between Duston and her captors, but that Mather himself "clearly relished the trope of the pious Indian" (127). Hawthorne turns Mather's trope, then, not only remaking Duston but also refashioning and redirecting the sympathies of the reader from her to her captors.

35. Many scholars have studied Thoreau's complicated relationship to historical writing and his attempts to forge a new historiographical practice in

both the published and unpublished work. My understanding of the Duston passage is especially indebted to the studies by Burbick and by Cameron. Although Cameron's study is not confined to Thoreau's historical vision, her arguments concerning his writing practices inform my view of the gendered history found in *A Week*.

36. See Cameron 163n24 and 167n36, and Miller 81. Miller goes on in his chapter "The Stratagems of Consciousness: Woman and Men" to examine the lore of the Ellen Sewall-Thoreau connection and intimates that there might be evidence for a consideration of Thoreau as homosexual: "Only within recent years have studies had the courage to call attention to the androgynous character of Thoreau's monomaniac discussions of friendship" (96). In 1958, Miller employs the evasive terms "androgynous" and the more clinically sinister "monomaniac," but his meaning is apparent. Though any discussion of Thoreau's sexuality is beyond the scope of this study, his conception of gender as a social construct, discussed below, is crucial to my understanding of the Duston passage. Michael Warner considers Thoreau's "emphasis on the subjective principle of modernity" (62), which Warner names the tradition of "liberal individualism." Within that model, Warner sees Thoreau attempting to produce a self/other construct in a discussion of sexuality and erotics in contradiction to gendered difference: "the othering of 'woman' is not the only way that people can become erotic objects to him. Gender difference and erotic difference are, so to speak, different differences" (54). Heterosexual models of self/other are always gendered, but Thoreau destabilizes this normative duality by introducing self-reflection as an interruption in the direct gaze between the subject and object. (This corresponds to Cameron's reading of a second narrator; see discussion below.) Thus, Warner states, "We might think of Thoreau's scene of reflective desire as an organizing problematic through which the dispersed erotics of the body come to be centralized as a sexuality of self/other relations. Not all erotic desires must have their source in self/other relations in order for them to be understood" (67). Thoreau's alternative erotics, like his alternative history, cannot fully escape the social organization of gender; however, in becoming Hannah Duston, Thoreau replaces the specifically (hetero)sexual relation between a man (the *Week*'s narrator) and a woman (Duston) with an identity that is nothing if not desexualized. See Warner's "Thoreau's Bottom" (53–79). Thus, Thoreau's enactment of drag emerges from an "erotics" that transcends heterosexual duality by deferring a strictly dyadic gender regime, at least in this episode of *A Week*.

37. Even in his most willing mode, Thoreau disapproves of a life too engaged with society. See, for example, his condescension regarding social reformers, "the earnest reprovers of the age," who require "charitable" understanding because "their errors are likely to be generous errors" (*Journal* 2, 117).

38. Roland Barthes's consideration of the preterite as the instrument of both history and novel writing characterizes the problems Thoreau attempts

to solve with his tense shifts in the Duston passage. Barthes notes, "Its function is no longer that of a tense. The part it plays is to reduce reality to a point of time, and to abstract, from the depth of a multiplicity of experiences, a pure verbal act, freed from the existential roots of knowledge, and directed towards a logical link with other acts, other processes, a general movement of the world. . . . Behind the preterite there always lurks a demiurge, a God or a reciter. The world is not unexplained since it is told like a story" (30). This relentlessly social and historical quality of the past tense would preclude the immediacy of personal testimony, but the language of the Duston passage passes through many different tenses and verb forms in an attempt to escape the formal aspects of conventional historiography. Through them, Thoreau seeks to reinstate "the multiplicity of experiences" so that the narrative obscures neither Duston's nor the narrator's experiences. The result is a prose palimpsest of that stretch of the Merrimack River.

39. In September 1850, Thoreau visited the Duston homestead in Haverhill, "now but a slight indentation in a cornfield. . . . The apple tree . . . is gone." He remarks, "It is a question with some which is the true site of the Dustin house" (*Journal 3*, 64). Again, on 27 April 1853, Thoreau finds himself pondering Duston: "It is along the east side of this pond that the Indians are said to have taken their way with Hannah Dustin and her nurse in 1697 toward the Merrimack. I walked along it and thought how they might have been ambuscaded" (quoted in Arner 22).

40. Gossip, traditionally represented as a woman's medium, derives from a corruption of "godparent." Thus Thoreau retains not only the gendered but also the genealogical connotations in the image. The definition in the *American Heritage Dictionary* (1992) also emphasizes the private nature of gossip: "a person who habitually spreads intimate or private rumors or facts."

41. Thoreau, "Died . . . Miss Anna Jones" (121). In an unpublished variant of the obituary, Thoreau writes, "And who shall say that under much that was conventional there burned not a living and inextinguishable flame?" (378n). Thoreau's vision that the conventional image obscured a secret "inextinguishable" function contributes to the notion that he perceived women as "unread" by the public eye of the historian.

3. "The Original Copy and the Mistake of the Transcriber"

1. Vail notes that "there are two versions of the text of this narrative, both based on the same original manuscript. The English editions follow one version and the American editions the other" (216); however, Vail does not discuss this original manuscript or its provenance.

2. See Vail 217 and VanDerBeets 131. VanDerBeets reprints the text of the "improved" London edition of 1760 and provides footnote comparisons

with the 1754 Philadelphia edition. For example, in comparing the diction and syntax of the opening pages in each edition, VanDerBeets argues that changes in the English edition "not only spoil the immediacy and naturalness of the earlier version but actually render it ambiguous in one instance and distorted in another" (133n).

3. The account of Hanson's captivity in Bownas's *Journals* appears within quotation marks and in the third person, in the same way that Duston's story was printed in Mather's *Humiliations,* and therefore implies that Bownas received the story from an informant other than Hanson. As well, the Bownas version, though quite short, imports phrases from the 1728 narrative, such as in the explanation for the first child's murder, which was meant "to strike the greater Terror upon those in the House" (179–80), and his text repeats the narrative's description of the beaver match-coats that the captives ate to ward off starvation. This evidence supports Vail's and VanDerBeet's contentions that Bownas was not the author; however, it does not throw light on the actual author or authors either. The 1760 edition postscript, quoted by VanDerBeets, asserts that "the foregoing account was taken from her own mouth by Samuel Bownas. . . . Samuel Hopwood was with her, and received the relation much to the same purpose" (149–50). Hopwood's presence might indicate that he had a hand in the composition of the narrative.

4. *The Short-Title Evans* ascribes the 1728 Philadelphia edition (Evans #2996) and the 1754 Philadelphia edition (Evans #7160) to Elizabeth Meader Hanson.

5. Strong, for example, considers Elizabeth Hanson's "interpretive style" as a mode of proto-ethnographic writing: "She characteristically offers an explanation for why her captors do what they do, even if these actions have come to be conventional in captivity" (162). Significantly, Strong notes at the end of that paragraph that Hanson "mention[s] dispassionately that the children were scalped (or her editor, for this was a more didactic voice)" (162). This easy shift from Hanson's "style" to an editor's "more didactic voice" suggests that Strong can discern distinctive rhetorical strategies and assign them either to Hanson or to her putative editor. This discernment is further problematized when Strong, too, posits Bownas as "the anonymous 'friend' who, as the title page states, took down Hanson's relation 'from her own mouth' and published it, 'almost in her own words'" (163). Ulrich is somewhat of an exception to the readings of Hanson as simply a passive Quaker. In the "Daughters of Zion" chapter of *Good Wives,* she conducts an extended comparison of the Rowlandson and Hanson texts. Ulrich notes the "strikingly different responses to pain and death, suffering and sorrow, anger and fear, but especially to the experience of subjection" (226) in the narratives of Rowlandson and Hanson, and she argues that "the primary social category in Mary Rowlandson's tale is race, in Elizabeth Hanson's gender"

(227). Yet for Ulrich the Hanson narrative ultimately defers or even erases the question of gender in order to represent passivity as a religious, not a gendered, trait: "In a Quaker narrative of 1729 [*sic*] submissiveness is a Christian rather than a peculiarly feminine quality, though the alignment of the poor captive and the equally downtrodden Indian women against the single abusive male is striking" (232). By not interrogating the Quaker context of the narrative, Ulrich subsumes gender under religion in her interpretation. As I will argue, Hanson's gender is precisely the reason for her text's publication, and the passivity of her character serves a Quaker goal of domesticating the public image of Quaker *women* in particular.

6. Worrall notes that "few Quakers from Salem had significant wealth. . . . Friends of Hampton and Dover were farmers, probably a good deal like the folk John Greenleaf Whittier later remembered and quite unlike wealthy merchants of urban centers" (174). Similarly, in his *Journals,* Bownas described the Dover Monthly Meeting in 1727 in such a way as to cast doubt on the likelihood of Hanson's literacy: "They were very raw and managed their Affairs but indifferently, chiefly occasioned for want of some better Hands to write and keep their Books in Order" (177). It is probable as well that Hanson, like Swarton, did not have an elevated social status, and therefore the publication of her experiences conferred on her what reputation she thereafter enjoyed. For both Swarton and Hanson, however, relative obscurity meant that issues of social credit, such as those that Toulouse traces in Rowlandson's narrative, do not appear in their narratives. This is especially true for Hanson as a Quaker because a higher social status purportedly did not grant a greater personal or spiritual authority among Friends.

7. For a detailed account of Sarah's marriage and children, see Coleman 2: 161–66. Coleman also reproduces the texts of contemporary accounts of Hanson's capture and return as well as the baptismal record of Hanson's infant (called Mary Ann Frossways in the narrative; probably Marianne Françoise), who was christened by the family who ransomed them.

8. See "Relation II" and "Relation III" in article 7 of *Decennium Luctuosum,* in which both Mehetabel Goodwin and Mary Plaisted see their infant children murdered by their captors.

9. Mary Anne Schofield argues for an authentic and "distinct" voice of the Quaker woman: "It is the voice of liminality. Poised on the threshold, the chroniclers and confessionalists tell a story of heroism and salvation, of feminine servitude and male rescue, but, read parenthetically, these same accounts tell of female despair, torture, harassment, and insecurity. It is only by examining the gaps, by analyzing the interstices, that a true portrait of the voice and the person behind the voice can be gleaned" (63). Schofield's study concerns what she characterizes as autobiographical writing, such as the testaments of English Quaker women who traveled as missionaries. Reading the

interstices, Schofield finds that these women were "unwilling to alienate their readership, [and so] the journalist-chroniclers learned to couch their stories in the fictional coverings approved of by the male world, yet understood in their true, revolutionary sense by the female audience" (64). This critical position not only posits a sisterhood of decoding readers that is almost impossible to document but, significantly for the purposes of my study, elides any intervention by the elaborate Quaker publishing establishment. That male world had a great deal to say about the form of any Quaker publication, whether it appeared under the name of a man or a woman. Thus, arguments about agency—found in the interstices or otherwise—require contextualization within this regulatory publishing environment.

10. Wright describes "sufferings" as "a term employed by the Friends to indicate any infringement upon property rights, or loss of health or life incurred through adherence to their beliefs and practices. Records of 'sufferings for the sake of conscience' include 'the taking of an iron pot from a poor man' in New England; the confiscation of quantities of sugar owned by Friends in the West Indies; imprisonments, lasting from a few hours to twenty years; and sickness, banishment, or death resulting from injury and from penal confinement" (87).

11. The Rowlandson text explicitly castigates the militia for delaying the deployment that could have prevented the attack on Lancaster, and the Swarton narrative criticizes Puritan laxity in allowing outlying areas to remain "ungospelized" and in relinquishing conversion opportunities among the Indians to the French priests.

12. For an overview of the differences between women's roles in Quaker and Congregationalist communities, see Dunn, "Saints and Sisters" and "Latest Light on Women of Light" (71–89).

13. Compare representations of other captives' responses to the men who held the power of life or death over them: Rowlandson had conversations with King Philip in which she clearly portrays herself as his equal; Swarton disputed theology with her French captors, and Duston killed and scalped hers.

14. Following Strong, we might note the proto-ethnographic characteristics of these passages and read them with an eye toward a Quaker audience in England as well, where scalping and other Indian practices were not as familiar as they were to some of the colonists. Colley's point regarding the "experiential and knowledge gap between the colonies and the mother country" is useful here. Although she argues that this gap became much wider after 1750, she notes, "British-based writers on captivity and other contacts with Indians during the Seven Years War, who had their own compatriots in mind as an audience, sometimes felt obliged to devote space to very rudimentary information" such as definitions and descriptions of Native American terms and artifacts (176).

15. The full quotation as it occurs in *God's Mercy* is "By the Rivers of Babylon there we sat down, yea we wept when we remember'd Zion, we hanged our Harps on the Willows in the midst thereof. For there they that carried us away captive, required of us a Song; and they that wasted us, required of us Mirth" (10). The fuller quotation reinforces the sense of victimization and helplessness.

16. That Dickinson and Hanson were not, by some fluke, the only Quaker captives is indicated by Worrall's contention that Quakers in the northern settlements had abandoned their earlier sympathy for Indians because of the attacks they themselves sustained: "The 1706 New England Yearly Meeting epistle to the London Yearly Meeting showed little affection for 'The Barbarous Indians—assaulting, Killing and Captivating' English colonists [and] thereby ending the growth of Quaker numbers north of Salem for the time being" (184).

17. The editors of the 1945 edition argue that Dickinson was not even immediately aware of the text's publication: "That he was not writing for publication is evident from the fact that his *Journal* was not printed until 1699 and then probably by a group of the Philadelphia Society of Friends without his knowledge when he himself was taking one of his many voyages from Philadelphia to Jamaica" (18).

18. Mack maintains that the writings of the second generation of female Quaker ministers abandoned the practices of first-generation women, who, in their "gender fluidity," employed "traditional male language," which included "negative female symbols and stereotypes." The later women "based their public authority not only on their conviction of being 'in the light' but on their competence and integrity as daughters, as mothers, and as heads of families." She adds that "their dignity as women was linked not only to a new appreciation of 'feminine qualities' but to an emphasis on the specifically bourgeois qualities of moderation, competence in business and in the home, and personal self-control" (10).

19. Significantly, although Dover had been an early center of Quaker activity, Elizabeth Meader Hanson (1684–1737) was not born into the faith. Her father, John Meader, was a devout Congregationalist who petitioned for a minister when Cocheco had none. Her husband, John Hanson, was, however, a second-generation Quaker.

20. The statistics detailing Quaker publications are startling, as are the numbers of women publishing them. Lloyd notes that "by the opening of the eighteenth-century, more than 2500 books and pamphlets had been published by the Quakers, an average of one new title every week since the rise of the Society" (147). See also Tarter, who states that "by 1700 [Quaker women] had published over 20% of *all* English women's writing for the entire century" (22–26).

21. Wright describes this censorship in the best light by arguing that "certain Friends early saw that the integrity of the Society could easily be endangered through the unrestricted use of the press. They, therefore, sought means for checking what they termed 'unwise printing'" (97). See her chapter entitled "Quaker Censorship" for the development of the censorship process from a "semi-official" board of ten Friends to its later institutionalization within the purview of the Second Day Morning Meeting.

22. Much of the following discussion of Quaker censorship practices and their consequences for women who wished to assert a public authority relies on Mack's chapter on "Quaker Preaching and Discipline." In particular, Mack's understanding of the increasing reliance on conventional gender roles to supplant the "genderlessness" of the early female preachers and writers informs my understanding of the extreme submission figured by Hanson, as well as my interpretation of those passages in which Hanson exhibits her concern as mother and wife.

23. J. William Frost in fact cautions students of Quaker history in this period "not to treat American Quakers in isolation," because "colonial Quakers retained close contacts with Friends in the British Isles." As well, Frost notes that "because of the frequent sending of epistles, disciplines, and tracts and the close relationship between Friends in England and America in the eighteenth-century, books written in England can be used as sources for Quaker thought everywhere" (224). An instance of the close connection in publication concerns is detailed by the editors of *God's Protecting Providence* in their discussion of the London reprints of the narrative in 1700 (cf. 177–78).

24. See Soderland 123–24 for the rationales and consequences of gender segregation among the Quakers.

4. *"Affecting History"*

1. Uncharacteristically, Linda Colley writes about the Johnson narrative without noting this historical dimension. Rather, Colley, like many contemporary captivity scholars, responds to the immediacy and drama of the text and does not attend to the rhetorical complexities that indicate its checkered origins. For example, after introducing her chapter on "War and the New World" with a present-tense reconstruction of the attack and capture, Colley writes that "Susannah Johnson's narrative reveals the extent to which, by the 1750s, this kind of captive-taking possessed, for all its violence, an almost routine quality" (169). The forty years between event and publication go unremarked in this formulation.

2. The major critical texts that interpret the early Republic public sphere through the processes of print culture are those of Warner and Ziff. Fliegel-

man's and Looby's studies challenge these print-based models (that is, *text*) with an emphasis on physicality and performance (that is, *voice*).

3. This study does not argue that actual bodies anchor each end of the axis; rather it seeks to deconstruct the apparent two-gender model that grounds—as well as confounds—the representations of sex and gender in early women's texts. See Guruswamy for a clear and persuasive argument concerning feminist rereadings of Anne Bradstreet. Sharon Harris offers a catalog of critical inquiries in the field that have been engaged largely as the result of feminist and queer theory.

4. Of these three questions, this one, concerning the erotics of gender impersonation, indicates the broad cultural significance latent in the phenomenon. See below, for example, the discussion of Susannah Johnson's viewing of her own body as well as the titillating episode when Howe's French master attempts to seduce her.

5. Major studies of captivity narratives that consider the Johnson narrative treat the text as the production of Susannah Johnson: "Johnson writes with confidence" (Castiglia 67–68) and "what Susannah Johnson described" (Namias 262–63). Ebersole refers to Johnson as "the author" (147–48). I do not intend, by quoting these studies, to impeach these readings of the *Narrative*, especially because my own theorizing about voice and identity does not exclude this kind of figurative reading; rather I seek to extend (and complicate) specifically the value of female agency that these scholars discuss, within the frame of gender impersonation.

6. Derounian-Stodola's categorization of Indian captivity narratives into "factive" and "fictive" provides one heuristic by which we may interpret the women's texts. In discussing Mary Rowlandson's narrative, she argues that Rowlandson's text is factive because it is "told in the first person and tend[s] towards veracity" ("Rowlandson and Oatman" 43). This *construction* of veracity (and, therefore, credibility) *lies at the heart* of the Johnson narrative. Like Derounian-Stodola, Gherman proposes that women's captivity narratives fall into two categories, "documentary" and "sentimental" (133–40). Johnson's *Narrative* and the Howe accounts discussed below demonstrate that the *dialogue* between these modes generates the meanings and cultural values in the texts.

7. Mark Kamrath's study of Charles Brockden Brown's theories of historiography provides a good overview of late eighteenth- and early nineteenth-century debates about content and method in historical writing.

8. My argument depends, in some measure, on Warner's reassessment of the meaning of print in the early Republic. In particular, Warner's concepts of the "supervisory" and "self-negating" characteristics of print culture inform my argument about the uses of female authorship in this period insofar as that authorship is grounded in a positive embodiment of the female over against the supervisory and hidden (here by impersonation) male.

9. I am grateful to the anonymous reader of an earlier version of this study for clear and useful suggestions that helped me to elaborate my consideration of Warner's theories.

10. The debate about women's roles in the new nation as it appears in print (specifically, magazines) and is engaged by women writers is detailed in Branson. Branson's study of women and print culture in the early national period necessarily focuses on the writing of privileged women: "Class plays a defining role in the practices and activities [of the women discussed in her study]. It is the ideas articulated by middle class and elite women that have survived in letters, diaries, essays, and novels" (7). There is no evidence that Susannah Johnson's life in Walpole, New Hampshire, included the kind of literary community that sustained the writings of Annis Boudinot Stockton or Elizabeth Graeme Fergusson: we have only one text and no manuscripts attributed to Johnson.

11. I wish to thank Professor Craig for sharing these insights. His acute analysis of "utterance" as a "part of the text's interpersonal meaning" has informed my theorization of the meanings of gender impersonation in the debate about vocality and textuality.

12. Mercy Otis Warren, in "An Address to the Inhabitants of the United States," the preface to her *History of the Rise, Progress, and Termination of the American Revolution,* speaks from her position in proximity to the events she describes, experiences she had specifically because she was "connected by nature, friendship, and every social tie, with many of the first patriots, and most influential characters on the continent" (xli). Warren displays a strong anxiety about assuming the role of (female) historian: "It is true there are certain appropriate duties assigned to each sex; and doubtless it is the more peculiar province of masculine strength, not only to repel the bold invader of the rights of his country and of mankind, but in the nervous style of manly eloquence, to describe the blood-stained field, and relate the story of slaughtered armies" (xli–xlii). The "Address" repeatedly manifests this concern with her gender transgression, even as Warren goes on to compose a three-volume history.

13. Brockden Brown's 1800 essay, "The Difference between History and Romance," quoted in Kamrath, explicates the problem of writing history dependent on anecdote: "Useful narrative must comprise facts linked together by some other circumstance. They must, commonly consist of events, for a knowledge of which the narrator is indebted to the evidence of others. This evidence, though accompanied with different degrees of probability, can never give birth to certainty" (246). Assuming the informant's "I" is an attempt to erase the gap between "evidence" and "certainty," this is the gesture made in the *Manheim* claim, and, as Brown theorized, a failed gesture. When the "I" speaks from female experience, however, another gap appears, between the affective and the rational, a gap that the composers of the Johnson narrative

bridge with supplementary genres: documentation and third-person historical interpretation.

14. Kamrath, in discussing the "historical veracity" invoked by Rowson and Foster in the prefaces to their novels, argues that these female novelists, too, recognized and manipulated the factive-fictive dyad; their novels, he asserts, "were efforts to participate successfully in the public and economic spheres of the early republic: to use history as a means of writing fiction" (237). Efforts such as those of Rowson and Foster are made possible by the gendering of specific modalities and genres within print culture.

15. Evans' *American Bibliography* lists Chamberlain as author of the 18mo 1796 Walpole edition (item #30180). However, the *American Bibliography* (item #30641) lists Susanna (note the variant spelling) Johnson as author of a 1796 12mo edition with the note: "17th New-Hampshire District Copyright, issued to George Kimball, as Proprietor, 16 September, 1796." Kimball was Elizabeth Captive Johnson's husband. Farmer and Moore's *Collections* includes a reprint of the 1814 edition with an introductory note stating that "The work was written many years since by a gentleman of distinguished literary reputation, and though a work of his early years, contains many just and accurate observations, on the dangers and hardships of settling a new country, and the cruelties which awaited those who were taken into captivity by the Indians" (177). Others who attribute Susannah Johnson's *Narrative* to John C. Chamberlain include Saunderson (304–5), Bell (247), Ellis (96), and Tanselle ("Attribution" 176). R. W. G. Vail reprints the note on the verso of the introduction (discussed below) but inserts "to John C. Chamberlain" in brackets between "dictated" and "by Mrs. Johnson" without explaining why he does so (415, item 1074). Yet most contemporary captivity theorists leave this question of attribution unremarked. See, for example, Castiglia, Ebersole, and Derounian-Stodola and Levernier. Castiglia's discussion of Jemima Howe, however, problematizes the editorial apparatus in that narrative to initiate a study of "the history of appropriation and resistance" in Mary Rowlandson and the nineteenth-century captivity anthologies (79–86). Frances Roe Kestler's study is the only contemporary source that lists Chamberlain as the author of the Johnson narrative.

16. Joseph Buckingham's reminiscences offer an entire chapter on the *Farmer's Weekly Museum*, including a discussion of the permutations of the newspaper's name, as noted below (174ff v.2).

17. Ellis, Dennie's biographer, and Tyler scholars Péladeau and Tanselle agree that "Spondee" generally referred to Tyler, and "Colon" to Dennie, but they note the difficulty of attributing much of this pseudonymous publication. See Ellis 66–67; Péladeau 192; and Tanselle, "Attribution" 172.

18. This episode is retold in a "fugitive" piece entitled "The Life of Dennie," published in the *Philadelphia Souvenir* of 1826. According to this "biographical note," Dennie considered the completion of his Lay Preacher essay

"a gross insult," although this source also states that the person who finished the essay (not identified as Tyler in this account) was "the only person who was awake and capable of writing" when copy was called for.

19. Ellis describes each of the contributors in detail (87–88, 94–110) and notes that members of the circle wrote essays for the *Eagle,* the magazine in which Dennie and Tyler first opened their "shop." John C. Chamberlain, according to Ellis, "may have contributed some of the *Vigil* essays . . . from 19 September, 1794, to the spring of the following year" (67). Ellis also maintains that when Dennie began a series entitled "The Saunterer" in the *Farmer's Weekly Museum,* "Royall Tyler and John C. Chamberlain were the chief contributors" (85). He further notes the difficulty of assigning authorship to any one of the circle; this may be due to the collective composition model described by Buckingham and to Dennie's editorial practices. Tanselle delineates the dangers of hasty attribution, especially in this period: "Contributions to newspapers and magazines at this time were generally anonymous or pseudonymous, and, in the absence of a record kept by the author himself or by the editor, it is now virtually impossible to establish the complete canon of any particular writer's periodical work." See Tanselle, *Royall Tyler* 109ff.

20. The Boston Public Library owns a copy of *The Spirit of the Farmers' Museum* (a compilation of selections from the newspaper) that Dennie presented to a friend upon its publication in 1801. Dennie obligingly penciled in the initials of the actual writers next to their pseudonymous pieces. So, we now know that John C. Chamberlain wrote the Hermit piece entitled "Description, in the manner of Mrs. Radcliffe," and in an untitled Hermit, he wrote, "Sometimes, with the taciturnity of Addison, I stand incog. among the crowd" (168, 171).

21. Like the narratives of Hannah Swarton, Jemima Howe, and Elizabeth Hanson, Susannah Johnson's tale offers descriptions of captivity in the French settlements in Canada as well as with Indians in the wilderness. They exhibit many details of race differentiation, but they are as likely to include extensive discussion of intra-European distinctions, and the Johnson narrative dwells on the differences between British and French (and later, American) social practices.

22. Johnson's journals were themselves later published as *Scout Journals.*

23. The *Narrative* was republished several times; a 1797 pamphlet, published by M. Augus in Newcastle, and an 1802 pamphlet issued by J. and P. Wilson were the first English reprints. Kestler provides information on all subsequent editions, including what she deems the second (1814) edition, which, she states, "was revised by the authoress" (although Kestler lists the *Narrative* under Chamberlain's name in her bibliography), and a third (again, 1814) edition "enlarged according to [Hastings's] request" (161–62). An inquiry into Susannah Johnson Hastings's further connections with her

story is beyond the scope of this study, the object of which is the production and representation of authorship in the first edition. There is, however, evidence indicating that Susannah Johnson had always considered her story in some ways "monumental." Saunderson notes that in 1787, 1790, and 1799, she made journeys to ascertain where her daughter was born on the trail. In 1799, accompanied by Peter Labarree, she "determined to erect two stones: one on the spot where Elizabeth Captive was born and the other on the spot where the Indians encamped" (456).

24. See Crèvecoeur 201, and note the emphasis on the "unmanning" accomplished by the sentimental discourses in both texts: "Sometimes feeling the spontaneous courage of a man, I seem to wish for the decisive minute; the next instant a message from my wife, sent by one of the children, puzzling me beside with their little questions, unmans me" (202).

25. See Sieminski 35–56. Mary Lawlor argues that the idea of authenticity is claimed by male figures as well: "The history of Daniel Boone is the history of a cultural figure and a literary character whose claim to authenticity is one of its most dominant components" (29). For Lawlor, Boone "duplicates the ideal, unmarked tabula rasa of the wilderness that he inscribes." Female captives, conversely, often exhibit alienation from their forest surroundings, as we see in the Johnson narrative.

26. Elaine Hadley's succinct catalog of the defining features of melodrama appears in almost all captivity narratives by women, but they are writ large in the Johnson narrative: "Melodrama's familial narratives of dispersal and reunion, its emphatically visual renderings of bodily torture and criminal conduct, its atmospheric menace and providential plotting, its expressions of highly charged emotion, and its tendency to personify absolutes like good and evil were represented in a wide range of social settings, not just on the stage" (3). Although Hadley's study is confined to nineteenth-century England, the characteristics she delineates are evident in these earlier American captivity narratives, and they signal a feminized discourse even in this period, one marked by the popularity of women's seduction novels.

27. Castiglia argues that in moments when white men fail to save white women from attack, the women's captivity narratives demonstrate a subversive, antipatriarchal gesture, a "lack of confidence in masculine agency" (67). In the case of the Johnson narrative, the male authors' concerns must be considered; however, the combination of James Johnson's heedless opening of the door and the subsequent capture of all the men, standing bound in the presence of Susannah Johnson's nakedness, may be read as both an indictment of male protection and a sensationalized focus on the narrator's body, the source of the text's credibility. That is, the men must be immobilized for the woman's body to take center stage. Otherwise, the men, presumably, would be the leading actors in the scene.

28. See Burke 164–65.

29. My many rereadings of the Johnson narrative, and of earlier women's captivity narratives, have led me back again and again to this strange formulation: "on viewing myself." The moment of seeing one's self becomes in this narrative, as in others, a moment of spectacular embodiment, a compelling emblem of the narrated atrocity. The narrator's display of her body disrupts the active telling of the tale: these images stop action and compel the reader to rethink her relationship to the "I" who transforms herself into a "me" and thereby blurs the subject-object categories that underwrite traditional historiography.

30. Two specimens from the *Farmer's Weekly Museum* indicate that the Johnson narrative is suffused with language similar to that found in reports on western battles. A reprint of a letter by Henry Knox, then secretary of war, notes "the encroachment of white people is incessantly watched, and in unguarded moments, they are murdered by Indians. Revenge is sought, and the innocent frontier people are too frequently involved, as victims in the cruel contest" (*FWM* 27 January 1795). In an "extract of a letter from an officer in the western army" (*FWM* 6 October 1795), readers found the "pleasing scene" of children "who have been absent 15 or 16 years" returned to their parents, although some of these children no longer could speak English.

31. See, for example, Dennie's Lay Preacher sermons: "Daring and impudent as it may appear in this leveling age to avow respect for birth or talents, I confess, as little of the aristocratical leaven has possibly leavened the whole lump, that my notions on this subject are very old-fashioned" (Sermon 15); "That animal, more restless than a hummingbird, called a Democrat or Jacobin. . . . I would interdict him from reading French gazettes, forbid his pronouncing the word 'Robespierre,' and debar him from nocturnal clubs or speeches. The man would infallibly become a good federalist" (Sermon 27); "Whether it proceeds from the warm climate in which they live, or the brisk champagne they drink, I know not, but the French are singularly prone to momentary fits of enthusiasm, almost bordering on convulsions. They are a very voluble and clamorous race. . . . those sanguinary craftsmen, Marat and Robespierre" (Sermon 37).

32. The proposal advertises that "the character of the Indians, the Manners of the French, and the poignancy of her Sufferings, render the narrative peculiarly interesting." The 1 November 1796 *FWM* printed a notice from the clerk of the district of Newhampshire attesting that George Kimball is the proprietor of the title of the book. He is described as an "innholder" of Charlestown.

33. See Derounian-Stodola and Levernier 46–50 and Slotkin 256–59 for a discussion of the mythological uses of the captivity narrative based on a reading of the Panther Captivity and its influence on Brockden Brown's *Edgar Huntley*.

34. Johonnot's narrative was later published as a single text by Carlisle and his then-partner, Isaiah Thomas, one year before the Johnson narrative. Johonnot fought in the "western army" and was captured by Kickapoos.

35. The exception to the short narratives is "Adventures and Sufferings of Peter Wilkinson," a seventeen-page first-person account of an indentured servant. According to Alden Vaughan's bibliography, the Wilkinson narrative was first published in York, England, in 1757. This narrative contains an expanded consideration of "captivity" beginning with his kidnapping at the age of eight from Scotland. See Colley's discussion of the Wilkinson narratives, in which she argues that Wilkinson (called Williamson in the text) was "someone who repeatedly re-invented himself and his life-story" (188).

36. The Panther Captivity was originally advertised in the 21 May 1787 edition of *Middlesex Gazette*, but no extant edition precedes the narrative's appearance in *Bickerstaff's Almanack for 1788*. Several editions were issued in Windsor, Vermont, in 1794. *Manheim*, at sixty-six pages a lengthy text, is an anthology composed of short, previously published sources such as Massey Herbeson's "Deposition." In its 1799 edition (Boston, printed by J. White), several of the earlier selections are deleted. As many scholars of these texts have noted, the numerous reprints and editions of Indian captivity narratives testify to their popularity. Significantly, the texts also may be seen as avenues to authorship, easy gambits for becoming, as Dennie hoped to be, "a man of letters." In the 16 August 1796 edition of *FWM,* above "Reason" and next to "Marie Antoinette," there is a call for "Authors" who "should take their first steps towards Parnassus warily, and prudently tempt the publick favor. Even if conscious of superior powers, let them exhibit them first in solitude. Men of letters, publish at a country press."

37. Up to now, most scholars have considered *Kittle* a work of fiction, but Sharon Harris, in a private conversation, indicated that she has found evidence that Bleecker's text is based upon actual events and that Maria Kittle was a real woman who experienced Indian captivity, and Miss Ten Eyck was most likely her relative. I am indebted to Professor Harris for generously sharing her research findings with me. See the note on Vail's characterization below.

38. Davidson notes that "almost one third of the novels written in America before 1820 were epistolary" (*Revolution* 14).

39. Vail states that the letter is to Bleecker's half-sister. Interestingly, although Vail argues that *Kittle*'s status as a factual account is belied by Bleecker's "not too unskilled imagination," he notes that Bleecker, whose husband was captured by Indians and who herself, in fleeing from invasion, lost her youngest daughter, was a victim of Revolutionary War fighting in 1777 (Vail 54–55).

40. See Bleecker 3.

41. Derounian-Stodola lists Kollock as the author of this narrative (*Women's Indian Captivity Narratives* 108).

42. Later editions of the *Narrative* include more details relating to her children's individual experiences with their captors, and Susannah Johnson has a dream she interprets in terms of her captivity. A noteworthy passage occurs in the last pages of the *Narrative*, where the narrator traces her misfortune to the time "when New-England was ruled by a few men who were the creatures of a king, the pleasures of dissipation were preferred to the more severe attention to business, and the small voice of a woman was seldom heard" (Farmer and Moore 1: 236–38). One subsequent edition was published by Alden Spooner in Windsor, Vermont, in 1807. The 1814 edition, also published in Windsor, but by Thomas Pomroy, is the "third edition, corrected and considerably enlarged," over which Elizabeth Captive Kimball, Johnson's daughter who was born on the trail, claims proprietorship. This edition begins with "Notices of the Willard Family" and decries the "deficiency, which at present exists in American genealogy" (4). Therefore the 1814 edition begins with a nod to the final pages of the 1796 text, with a focus on the "numerous progeny" of the Willard-Johnson families, and underscores the *Narrative*'s authentic, historically accurate status. A fourth edition was published by Daniel Bixby in Lowell, Massachusetts, in 1834.

43. See the note on Sieminski and Lawlor above, and for the wild and crazy Ethan Allen, see Ziff and Colley.

44. Although Susannah Johnson was not accused, she soon joined her husband in prison, as was the custom.

45. Vaudreuil, misspelled "Vaudrieul" throughout, at first would not hear any exculpating evidence from James Johnson, but in January 1756, James sent a letter to him from the criminal prison, where the family had contracted smallpox, and received an obsequious reply stating that Vaudreuil had ordered them to the civil jail, where conditions were somewhat better: "If it is some opportunity of doing you some pleasure, I will make use of it; unless some reason might happen, that hinder and stop the effects of my goodwill. If you had not before, given some cause of being suspected, you should be at liberty" (106). This appears under the heading "Translation," which may account for the ungrammatical English. No translator is identified in the text.

46. As well, as Colley notes, the Johnson narrative displays "multiple transatlantic crossings and confrontations of a new type all brought about by the onset of seismic imperial warfare" (171). It is important to note that Colley drew on 1797 and 1834 editions of the narrative, the latter of which "includes additional material" (404n1), although it is unclear who added that material.

47. In his manuscript memoir of his father, Royall Tyler, Thomas P. Tyler recounts the meeting: "They [Royall Tyler and his wife] crossed the Con-

necticut, on the ice, near the site of old Fort Dummer; and stopped for supper at Squire Howe's, in Vernon. This man was a baby at the time of the Massacre by the Indians, during the French war. His father was killed, and the whole family carried captive to Canada. They were subsequently ransomed. The mother, known in story as the 'fair captive,' married a Mr. Tute; but was now once more a widow, and residing with her son, Squire. She was, of course, one of the celebrities of the country; and the travellers enjoyed, not only a good fire and substantial supper, but an account, from the heroine's own lips, of the terrible sufferings of that march through the woods to Quebec" (83). The typescript of the Thomas Tyler manuscript is deposited in the collections of the Vermont Historical Society. I am indebted to John Lovejoy for alerting me to this text and generously sharing his notes on it with me.

48. Tyler subsequently superseded this model by creating a fictional captive, rather than appropriating the voice of an actual one. His *Algerine Captive,* now a key text of the early Republican period, was published, anonymously, one year later, also by David Carlisle. The Johnson *Narrative,* in its topic and authorial imposture, is clearly an important source for Tyler's novel.

49. The lapse, too, permits the author(s) of the Johnson *Narrative* to produce a historical woman in the sense that Johnson, "speaking" about herself forty years ago, produces a female figure that predates contemporary debates about women's roles in the public life of the nation. This case of gender impersonation in historiography, then, substantiates a conservative gender politics that severely constrains possibilities for women's political participation in the new Republic.

50. Humphreys' statement implies that for his readers, the line between "fiction" and "annals" is ambiguous, and therefore, it initially produces a complete lack of faith in historiography. That is, the rise of fiction generates a crisis in the credibility of historical writing (10).

51. Castiglia cites Eve Kosofsky Sedgwick's theory of patriarchal power as the product of male homosocial desire: "Through their traffic in the shared female object, the men ensure their own position as subjects in control of a symbolic economy in which the women figures only as a prized commodity" (206n20).

52. Because the erotics—the textual pleasure—I find here relies on the objectification of others, the depiction of the helpless frontier farmers extends the erotic effects of rhetorical drag to the subjection of *classed* others. The portrayal of the Indians as dehumanized brutes completes this vision of silenced others, whose meanings need to be explained by the historical writers.

53. Bottorff's introduction notes this incredible claim and discusses its "patriotic purposes" (x).

54. Tucker 32. My discussion of Belknap relies extensively on Tucker's study, especially his chapter on "The Historian" (27–58), which traces both

Belknap's development as a historiographer and the contemporary critical responses to his work.

55. The letter, dated 18 May 1787, is quoted at length in Tucker (47–48) and is useful for its delineation of Belknap's methodologies, including his reliance on "some intelligent and faithful correspondent in each of the States" (47).

56. Belknap, volume 1 [n.p., but actually v]. Each volume was issued by a different printer (vol. 1 [1784]; vol. 2 [1791]; vol. 3 [1792]). See Tucker 36n30.

57. The full title page reads "Taken from her own mouth, and written, by the Rev. Bunker Gray [*sic*], A. M. Minister of *Hinsdale*, in a letter to the Author of the *History of New-Hampshire,* extracted from the third volume of said History, by consent of the Author . . . In this account the mistakes of Col. Humphreys, relating to Mrs. Howe, in his 'life of General Putnam,' are rectified."

Epilogue

1. Schultz's study of the Watertown convent burning, *Fire and Roses,* provides rich detail and historical background of the major actors and their relationship with Reed, the "escaped" nun.

2. For example, Castiglia reads Bunker Gay's parenthetical in the first sentence of Jemima Howe's narrative ("The Indians [she says] having plundered . . .") as a representation of Howe's "liminal position, not entirely with the Indians any longer but not assimilated into her editor's culture either. Within her separate space—a space figured by the parentheses—Howe gains the distance from the discourse of two cultures which grants her a critical insight and also, therefore, a voice" (80). A reading of this passage through the lens of rhetorical drag, however, sees the parenthetical as Gay's slippage, his attempt to signal that the "embodied" Howe ("she says") underwrites his impersonation of her for insertion into Belknap's authoritative history. I agree with Castiglia that many (especially nineteenth-century) women's captivity narratives do resist the "social status quo" of the ministers and editors who sponsored them, but in the cases of impersonation, especially in oft-cited narratives such as the ones examined here, the historiographical imperatives trump gender resistance.

3. Namias uses this term to describe the processes that produced the Jemison text. Quoting Gretchen M. Bataille and Kathleen Mullen Sands's studies of Indian women's autobiographies, Namias writes, "Like Indian women's autobiographies, these accounts 'tend to be retrospective rather than introspective' and develop through a process involving both teller and editor in 'selection and recollection, structuring, and expression.' The 'possibilities of error are great, and distortion and misrepresentation are confronted at every moment because two creators are at work simultaneously'" (151). Note the

presumption, implicit in likening the Jemison text to these autobiographical works, that the collaboration is between two creators—"teller" and "editor"—who seem to have equivalent cultural authority and similar, if not identical, aims. That is, there is no sense here that Jemison, in the collaboration, had the distinct disadvantage of not writing English nor having direct access to the processes of publication.

4. Wilcomb Washburn states that Olive Oatman, who bore facial tattoos from the time of her captivity, later gave lectures. Her lecture notes apparently survive. See Washburn's introduction and especially note 16 (xv). As to other, illegible, marks, Washburn states, "Skepticism concerning Olive's virginal state . . . arose following her release" (xiii).

5. By describing the artifice and performance in all these impersonated texts, I do not argue that they cannot be read as historical documents as well. Colley, for example, believes that even captivity texts "intercut with fictional or pirated passages" can provide historians with valuable information. She argues convincingly that "captivity narratives are fractured, composite sources, but it is inappropriate—indeed it is something of a cop-out—to analyse them textually but not contextually. Too much gets lost along the way" (93).

6. Laura Browder's work on ethnic impersonators employs similar investigatory methods. Significantly, Browder argues that race (and ethnicity), like gender, is not an essentialized category but a performance. She argues that "the performance of gender or race insists on its own reality" (9) and achieves its power through reiterated acts.

7. McDaniel offers an intriguing argument that *reading* practices form the basis for comparison between eighteenth- and nineteenth-century journal writers and contemporary bloggers.

8. As Myles notes, Melanie McAlister's 6 April 2003 *New York Times* op-ed piece initiated the published comparison, but many scholars of early American studies had been discussing the resemblances from the moment the story emerged.

9. A remarkably persistent, even relentless, motif in Bragg's book, Lynch's girlishness, her diminutive stature, and her prissiness combine to ensure that Lynch's gender is performed in a most reductive and sentimental version of femininity. It is important to note, however, that Bragg represents Lynch as insistently deferring the role of heroine. This honorific is assigned to her colleague and friend, Lori Piestewa, who was killed in the same attack in which Lynch was injured. *I Am a Soldier, Too* thus disrupts both the Pentagon version and the conservative backlash version of Lynch's experiences.

Works Cited

The Affecting History of the Dreadful Distresses of Frederic Manheim's Family . . . Garland Library of Narratives of North American Indian Captivities 21. Ed. Wilcomb E. Washburn. New York: Garland, 1977.

Andrews, William. "The Printed Funeral Sermons of Cotton Mather." *Early American Literature* 5 (1970): 24–44.

Arner, Robert D. "The Story of Hannah Duston: Cotton Mather to Thoreau." *American Transcendental Quarterly* 18 (1973): 19–23.

Bacon, Margaret Hope. *Mothers of Feminism: The Story of Quaker Women in America.* San Francisco: Harper & Row, 1986.

Barthes, Roland. *Writing Degree Zero.* Trans. Annette Lavers and Colin Smith. New York: Hill and Wang, 1983.

Baym, Nina. "Thwarted Nature: Nathanial Hawthorne as Feminist." *American Novelists Revisited: Essays in Feminist Criticism.* Ed. Fritz Fleischman. Boston: G. K. Hall, 1982.

Belknap, Jeremy. *The History of New-Hampshire.* 3 vols. Boston, 1791–92.

———. "The Subscriber, Being Engaged. . . ." Boston, 1790.

Bell, Charles H. *The Bench and Bar of New Hampshire.* Boston, 1894.

Bleecker, Ann Eliza. *The History of Maria Kittle.* Garland Library of Narratives of North American Indian Captivities 20. Ed. Wilcomb E. Washburn. New York: Garland, 1978.

Bottorff, William K. Introduction. *The Miscellaneous Works of David Humphreys.* Gainesville, FL: Scholars' Facsimiles and Reprints, 1968.

Bownas, Samuel. *Journals of the Lives and Travels of Samuel Bownas and John Richardson.* Philadelphia, 1759.

Bragg, Rick. *I Am a Soldier, Too: The Jessica Lynch Story.* New York: Knopf, 2003.

Branson, Susan. *These Fiery Frenchified Dames: Women and Political Culture in Early National Philadelphia.* Philadelphia: University of Pennsylvania Press, 2001.

Browder, Laura. *Slippery Characters: Ethnic Impersonators and American Identities.* Chapel Hill: University of North Carolina Press, 2000.

Buckingham, Joseph T. *Specimens of Newspaper Literature.* 2 vols. 1850. Freeport, NY: Books for Libraries Press, 1971.

Burbick, Joan. *Thoreau's Alternative History: Changing Perspectives on Nature, Culture, and Language.* Philadelphia: University of Pennsylvania Press, 1987.

Burke, Edmund. *Reflections on the Revolution in France.* London: Penguin, 1982.

Burnham, Michelle. *Captivity and Sentiment: Cultural Exchange in American Literature, 1682–1861.* Hanover, NH: University Press of New England, 1997.

Butler, Judith. *Bodies That Matter: On the Discursive Limits of "Sex."* New York: Routledge, 1993.

——. *Gender Trouble: Feminism and the Subversion of Identity.* New York: Routledge, 1990.

Cady, Edwin Harrison, and Harry Hayden Clark. *Whittier on Writers and Writing.* Syracuse, NY: Syracuse University Press, 1950.

Cameron, Sharon. *Writing Nature.* Chicago: University of Chicago Press, 1985.

Castiglia, Christopher. *Bound and Determined: Captivity, Culture-Crossing, and White Womanhood from Mary Rowlandson to Patty Hearst.* Chicago: University of Chicago Press, 1996.

Catapano, Terry. "Corrective Notes to Lorrayne Carroll's 'My Outward Man': The Curious Case of Hannah Swarton." *Early American Literature* 33 (1998): 315–21.

Cohen, B. Bernard. "The Composition of Hawthorne's 'The Duston Family.'" *New England Quarterly* 21 (1948): 236–41.

Coleman, Emma L. *New England Captives Carried to Canada between 1677 and 1760.* 2 vols. Portland, ME: Southworth Press, 1925.

Colley, Linda. *Captives: Britain, Empire, and the World, 1600–1850.* New York: Anchor Books, 2002.

Cowell, Pattie. Introduction. *Ornaments for the Daughters of Zion, or The Character and Happiness of a Virtuous Woman: A Facsimile Reproduction.* By Cotton Mather. Delmar, NY: Scholars' Facsimiles and Reprints, 1978.

Craig, Raymond. "Carping Tongues and Censorious Poets: The Construction of Readers in Seventeenth-Century America." American Literature Association Conference. Cambridge, MA. 24 May 2001.

Crèvecoeur, J. Hector St. John. *Letters from an American Farmer and Sketches of Eighteenth-Century America*. New York: Penguin, 1981.

Davidson, Cathy. Introduction. *The Coquette*. By Hannah Webster Foster. New York: Oxford University Press, 1986.

——. *Revolution and the Word: The Rise of the Novel in America*. New York: Oxford University Press, 1986.

Dennie, Joseph. *The Lay Preacher*. Ed. Harold Milton Ellis. New York: Scholars' Facsimiles and Reprints, 1943.

Derounian, Kathryn Zabelle. "The Publication, Promotion, and Distribution of Mary Rowlandson's Indian Captivity Narrative in the Seventeenth Century." *Early American Literature* 23 (1988): 239–61.

Derounian-Stodola, Kathryn Zabelle. "Indian Captivity Narratives of Mary Rowlandson and Olive Oatman: Case Studies in the Continuity, Evolution, and Exploitation of Literary Discourse." *Studies in Literary Imagination* 27 (1994): 33–46.

——. *Women's Indian Captivity Narratives*. New York: Penguin, 1998.

Derounian-Stodola, Kathryn Zabelle, and James Levernier. *The Indian Captivity Narrative, 1550–1900*. New York: Twayne, 1993.

Dickinson, Jonathan. *Jonathan Dickinson's Journal, or God's Protecting Providence*. Ed. Evangeline Walker Andrews and Charles McLean Andrews. New Haven, CT: Yale University Press, 1945.

Dunn, Mary Maples. "Latest Light on Women of Light." *Witnesses for Change: Quaker Women over Three Centuries*. Ed. Elizabeth Potts Brown and Susan Mosher Stuard. Brunswick, NJ: Rutgers University Press, 1989.

——. "Saints and Sisters: Congregational and Quaker Women in the Early Colonial Period." *Women in American Religion*. Ed. Janet Wilson James. Philadelphia: University of Pennsylvania Press, 1982.

Dwight, Timothy. *Travels in New England and New York*. Ed. Barbara Miller Solomon. 4 vols. Cambridge, MA: Belknap Press of Harvard University Press, 1969.

Ebersole, Gary. *Captured By Texts: Puritan to Post-Modern Images of Indian Captivity*. Charlottesville: University Press of Virginia, 1995.

Egan, Jim. *Authorizing Experience: Refigurations of the Body Politic in Seventeenth-Century New England Writing*. Princeton, NJ: Princeton University Press, 1999.

Ellis, Harold Milton. *Joseph Dennie and His Circle*. 1915. New York: AMS Press, 1971.

Ellis, John Harvard. *The Works of Anne Bradstreet in Prose and Verse, 1867*. Gloucester, MA: Peter Smith, 1962.

Ernest, Joseph M., Jr. "Whittier and the 'Feminine Fifties.'" *American Literature* 28 (1956): 184–96.

Evans, Charles. *American Bibliography* 10. New York: Peter Smith, 1942.

Works Cited

Faery, Rebecca Blevins. *Cartographies of Desire: Captivity, Race, and Sex in the Shaping of an American Nation.* Norman: University of Oklahoma Press, 1999.

Farmer, John, and Jacob Moore. *Collections, Topographical, Historical, and Bibliographical, relating Principally to New-Hampshire.* 3 vols. Concord, NH, 1822.

Farmer's Weekly Museum. Walpole, NH, 1793–1796.

Fitzpatrick, Tara. "The Figure of Captivity: The Cultural Work of the Puritan Captivity Narrative." *American Literary History* 3 (1991): 1–26.

Fliegelman, Jay. *Declaring Independence: Jefferson, Natural Language, and the Culture of Performance.* Stanford, CA: Stanford University Press, 1993.

Foster, Hannah Webster. *The Coquette.* New York: Oxford University Press, 1986.

Foster, William Henry. *The Captor's Narrative: Catholic Women and Their Puritan Men on the Early American Frontier.* Ithaca, NY: Cornell University Press, 2003.

Frost, J. William. *The Quaker Family in Colonial America: A Portrait of the Society of Friends.* New York: St. Martin's Press, 1973.

Foucault, Michel. "What Is an Author?" *The Foucault Reader.* Ed. Paul Rabinow. New York: Pantheon Books, 1984.

Garber, Marjorie. *Vested Interests: Cross-Dressing and Cultural Anxiety.* New York: Routledge, 1997.

Gay, Bunker. *A Genuine and Correct Account of the Captivity, Sufferings and Deliverance of Mrs. Jemima Howe.* Boston, 1792.

Gherman, Dawn Lander. "From Parlour to Tepee: The White Squaw on the American Frontier." Diss., Amherst: University of Massachusetts, 1975.

Gilmore, Leigh. *Autobiographics: A Feminist Theory of Women's Self-Representation.* Ithaca, NY: Cornell University Press, 1994.

Goldberg, Jonathan. *Writing Matter: From the Hands of the English Renaissance.* Stanford, CA: Stanford University Press, 1990.

"Gossip." *American Heritage Dictionary.* 3rd ed., 1992.

Guruswamy, Rosemary Fithian. "Queer Theory and Publication Anxiety: The Case of the Early American Woman Writer." *Early American Literature* 34 (1999): 103–13.

Hadley, Elaine. *Melodramatic Tactics: Theatricalized Dissent in the English Marketplace, 1800–1885.* Stanford, CA: Stanford University Press, 1995.

Hanson, Elizabeth. *God's Mercy Surmounting Man's Cruelty, Exemplified in the Captivity and Redemption of Elizabeth Hanson.* Philadelphia, 1728.

Haraway, Donna J. *Simians, Cyborgs, and Women: The Reinvention of Nature.* New York: Routledge, 1991.

Harris, Sharon. "Feminist Theories and Early American Studies." *Early American Literature* 34 (1999): 86–94.

Hawthorne, Nathaniel. "The Duston Family." *The Complete Writings of Nathaniel Hawthorne.* Vol. 17. Boston: Houghton Mifflin, 1900.

———. "Mrs. Hutchinson." *Selected Tales and Sketches.* Ed. Michael Colacurcio. New York: Penguin, 1987.

Hensley, Jeannine. *The Works of Anne Bradstreet.* Cambridge, MA: Belknap Press of Harvard University Press, 1967.

Herbert, T. Walter. *Dearest Beloved: The Hawthornes and the Making of the Middle-Class Family.* Berkeley and Los Angeles: University of California Press, 1993.

Holmes, Thomas J. *Cotton Mather: A Bibliography of His Works.* 3 vols. Cambridge, MA: Harvard University Press, 1940.

Hosmer, James Kendall. *Winthrop's Journal: "History of New England" 1630–1649.* 2 vols. New York: Barnes and Noble, 1908.

Humphreys, David. *An Essay on the Life of the Honorable Major-General Israel Putnam.* Hartford, CT, 1788.

Hutchinson, Thomas. *The History of Massachusetts, from the First Settlement Thereof in 1628, until the Year 1750.* 3rd ed. 2 vols. Boston, 1795.

"Instructions to Matthew Cary about Bringing Prisoners from Canada; Information Obtained by Him in Quebec, and Lists of the Prisoners Redeemed and Left in Canada—1695." *New England Historical and Genealogical Register* 24 (1870): 286–91.

Jameson, Frederic. "Postmodernism and Consumer Society." *The Anti-aesthetic: Essays on Postmodern Culture.* Ed. Hal Foster. Seattle, WA: Bay Press, 1983.

Johnson, James. *Scout Journals.* Garland Library of Narratives of North American Indian Captivities 104. Ed. Wilcomb E. Washburn. New York: Garland, 1976.

Johnson, Linck C. *Thoreau's Complex Weave: The Writing of A Week on the Concord and Merrimack Rivers.* Charlottesville: University Press of Virginia, 1986.

Johonnot, Jackson. *The Remarkable Adventures of Jackson Johonnot, of Massachusetts.* Walpole, NH, 1795.

Jones, Rufus M. *The Quakers in the American Colonies.* New York: Russell & Russell, 1962.

Kamrath, Mark. "Charles Brockden Brown and the 'Art of the Historian': An Essay Concerning (Post)Modern Historical Understanding." *Journal of the Early Republic* 21.2 (2001): 231–62.

Kestler, Frances Roe. *The Indian Captivity Narrative: A Woman's View.* New York: Garland, 1990.

Kinnan, Mary. *A True Narrative of the Sufferings of Mary Kinnan.* Elizabethtown, 1795.

Koehler, Lyle. *A Search for Power: The "Weaker Sex" in Seventeenth-Century New England.* Urbana: University of Illinois Press, 1980.

Kolodny, Annette. *The Land Before Her: Fantasy and Experience of the American Frontiers, 1630–1860.* Chapel Hill: University of North Carolina Press, 1984.

———. "Turning the Lens on 'The Panther Captivity': A Feminist Exercise in Practical Criticism." *Critical Inquiry* 8 (1981): 329–45.

Lang, Amy Schrager. *Prophetic Woman: Anne Hutchinson and the Problem of Dissent in the Literature of New England.* Berkeley and Los Angeles: University of California Press, 1987.

Lawlor, Mary. "The Fictions of Daniel Boone." *Desert, Garden, Margin, Range: Literature on the American Frontier.* Ed. Eric Heyne. New York: Twayne, 1992.

Levernier, James, and Hennig Cohen. *The Indians and Their Captives.* Westport, CT: Greenwood Press, 1977.

Lincoln, Charles H., ed. *Narratives of the Indian Wars, 1675–1699.* New York: Barnes and Noble, 1966.

Lloyd, Arnold. *Quaker Social History, 1669–1738.* Westport, CT: Greenwood Press, 1979.

Looby, Christopher. *Voicing America: Language, Literary Form, and the Origins of the United States.* Chicago: University of Chicago Press, 1996.

Mack, Phyllis. *Visionary Women: Ecstatic Prophecy in Seventeenth-Century England.* Berkeley and Los Angeles: University of California Press, 1992.

Mather, Cotton. *Decennium Luctuosum.* Boston, 1699.

———. *Diary of Cotton Mather.* 2 vols. New York: Frederick Ungar, 1957.

———. *Humiliations Follow'd with Deliverances.* 1697. New York: Garland, 1977.

———. *A Letter to Ungospelized Plantations,* 1702.

———. *Magnalia Christi Americana.* London, 1702.

———. *Ornaments for the Daughters of Zion, or The Character and Happiness of a Virtuous Woman: A Facsimile Reproduction.* Delmar, NY: Scholars' Facsimiles and Reprints, 1978.

———. *Pillars of Salt.* Boston, 1699.

———. *Souldiers Counselled and Comforted.* Boston, 1689.

———. *Warnings from the Dead.* Boston, 1693.

Mather, Increase. *The Doctrine of Divine Providence.* Boston, 1684.

McDaniel, W. Caleb. "Blogging in the Early Republic." *Common-Place* 5.4 (2005). 6 April 2006. http://www.common-place.org/vol-05/no-4/mcdaniel/index.shtml.

Miller, Perry. *Consciousness in Concord.* Boston: Houghton Mifflin, 1958.

Mirick, B. L. *The History of Haverhill, Massachusetts.* Haverhill, MA, 1832.

Myles, Anne G. "Slaves in Algiers, Captives in Iraq: The Strange Career of the Barbary Captivity Narrative." *Common-Place* 5.1 (2004). 6 April 2006. http://www.common-place.org/vol-05/no-01/myles/index.shtml.

Namias, June. *White Captives: Gender and Ethnicity on the American Frontier.* Norman: University of Oklahoma Press, 1993.

A Narrative of the Captivity of Mrs. Johnson. Containing an Account of Her Sufferings, during Four Years with the Indians and French. Garland Library of Narratives of North American Indian Captivities 23. Ed. Wilcomb E. Washburn. New York: Garland, 1976.

Neal, Daniel. *The History of New-England.* 2nd ed. 2 vols. London, 1747.

Newton, Esther. *Mother Camp: Female Impersonators in America.* Chicago: University of Chicago Press, 1979.

Panther, Abraham. *A Very Surprising Narrative. . . .* Fairfield, WA: Ye Galleon Press, 1972.

Pedder, Laura Green. *The Letters of Joseph Dennie.* Orono: University of Maine Press, 1936.

Péladeau, Marius. *The Prose of Royall Tyler.* Montpelier: Vermont Historical Society, 1972.

Penhallow, Samuel. *The History of the Wars of New-England.* Boston, 1726.

Person, Leland S., Jr. *Aesthetic Headaches: Women and a Masculine Poetics in Poe, Melville, and Hawthorne.* Athens: University of Georgia Press, 1988.

"Petition of the Inhabitants of Maine." *The Andros Tracts.* Boston: The Prince Society, 1868.

Pickard, John B. *The Letters of John Greenleaf Whittier.* 2 vols. Cambridge, MA: Belknap Press of Harvard University Press, 1975.

——. *Memorabilia of John Greenleaf Whittier.* Hartford, CT: Emerson Society, 1968.

Poovey, Mary. "Aesthetics and Political Economy in the Eighteenth Century: The Place of Gender in the Social Construction of Knowledge." *Aesthetics and Ideology.* Ed. George Levine. New Brunswick, NJ: Rutgers University Press, 1994.

Rowlandson, Mary. *The Sovereignty and Goodness of God Together with the Faithfulness of His Promises Displayed.* Ed. Neil Salisbury. Boston: Bedford Books, 1997.

Rowson, Susanna. *Charlotte Temple.* New York: Oxford University Press, 1986.

Saltonstall, Leverett. *Sketch of Haverhill, Massachusetts.* Vol. 4 of *Collections of the Massachusetts Historical Society.* Boston, 1816.

Sanchez-Eppler, Karen. *Touching Liberty: Abolition, Feminism, and the Politics of the Body.* Berkeley and Los Angeles: University of California Press, 1993.

Saunderson, Henry H. *History of Charlestown, New Hampshire.* Claremont, NH: Claremont Manufacturing, 1876.

Sayre, Gordon. *American Captivity Narratives.* Boston: Houghton Mifflin, 2000.

Scheick, William J. *Authority and Female Authorship in Colonial America.* Lexington: University Press of Kentucky, 1998.

Schofield, Mary Anne. "'Women's Speaking Justified': The Feminine Quaker Voice, 1662–1797." *Tulsa Studies in Women's Literature* 6 (1987): 61–77.

Schultz, Nancy Lusignan. *Fire and Roses: The Burning of the Charlestown Convent, 1834.* Boston: Northeastern University Press, 2000.

——. *Veil of Fear: Nineteenth-Century Convent Tales.* West Lafayette, IN: Purdue University Press, 1999.

Scott, Joan W. "Experience." *Feminists Theorize the Political.* Ed. Judith Butler and Joan W. Scott. New York: Routledge, 1992.

Seaver, James E. *A Narrative of the Life of Mrs. Mary Jemison.* Syracuse, NY: Syracuse University Press, 1990.

Sewall, Samuel. *The Diary of Samuel Sewall (1674–1729).* Ed. M. Halsey Thomas. 2 vols. New York: Farrar, Straus and Giroux, 1973.

Shipton, Clifford K., and James E. Mooney, eds. *National Index of American Imprints through 1800: The Short-Title Evans.* 2 vols. Worcester, MA: American Antiquarian Society, 1969.

Sieminski, Captain Greg. "The Puritan Captivity Narrative and the Politics of the American Revolution." *American Quarterly* 42 (1990): 35–56.

Silverman, Kenneth, ed. *Selected Letters of Cotton Mather.* Baton Rouge: Louisiana State University Press, 1971.

——. *The Life and Times of Cotton Mather.* New York: Harper & Row, 1984.

Slotkin, Richard. *Regeneration through Violence.* Middletown, CT: Wesleyan University Press, 1973.

Smith, Grace. *A Dying Mother's Legacy.* Boston, 1712.

Soderland, Jean R. "Women's Authority in Pennsylvania and New Jersey Quaker Meetings, 1680–1760." *William and Mary Quarterly* 44 (1987): 722–49.

Sontag, Susan. *Regarding the Pain of Others.* New York: Farrar, Straus and Giroux, 2003.

The Spirit of the Farmers' Museum, and Lay Preacher's Gazette. Walpole, NH, 1801.

Stout, Harry S. *The New England Soul: Preaching and Religious Culture in Colonial New England.* New York: Oxford University Press, 1986.

Stratton, R. B. *Captivity of the Oatman Girls.* Lincoln: University of Nebraska Press, 1983.

Strong, Pauline. *Captive Selves, Captivating Others: The Politics and Poetics of Colonial American Captivity Narratives.* Boulder, CO: Westview Press, 1999.

Tanselle, G. Thomas. "Attribution of Authorship in 'The Spirit of the Farmers' Museum.'" *Papers of the Bibliographical Society of America* 59 (1965): 170–76.

————. *Royall Tyler.* Cambridge, MA: Harvard University Press, 1967.

Tarter, Michele Lise. "Nursing the Wor(l)d: The Writings of Quaker Women in Early America." *Women and Language* 16 (1993): 22–26.

Thoreau, Henry D. "Died . . . Miss Anna Jones." *Early Essays and Miscellanies.* Ed. Joseph J. Moldenhauer and Edwin Moser. Princeton, NJ: Princeton University Press, 1975.

————. *Journal 1: 1837–1844.* Ed. Elizabeth Hall Witherell, William L. Howarth, Robert Sattelmeyer, and Thomas Blanding. Princeton, NJ: Princeton University Press, 1981.

————. *Journal 2: 1842–1848.* Ed. Robert Sattelmeyer. Princeton, NJ: Princeton University Press, 1984.

————. *Journal 3: 1848–1851.* Ed. Robert Sattelmeyer, Mark R. Patterson, and William Rossi. Princeton, NJ: Princeton University Press, 1990.

————. "Love." *Early Essays and Miscellanies.* Ed. Joseph J. Moldenhauer and Edwin Moser. Princeton, NJ: Princeton University Press, 1975.

————. *A Week on the Concord and Merrimack Rivers.* Ed. Carl F. Hovde. Princeton, NJ: Princeton University Press, 1980.

Toulouse, Teresa. "'My Own Credit': Strategies of (E)valuation in Mary Rowlandson's Captivity Narrative." *American Literature* 64 (1992): 655–76.

Tucker, Louis Leonard. *Clio's Consort: Jeremy Belknap and the Founding of the Massachusetts Historical Society.* Boston: Massachusetts Historical Society, 1990.

Tyler, Royall. *The Algerine Captive, or, The Life and Adventures of Doctor Updike Underhill.* Ed. Caleb Crain. New York: Modern Library, 2002.

Ulrich, Laurel Thatcher. *Good Wives: Image and Reality in the Lives of Women in Northern New England, 1650–1750.* New York: Oxford University Press, 1983.

————. "'Vertuous Women Found': New England Ministerial Literature, 1668–1735." *A Heritage of Her Own.* Ed. Nancy Cott and Elizabeth H. Pleck. New York: Simon and Schuster, 1979.

Vail, R. W. G. *The Voice of the Old Frontier.* Philadelphia: University of Pennsylvania Press, 1949.

VanDerBeets, Richard. *Held Captive by Indians: Selected Narratives, 1642–1836.* Knoxville: University of Tennessee Press, 1973.

Vaughan, Alden T. *Narratives of North American Indian Captivity: A Selective Bibliography.* New York: Garland, 1983.

Vaughan, Alden T., and Edward W. Clark. *Puritans Among the Indians: Accounts of Captivity and Redemption.* Cambridge, MA: Harvard University Press, 1981.

Warner, Michael. *Letters of the Republic: Publication and the Public Sphere in Eighteenth-Century America.* Cambridge, MA: Harvard University Press, 1990.

————. "Thoreau's Bottom." *Raritan* 11 (1992): 53–79.

Warren, Mercy Otis. *History of the Rise, Progress, and Termination of the American Revolution.* 1805. Indianapolis, IN: Liberty Fund, 1994.

Washburn, Wilcomb. Introduction. *Narratives of North American Indian Captivity: A Selective Bibliography.* By Alden T. Vaughan. New York: Garland, 1983.

Waters, Thomas Franklin, ed. "The Copy of a Valedictory and Monitory Writing, Left by Sarah Goodhue." *Ipswich, in the Massachusetts Bay Colony.* Ipswich, MA: Ipswich Historical Society, 1905.

Whitford, Kathryn. "Hannah Dustin: The Judgement of History." *Essex Institute Historical Collections* 108 (1972): 304–25.

Whittier, John Greenleaf. *The Complete Writings of John Greenleaf Whittier.* 7 vols. 1894. New York: AMS Press, 1969.

———. *Leaves from Margaret Smith's Journal in the Province of Massachusetts Bay, 1678–79.* Boston, 1849.

———. *Legends of New England.* Gainesville, FL: Scholars' Facsimiles and Reprints, 1965.

———. *Letters of Lydia Maria Child, with a Biographical Introduction by John G. Whittier and an Appendix by Wendell Phillips.* Boston, 1883.

Worrall, Arthur. *Quakers in the Colonial Northeast.* Hanover, NH: University Press of New England, 1980.

Wright, Louella M. *The Literature of the Early Friends, 1650–1725.* New York: AMS Press, 1966.

Ziff, Larzer. *Writing in the New Nation: Prose, Print, and Politics in the Early United States.* New Haven, CT: Yale University Press, 1991.

Index